The Insecure Workforce

Edited by
Edmund Heery and John Salmon

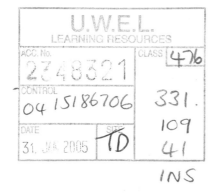

London and New York

First published 2000
by Routledge
11 New Fetter Lane, London EC4P 4EE

Simultaneously published in the USA and Canada
by Routledge
29 West 35th Street, New York, NY 10001

Typeset in Baskerville by RefineCatch Limited, Bungay, Suffolk
Printed and bound in Great Britain by
Biddles Ltd, Guildford and King's Lynn

British Library Cataloguing in Publication Data
A catalogue record for this book is available from the British Library

Library of Congress Cataloging in Publication Data
The insecure workforce / [edited by] Edmund Heery and John Salmon.
        p.   cm. – (Routledge studies in employment relations)
    Includes bibliographical references and index.
       1. Job security – Great Britain.   2. Unemployment – Great Britain –
Psychological aspects.   3. Labor market – Great Britain.   4. Trade-
unions – Great Britain.   5. Industrial relations – Great Britain.
6. Consumption (Economics) – Great Britain. 7. Great Britain –
Economic conditions – 1997–   I. Heery, Edmund.   II. Salmon,
John, 1946–   .   III. Series.
HD5708.45.G7157   2000
331.1′0941 – dc21   98–51651
                                                                  CIP

ISBN 0–415–18670–6 (hbk)
ISBN 0–415–18671–4 (pbk)

Contents

List of figures and tables

Figures

Tables

The Contributors

Brian Abbott is Senior Lecturer in Human Resource Management at Kingston University Business School.

Nigel Allington is Lecturer in Economics at Cardiff Business School and Fellow of Gonville and Caius College, Cambridge.

Brendan J. Burchell is University Lecturer in the Faculty of Social and Political Sciences, University of Cambridge and a Fellow of Magdalene College.

Paul Gregg is Senior Research Fellow at the Centre for Economic Performance at the London School of Economics and Political Science.

David Guest is Professor of Occupational Psychology at Birkbeck College, University of London.

Edmund Heery is Professor of Industrial Relations at Cardiff Business School.

Genevieve Knight works at the Policy Studies Institute and was previously Research Officer at the Centre for Economic Performance, the London School of Economics and Political Science.

Philip Morgan is Lecturer in Organisational Behaviour at Cardiff Business School.

Jane P. Nolan is an ESRC-funded postgraduate student in the Faculty of Social and Political Sciences at Cambridge University and a member of Newnham College.

Kate Purcell is Bristol and West Professor of Employment Relations at Bristol Business School, University of the West of England.

Peter Robinson is Senior Economist at the Institute for Public Policy Research and editor of *New Economy*, the IPPR's journal. He is also Research Associate at the Centre for Economic Performance at the London School of Economics and Political Science.

John Salmon is Lecturer in Industrial Relations and Japanese Management at Cardiff Business School.

Peter Turnbull is Professor of Human Resource Management and ESRC Senior Management Research Fellow at Cardiff Business School.

Jonathan Wadsworth is Research Officer at the Centre for Economic Performance, London School of Economics and Political Science, and Lecturer in Economics at Royal Holloway College, University of London.

Richard M. Walker is Lecturer in Housing and a member of the Centre for Housing Management and Development in the Department of City and Regional Planning, Cardiff University.

Victoria Wass is Senior Research Associate in Economics at Cardiff Business School.

Ines C. Wichert is an ESRC-funded postgraduate student in the Faculty of Social and Political Sciences at Cambridge University and a member of Hughes Hall.

Preface

In recent years there has been something of a moral panic over increased work-force insecurity, and the issue has featured prominently in media and political debate. It is widely believed that jobs have become less secure, that the life-time career is disappearing and that an expanding proportion of employment contracts are temporary, part-time and contingent. The blame for this state of affairs has been variously laid at the door of the global economy, the economic short-termism fostered by financial institutions and markets, and the deregulatory appetites of governments such as those of Margaret Thatcher and John Major in Britain. The consequences of the move to employee insecurity are felt to be a workforce which is more vulnerable to exploitation and a series of adverse changes, including the erosion of worker commitment within the workplace and political alienation and reduced consumer confidence beyond.

The purpose of this collection of essays is to test these and associated claims about the direction, causes and consequences of labour market change in the developed economies. It draws upon a number of academic fields (human resource management, industrial relations, labour economics, the sociology of employment, occupational psychology and social policy) and seeks to intervene authoritatively in the debate over insecurity through a review of available and relevant evidence. The collection originated in a conference with the same title organised by the Employment Research Unit at Cardiff Business School in September 1997, but each of the chapters has been specially commissioned for this volume and takes the form of a review essay dealing with a particular facet of the 'insecure workforce'. The result, we hope, is an integrated volume which brings together scholars from diverse backgrounds to address a common theme which has mounting salience in Britain, North America, the Far East, Australia, New Zealand and continental Europe.

In putting the collection together we have incurred a number of debts and owe thanks, first, to our contributors who have found time within busy schedules to devote attention to a project which lies slightly outside the mainstream of academic publication. Second, we would like to thank the staff of Cardiff Business School for their support, and offer particular thanks to Julie Roberts, who organised the original conference, and Donna Watson and Sarah Gape who helped with the editorial process. Thanks are also due to academic colleagues at Cardiff who have commented on a number of the chapters, including George Boyne, Philip Morgan, Paul Stewart, Peter Turnbull and Victoria Wass. Finally, we owe thanks to our families for being tolerant of the time, effort and anxiety absorbed by the writing and editing of the collection. Hopefully, next summer will be less fraught.

Edmund Heery and John Salmon
October 1998

1 The Insecurity Thesis

Edmund Heery and John Salmon

Introduction

Unease about the direction of labour market change pervades a wide range of opinion today and it is now commonplace for the workforce of the developed economies to be described as increasingly insecure. This view is global in scope and embraces international agencies and commentators in a range of countries (Barker and Christensen 1998; OECD 1997; Standing 1997) and is apparent across a spectrum of interests which, in Britain, includes government (DTI 1998: 13), policy makers (Fabian Society 1996; IER 1996), trade unions (TUC 1996) and management organisations (IPD 1996). For some, we live in an 'age of insecurity' (Elliott and Atkinson 1998; cf. Beck 1992) and risk and instability have become defining features of contemporary social life. Underlying this viewpoint is a coherent set of statements about the nature, causes and effects of recent change in employment relations which can be labelled the 'insecurity thesis'. This thesis informs a great deal of contemporary debate and commentary and includes amongst its key propositions: that economic risk is being transferred increasingly from employers to employees, through shortened job tenure and contingent employment and remuneration; that insecurity is damaging to long-term economic performance, through its promotion of an employment relationship founded on opportunism, mistrust and low commitment; and that the emergence of an insecure workforce imposes severe costs on both individuals and the wider society. These and associated claims constitute a deeply critical assessment of current labour market change, and adherents of the thesis have proposed a variety of radical reforms to reverse or mitigate the perceived slide towards insecure employment.

The purpose of this collection is to interrogate the insecurity thesis. Contributors from a range of academic disciplines, economics, sociology, psychology, social policy, management and industrial relations, have been brought together and have been asked to review the question of the insecure workforce from the perspective of their own field. The contributors encompass a variety of opinion and, while some subscribe to the insecurity thesis, other reactions range from mild to marked scepticism. In each case, however, they have been asked to summarise available research evidence in order to shed light on a series of questions which are more commonly the subject of assertion than empirical review. Their essays deal largely with four such questions: first, how can insecurity be defined and the insecure workforce be measured; second, what evidence is there that the insecure workforce is growing both in Britain and in other developed economies; third, to the extent that insecurity has grown, what are its causes; and fourth, what are the consequences of insecurity in the workplace and beyond? There has been a rough division of labour between the essays with the earlier contributions focusing more on the first pair of questions and the later contributions concentrating on the second pair; the collection has been conceived as a progression which extends outwards from the employment relationship to embrace a wider range of social experience as it proceeds.

Thus, the early chapters by Robinson, Gregg *et al.* and Turnbull and Wass examine change in the structure of jobs, and address the question of whether there has been an 'objective' rise in insecurity in Britain over the past two decades. They are followed by chapters by Morgan *et al.* and Purcell which deal, respectively, with the specific experiences of public sector workers and gender differences with regard to insecure employment. Guest and Heery and Abbott then consider the responses of managers and trade unions to the issue of insecurity. The collection ends with contributions from Nolan *et al.* and Walker which move beyond the world of work and which look, in turn, at the impact of insecure employment on personal well-being and family relationships and patterns of housing consumption.

The purpose of this introductory essay is to provide a general framework for interpreting the more specialised chapters which follow. It seeks to do this, in the first instance, by providing a stylised account of the insecurity thesis and its key propositions, as set out principally in recent British and American texts on employment change. It then considers critical responses to the thesis, which tend either to dispute its empirical validity or to accept the latter but offer a competing evaluation under the rubric of labour market flexibility. Finally, it reviews the main issues which have arisen in the emerging debate between adherents and critics of the insecurity thesis.

The insecurity thesis

One attraction of the insecurity thesis as a social theory is its breadth of coverage and the fact that it seeks to connect developments in the world of work with changes beyond. At its heart, however, is a basic claim about the changing nature of employment in developed economies, as follows:

Proposition One: Employment in the developed economies has become more insecure or unstable in the sense that both continued employment and the level of remuneration have become less predictable and contingent on factors which lie beyond the employee's control.

Cappelli *et al.* (1997: 4) characterise this shift in terms of a movement from a dominant pattern in which internal labour markets shielded workers from market forces, to 'a new employment relationship where pressures from product and labor markets are brought inside the organisation and used to mediate the relationship between workers and management'. At its most severe, this switch might be seen in the end of permanent, career-long employment and its replacement with contingent contracts and mobile workers. The measures of insecurity (or job instability, as it is sometimes called) which have been adduced to support this first proposition are various but include: a decline in median job tenure for at least some categories of employee since the mid-1980s (Gregg *et al.*, this volume); an increase in involuntary job separations due to greater resort by employers to redundancy (Turnbull and Wass, this volume); and a growth in the use of various forms of contingent labour, such as temporary workers, fixed-term contract staff, agency labour and freelancers (Appelbaum 1989; Allen and Henry 1997; Cappelli 1995; Purcell, this volume). Some have also remarked on the increased use of contingent remuneration and a trend towards greater use of 'variable pay', in which base salary is replaced by performance-linked cash payments which are neither consolidated nor pensionable (Cappelli *et al.* 1997: 189–93; Heery 1996; Morgan *et al.* this volume).

While the insecurity thesis is rooted in a claim about the changing nature of jobs, it is also argued that changes beyond the workplace have served to compound insecurity:

> *Proposition Two: The trend towards insecure employment has been compounded by changes in the external labour market and national systems of employment regulation which serve to exacerbate insecurity.*

These wider changes are believed to have assumed two forms. First, developments in labour markets have raised the costs of job loss and so not only have the risks of job separation increased but the impact of such an event has tended to become more severe. Thus, the OECD (1997: 147) presents an analysis for nine EU countries which reveals that the difficulty in finding replacement work has risen since the early 1980s, even when the effects of the economic cycle are taken into account. The OECD also notes that earnings when a new job is found may be substantially lower than in the previous job, and there is evidence from both Britain and the USA that this difference is substantial and enduring (Farber 1993; Gregg *et al.*, this volume) and may be increasing (OECD 1997: 149). Second, the deregulation of the labour market and the weakening or removal of institutions designed to protect employees are believed to have further contributed to insecurity. Key developments in Britain include changes in the benefit system which have 'increased the pressure on men, in particular, to accept flexible jobs' (Dex and

McCulloch 1997: 9), the attenuation of individual employment rights under the Conservatives and most notably the increase in the qualifying period for the right not to be unfairly dismissed, from six months to two years (Robinson, this volume), and the severe and continuing decline in trade union density and coverage by collective bargaining (Cully and Woodland 1998; Milner 1995).

These 'objective' changes in the structure of jobs and pattern of labour market regulation are believed to have stimulated a 'subjective' response from employees and the development of the insecurity thesis has been based in part on longitudinal survey data which point to rising popular concern with job security:

> *Proposition Three: Employees increasingly regard themselves as insecure and the issue of job insecurity has become more salient in recent years.*

Thus, the OECD (1997: 131, 134–5) reports a threefold increase in media references to insecurity in the G7 economies between 1982 and 1996 and an increase in 'perceived employee insecurity' in the 1990s 'in all OECD countries for which data are available'. Guest (this volume; see also Gallie *et al.* 1998: 142) points out, however, that it is important to draw a distinction between the cognitive dimension of people's attitudes, such as a perception of the probability of job loss, and the affective dimension, understood in terms of feelings of concern and anxiety. A strong statement of the insecurity thesis would suggest that along both dimensions employee attitudes are changing; that employees increasingly calculate that their jobs are insecure and that this is a source of concern.

A decline in the level of job security over time is the central claim of the insecurity thesis, but it is also argued that the distribution of insecure work is changing. In particular, adherents of the thesis have suggested that previously secure groups are either faced with greater job instability, or have come to regard their situation as more insecure:

> *Proposition Four: The incidence of both job instability and feelings of insecurity is changing and previously secure groups are now finding themselves in a precarious position.*

Among the groups identified as in transition from a more to a less secure status are: middle managers under threat from corporate delayering (Cappelli *et al.* 1997: 68–9; Hendry and Jenkins 1997); public service professionals, who have experienced an increase in the incidence of redundancy and contingent contracts (Keep and Sisson 1992; Morgan *et al.*, this volume); older workers, who have suffered a particularly sharp decline in job tenure and a more acute penalty for job loss (Gregg *et al.*, this volume); and male workers, for whom the rising incidence of part-time work is indicative of a more general threat to their breadwinner role (Gallie *et al.* 1998: 151; Purcell, this volume; Rubery 1996: 26). Each of these categories may on average continue to enjoy higher security than non-management employees, private sector workers, younger workers and women, but it is asserted that their relative position is becoming less favourable.

Supporters of the insecurity thesis have identified a number of causes, but are united in two claims: they regard the rise in insecurity as a secular trend and not a temporary or cyclical phenomenon, and they trace its origins to the actions of employers and governments, and downplay the free choices of employees. Cappelli *et al.* (1997: 206, 208–10), for instance, in their review of change in the American workplace, talk of a permanent shift in the nature of the employment relationship and state that this has been largely imposed on employees, who have borne the costs of structural adjustment. The explanations which are favoured by adherents of the insecurity thesis tend to fall into two categories, one of which places emphasis on the process of globalisation and the exposure of domestic markets to more intense competition (Standing 1997), while the other focuses on national institutions and identifies insecurity as a phenomenon of 'Anglo-Saxon' capitalism, with its active market for corporate control and systems of corporate financing and governance which accord priority to shareholder value in the shorter term (Dore 1997; Hutton 1995):

Proposition Five: The increase in workforce insecurity can be traced either to the globalisation of the world economy and resultant pressure for cost reduction within national economies, or to national systems of capitalism which promote the dominance of financial interests and the short-term management of company assets in the interest of 'shareholder value'.

The globalisation argument is often linked to the claim that the international capitalist economy is entering a new stage of development – Standing (1997: 11) refers to the 'era of market regulation' – at the heart of which is a new international model of management characterised by the identification of 'core competencies' and the use of market relationships to provide all operations and services which fall outside of this narrowly defined circle (Cappelli *et al.* 1997: 43–4). The argument from corporate financing and governance, in contrast, emphasises the differential experience across national capitalist economies and leaves room also for national systems of labour market regulation to either accentuate or moderate pressures for insecurity. A recent review of part-time work in Europe, for instance, has explained different national patterns in terms of variation in systems of corporate governance and the strategies of labour use which they engender and the strength or weakness of protective employment legislation (Wickham 1997).

With regard to the effects of insecurity, adherents of the thesis tend to emphasise a series of perverse consequences which rebound against employers.[1] While acknowledging the immediate benefits which can accrue to companies in terms of reduced costs, greater flexibility and worker compliance, they argue that a more insecure workforce is problematic for employers in several important respects. Indeed, this argument is encountered repeatedly and amongst sociologists and industrial relations specialists has become an almost routine accompaniment to discussion of workplace change. At its core is a belief that new forms of employment are altering the 'psychological contract' at work, such that the latter has come to resemble 'a spot market where workers are encouraged to focus on their immediate self-interest and employers promise to do the same' (Cappelli *et al.* 1997: 11; see also Beynon 1997: 38; Brown 1997: 83).[2] Specific disadvantages which are believed to flow from this kind of employment relationship include: low levels of employee commitment and an unwillingness to work 'beyond contract'; encouragement of opportunistic behaviour and the use by employees of their available bargaining power to maximise immediate wage returns; high transaction costs associated with the monitoring and enforcement of a more 'contractual' employment relationship; and the disincentive for employers to invest in training or employee involvement (Broadbent *et al.* 1998: 8; Cappelli *et al.* 1997: 212–15; Kelly 1997: 393–4; Legge 1998; Saundry 1998: 157; Walsh 1993: 425–6):

Proposition Six: The emergence of the insecure workforce is prompting a change in the balance of expectations within the employment relationship and is associated with the erosion of employee commitment, encouragement of opportunistic bargaining, higher transaction costs and a disincentive for employers to train.

These developments are believed to be particularly problematic because they contradict other trends within business and threaten to derail changes which are conducive to the long-term health of the economy. Cappelli *et al.* (1997: 8–10) argue that new forms of high-performance work organisation require committed, flexible and highly trained employees and their diffusion is hampered by the spread of worker insecurity, and it has been repeatedly argued that an essential precondition for business strategies which emphasise quality enhancement and productivity growth is a stable, secure and trained workforce (Brown *et al.* 1993; Edwards *et al.* 1998; Kochan and Osterman 1994).[3]

For a proportion of the insecure workforce, a looser, market-based pattern of employment relations will offer benefits in terms of reduced dependence on employers and the ability to exploit marketable skills. A cardinal assertion of the insecurity thesis, however, is that the shift to more insecure and contingent employment imposes costs on the majority of employees affected:

Proposition Seven: The spread of insecure employment imposes both economic and psychological costs on employees and has been associated with both the intensification of work and the widespread abuse of management authority.

These costs are held to assume a variety of different forms, though perhaps the most apparent and the most quantifiable are the financial penalties associated with both job instability and contingent contracts. With regard to the former, there is evidence (referred to above) that involuntary job separation in both Britain and the USA is associated with increased risk of unemployment and reduced earnings. With regard to the latter, there is again evidence from both countries that employees with non-standard employment contracts suffer in terms of reduced access to benefits such as holiday, sick pay and occupational pensions (Dex and McCulloch 1997: 16–19; Engberg 1993: 164) and many such workers fall beyond the protection of employment legislation.[4] It is also argued that insecure workers are vulnerable to exploitation and may experience abusive management and work intensification. Cappelli *et al.* (1997: 4; see also Rubery 1996: 35–6) summarise the American situation as one in which, '[j]obs demand more of workers but . . . offer them less', and in Britain the National Association of Citizens' Advice Bureaux has published a series of reports which highlight the abuse of contingent workers in the lower regions of the labour market (NACAB 1990, 1993, 1997; see also Kelly 1998: 44–5). Finally, it is claimed that the costs for employees of job insecurity extend beyond the workplace and include psychological stress and ill-health and, indeed, there is evidence that the adverse effect on well-being of perceived insecurity is as great as that which is associated with unemployment (Nolan *et al.*, this volume; see also Dex and McCulloch 1997: 74; Gallie *et al.* 1998: 232).

The alleged costs of rising insecurity for workers raise the issue of worker representation and in some quarters it has been suggested that change in the nature of employment relations is stimulating fresh demand for protection through trade unions. In Britain, Kessler and Bayliss (1995: 295) conclude their survey of contemporary industrial relations by predicting that, in a labour market in which 'isolated individuals [face] powerful and confident managers . . .', the value of collective organisation and representation will be 'relearned', while from a point further to the left, Kelly (1998: 130) has suggested that the current wave of economic restructuring is creating the basis for a renewed wave of worker mobilisation within trade unions. In America, similar predictions have been made and, according to Voos (1997: 333–4), the 'return to contract' in the US labour market, which is manifest in the growth of a contingent and insecure workforce, is producing 'a situation that is ripe for traditional labour unionism with a dual emphasis on economic gains for members and protection of individual employees in the employment relationship'.

> **Proposition Eight: The emergence of a more insecure workforce is stimulating demand from employees for protective regulation and is furnishing a new representative opportunity to trade unions.**

While insecurity might generate potential demand for trade unionism, it has been argued that unions must effect a realignment of their policies and internal structure if this potential is to be realised (Heery and Abbott, this volume). Two kinds of realignment have been proposed, each of which has its particular adherents and is advocated against the claims of the other. First, a change in union relations with employers through the embrace of 'social partnership' or 'mutual gains' and the pursuit of a bargain in which job security is exchanged for union cooperation in raising productivity and company performance. Second, a shift in union policy towards the organisation and representation of contingent workers in the new service industries which, given the demographic character- istics of this new workforce, must involve closer engagement with the interests of women, young workers and migrants (Wever 1998). This second response is also commonly believed to require a change in internal union government systems in order to allow the diversity of the new workforce to be adequately represented within union policy-making (Leisink 1997; Valkenburg and Beukema 1996).

   While employees may bear the brunt of rising insecurity, it is claimed repeat- edly by adherents of the insecurity thesis that there are wider costs borne by society at large. In some cases this complaint merges with a general attack on the corrosive effects on community and social solidarity of free market liberalism (Gray 1995), or with a broad defence of postwar social democracy and the high level of security it afforded citizens in the developed economies (Elliott and Atkinson 1998). More particularly, however, several negative consequences for economy and society have been identified in statements of the insecurity thesis. Within the economy, it is claimed that pressures for short-term flexibility in the employment relationship inhibit both long-term skill formation and the mainten- ance of consumer confidence in key markets, such as that for housing, which require long-term commitment by individual consumers. Insecurity has also been linked to widening inequality in the distribution of income and wealth which, in turn, has been connected with a decline in social cohesion and the exacerbation of a range of social problems, including criminality, family breakdown and political alienation:

Proposition Nine: The emergence of a more insecure workforce is associated with a range of wider social ills including barriers to skill development in the system of production, erosion of consumer confidence in the field of consumption, rising inequality in income and wealth and a reduction in social cohesion which is manifest in rising crime, family breakdown and political alienation.

Skill formation has been identified increasingly as 'the main collective goal of economic policy' (Crouch 1997: 370; see also Lane 1990; Streeck 1989) and an effective system of vocational education and training is viewed as a necessary condition for the maintenance of a high-wage economy in the context of increased global competition. It has also been suggested that the emergence of more flexible systems of production requires increased involvement of individual enterprises in the design and delivery of programmes of training and development. A more contingent employment relationship and the collapse of internal labour markets, however, threaten to inhibit the assumption of this role by individual employers and, according to some, the prime negative consequence of insecurity lies in its potential to undermine the necessary 'enskilling' of the workforce (Cappelli *et al.* 1997 122–5; Crouch 1997: 374–6). A similar problem of market failure has been identified in the sphere of consumption, where job insecurity may discourage individuals from making long-term investments in housing, pensions and the education of their children (Cappelli *et al.* 1997: 11; Gray 1996; Rubery 1996: 34).[5] Moreover, the restructuring of welfare systems and the increased requirement for individuals to make provision for their own personal security (through house purchase, personal pensions and private education and healthcare) can interact with employment change to generate new consumption problems such as mortgage arrears and house repossession and inadequate pension provision (Hutton 1995: 197–211; Walker, this volume).

Concern over workforce insecurity has risen alongside growing inequality in Britain, the USA and other countries, and for some analysts these trends are intimately related. The connection can arise through common origins, with the growth of both income inequality and job insecurity arising from reduced demand for unskilled, male labour and the decline of trade unions (Cappelli *et al.* 1997: 186–9; Goodman *et al.* 1997: 280), or through interaction, with the reduction in bargaining power attendant on growing insecurity preventing low-paid workers from maintaining their relative income. The connection might also be seen in outcomes, and the combined result of greater inequality and insecurity is widely believed to be a state of anomie, or declining 'social cohesion' (Kelly 1997: 394). The slackening of social constraints and erosion of commitments, which are the products of a more insecure and unequal labour market, are believed to provide ground on which a variety of social ills can flourish. Commonly mentioned are criminality, family breakdown and political alienation (Beynon

1997: 53; Gray 1995: 96–9; Hutton 1995: 323; Nolan *et al.*, this volume). With regard to the latter, Luttwak (1994), in a particularly trenchant statement of the insecurity thesis, has suggested that 'the central problem of our days: the personal economic insecurity of working people . . .' is distancing a growing percentage of the population from conventional politics and political parties and fostering support for the extreme right. The insecure workforce, in other words, provides a breeding ground for the populist politics of Le Pen in Europe and the anti-federal militias in the USA.

Exposition of the insecurity thesis ends typically in calls for reform and proposals either to reverse the trend towards insecure employment or to mitigate the adverse effects on individuals, companies and the wider society. These proposals vary in focus and in their degree of radicalism, and would-be reformers have produced a bewildering variety of recommendations for change. The latter include: the establishment of a 'citizen's income', to detach economic security from the functioning of the labour market (Standing 1997: 30); the refashioning of the welfare state to reflect new patterns of employment and associated family structures (Crompton *et al.* 1996: 7; Rubery 1996: 36); and the strengthening of national systems of vocational education and training to compensate for the reduced incentive to train (Cappelli *et al.* 1997; Crouch 1997). Within the field of employment relations, proposals to counter insecurity have fallen into three categories: those which emphasise voluntary action by managers either to rebuild job security or promote 'employability' (Guest, this volume; Kochan and Osterman 1994: 52–5; Warren 1996); those which emphasise legal regulation of the labour market and seek to constrain employers' use of flexible or insecure labour (Rubery 1996: 37; Turnbull and Wass, this volume); and those which focus on the systems of corporate financing and governance and advocate some form of 'stakeholder capitalism' (Hutton 1995):

Proposition Ten: The emergence of the insecure workforce necessitates action to reform the system of employment, which may take the form of voluntary action by employers to rebuild job security or promote 'employability', legal regulation to eliminate insecure work, or the reform of corporate governance to ensure companies become more responsive to the interests of employees.

With regard to management action, it has been suggested that more contingent employment requires a 'new deal', in which compensation for reduced tenure is made through payment for performance and the opportunity to develop marketable skills. Even those who are sympathetic to this prescription, however, concede that management commitment to 'employability' may be largely rhetorical and, if the argument about reduced incentives to train is correct, economic pressures on managers may preclude the emergence of such a new deal in all but a minority of firms (Hendry and Jenkins 1997; Herriot and Pemberton 1997). Proposals to re-regulate the labour market have assumed two main forms: those which seek to make labour less disposable, either by restricting the use of contingent labour or by making it more difficult for employers to resort to dismissal and redundancy; and those which seek to harmonise the treatment of standard and non-standard labour, so that the penalties associated with the latter are reduced (Fredman 1997; Morgan 1998). Increasingly, it is recognised that such regulation must be inter-national in scope in the manner of the recent part-time workers' directive adopted by the European Union (Crompton *et al.* 1996: 17). Finally, it is increasingly common to suggest that employment relations reflect wider patterns of corporate financing and governance (Sisson 1995), with the implication that reform of employment should begin with the regulation of these systems, perhaps by provid-ing new statutory channels for employee voice or imposing an obligation on managers (akin to their fiduciary duty to shareholders) to consider the needs of employees in decision-making.

Critique

The stylised version of the insecurity thesis presented above can be found in no single text, but its constituent propositions are encountered widely in both media and academic output. As they have diffused, moreover, they have become the object of criticism, and two primary reactions have emerged. The first of these attacks the root proposition at the core of the thesis, that the labour market is changing in a fundamental way and employment is becoming more insecure, particularly in an objective sense. This argument comes in both strong and weak forms, with the latter conceding that some modest change has occurred, and is associated with a belief that there is a moral panic over insecurity which is tem-porary and stimulated by media coverage of the issue. Insecurity sceptics write from a range of perspectives and disciplines, and include Burgess and Rees (1996) Godard (1998), Guest (1997), Rainnie (1998) and Spencer (1996). In many cases their critique stops short at a statement of the limited empirical support for growing job instability; for some, however, the argument extends further to include a defence of flexible labour markets and government policies of deregula-tion (Smith 1997). A critique of the insecurity thesis in this case is linked to defence of a neo-liberal economic position, essentially by denying that the emer-gence of more flexible labour markets is associated with significant costs for the majority of employees.

The second line of criticism is less frequently articulated, though we suspect it is adhered to widely amongst economists and policy makers. Essentially, it comprises a restatement of classic utilitarianism and accepts that, yes, job insecurity is rising and imposes a cost on a portion of the workforce, but that there are compensatory benefits which outweigh these costs in the scales of utility. The OECD (1997: 129), for instance, reports that Alan Greenspan, Chairman of the US Federal Reserve Board, is 'on record as attributing the fact that the USA has been experi-encing a prolonged upswing in the 1990s without any noticeable inflationary pressures to a growing sense of insecurity in the USA workforce'. Very similar claims have been made in Britain, where the success of the Conservatives' labour market reform of the 1980s is adjudged to have resulted in the 'death of inflation', in large part through the removal of the protective shield of trade unionism from a large percentage of the labour force (Bootle 1996). The central argument for those who develop this position is that rising job insecurity has eroded workers' bargaining power and thereby reduced inflationary pressure within the labour market (Robinson, this volume). As a consequence, macroeconomic policy can be set within a looser framework, with lower interest rates, and the NAIRU (non-accelerating inflation rate of unemployment) will stabilise at a lower level. Insecurity, therefore, is unpleasant medicine, but in the longer term it serves to improve the health of the economy and, paradoxically, benefits even those who fear for their jobs.

Debate

The emergence of these critical responses to the insecurity thesis has stimulated debate between adherents and critics and a number of the propositions sketched out above are now the focus of academic research and controversy. The chapters below contribute to this debate and there is insufficient space here to review all the questions which have come under scrutiny. What we do want to do, however, is to describe briefly the critical issues which separate adherents to the insecurity thesis from their two sets of critics. With regard to the division between adherents and sceptics, these critical issues include the definition of insecurity, its measurement and the direction of current trends. With regard to that between adherents and those who perceive benefits in a more insecure workforce, the central focus of debate is the degree to which worker insecurity (however defined) produces perverse or beneficial effects on business performance and the wider economy.

Insecurity sceptics are often economists and tend to favour fairly narrow and 'objective' definitions of insecurity in terms of changes in job tenure, the use of temporary labour and employment legislation regulating the dismissal of employees. The value of such an approach is that it allows measurement of the 'ill-defined' (Robinson, this volume), but arguably its weaknesses are that the reports of employees themselves are dismissed as 'mass hysteria' (Smith, quoted in Gregg *et al.*, this volume) and the possibility that insecurity is multidimensional is downplayed. Adherents, in contrast, tend to consider a broader range of evidence but, in some cases, either end up with definitions of insecurity which are too encompassing (Standing 1997) or fail to define the term at all. The latter is particularly likely where authors engage in polemic and make use of the insecurity thesis to mount a broad attack on free markets and deregulation (Gray 1995). In our view, insecurity should be defined broadly but nevertheless precisely along three dimensions. First, it can be seen as a property of jobs, understood in terms of increased risk of involuntary job loss and unpredictability of earnings which can be measured through a combination of indicators, including job tenure, compulsory redundancy, the incidence of contingent contracts and the use of variable pay. Second it can be viewed as a property of the environment in which jobs exist, understood in terms of the penalties associated with job loss and the degree of protective regulation of the labour market through employment law, trade unionism and welfare support for workers who lose their employment. Third, it can be viewed as a property of the subjective experience of employees, understood in terms of cognitive and affective attitudes towards security of employment.

If this framework is applied to Britain, does it demonstrate the emergence of a more insecure workforce in the last two decades? Below is a summary of what we feel is the key evidence which, although it does not point to catastrophic change, indicates a fairly consistent pattern of development across a range of indicators. British workers, we believe, can accurately be described as increasingly insecure.

- It is acknowledged widely that job tenure is a weak measure of insecurity, but nevertheless there is evidence of a modest decline in aggregate job tenure over the past twenty years, and experience of more substantial decline for particular groups within the labour force. According to Gregg *et al.* (this volume; see also Dex and McCulloch 1997: 100–1; Gallie *et al.* 1998: 119–22), nearly three-quarters of the workforce have experienced greater 'job instability' in the past ten years, with the largest rise amongst men, for whom median job tenure has fallen by 12 per cent in a decade. Job tenure is also declining for childless women; the modesty of the aggregate decline is explained in part by increasing tenure amongst women with children, who have availed themselves of enhanced maternity provisions.

- Over the past twenty years the risk of becoming unemployed has risen for both men and women. According to Gallie *et al.* (1998: 124), 5.6 per cent of British employees experienced a spell of unemployment in the period 1973–77, a figure which rose to 9.6 per cent in 1978–82, 11.6 per cent in 1983–87 and 15.0 per cent in 1988–92. Although this pattern of increased risk of unemployment was experienced by both sexes, it was particularly marked for men, more than a fifth of whom experienced unemployment in the period 1988–92. A parallel change has been a secular increase in involuntary job loss in Britain, measured in absolute terms and as a proportion of all job losses across the economy (Turnbull and Wass, this volume).

- The structure of employment is changing, with a modest but nevertheless clear decline in the percentage of employees in full-time permanent employment (from 67.4 to 61.7 per cent between 1984 and 1997), and an increase in various forms of non-standard employment. According to Dex and McCulloch (1997: 173), at least one quarter of British men and one half of British women held non-standard jobs by 1994 (see also Purcell, this volume). The increase in the incidence of these forms of employment, moreover, is due primarily to changes in patterns of labour use by employers, with changes in industrial or occupational structure playing a much less significant role (Casey *et al.* 1997: 35).

- The extent to which non-standard jobs are more 'insecure' than full-time permanent employment is a matter of debate, though Dex and McCulloch (1997: 35), on the basis of Labour Force Survey data, note that 'all of the non-standard types of employment, with the exception of the self-employed with employees, [have] considerably higher proportions with short tenure than [is] the case for full-time permanent jobs'. Temporary employment is the non-standard form which is most obviously insecure and, after a long period of stability, has grown from 4.5 to 6.5 per cent of total employment since 1991, a change which is registered across all sectors apart from distribution (Robinson, this volume; see also Casey *et al.* 1997: 34). Another indicator of recent change is the emergence of zero-hours contracts; a new form, the incidence of which is as yet unmeasured (Dex and McCulloch 1997: 26).[6]

- Within organisations, there is evidence of a growth in the use of performance management and performance pay systems which arguably reinforce other trends in the structure of jobs (Beatson 1995: 74–7; Morgan *et al.* this volume). These management systems are intended to impose risk on individual employees in order to elicit higher performance and seek to make future earnings contingent while introducing a more exacting scrutiny of employee behaviour.

- Changes in the structure of jobs over the past two decades have occurred against a background of continual high unemployment and have partly been caused through the impact of two severe recessions. This context means that the penalties for involuntary job loss have risen and there is evidence that redundancy increases the likelihood of unemployment, occupational downgrading and inferior terms and conditions of employment (Turnbull and Wass, this volume; see also Gallie *et al.* 1998: 146–51). According to Gregg *et al.* (this volume), the penalty for job loss is particularly severe for older workers and the less educated.

- Other contextual changes have also compounded rising job instability: first, a series of welfare changes in the 1980s cut financial support to the unemployed and reduced 'replacement ratios' (the ratio of income while out of work to income whilst in work) for most groups in the labour market (Mayhew 1991: 4); secondly, changes to employment legislation have reduced the percentage of the workforce who possess rights in the areas of redundancy and dismissal and, though a recent House of Lords judgment has improved the position of part-time workers, Smith (1997: 18; see also Gallie *et al.* 1998: 169) estimates that 74 per cent of full-timers and 57 per cent of part-timers were covered by protective legislation in 1995, compared with 94 per cent and 77 per cent in 1975; thirdly, the withdrawal of trade unionism and collective bargaining from much of the UK economy has further weakened protective regulation and, where unions are absent, there tends to be shorter job tenure, increased risk of dismissal and compulsory redundancy and greater likelihood that pay will be set unilaterally by management on the basis of an assessment of individual performance (Millward *et al.* 1992: 363–4).

- While not all research indicates a growth in employee concern over job insecurity (Felstead *et al.* 1998), a number of longitudinal studies do demonstrate such an increase. Details of some are provided by the OECD (1997) and indicate that between 1992 and 1996, a period of economic recovery, the percentage of British workers not worried about the future of their company dropped from 52 to 47 per cent, while the percentage reporting satisfaction with their job security fell from 52 to 43 per cent. Between 1985 and 1995, moreover, British workers registered the sharpest decline of confidence in employment security in Europe.

- Another source which indicates rising employee perceptions of insecurity is the regular *British Social Attitudes* survey. The most recent report concludes that, while perceptions of insecurity increase when unemployment is high, there has been an underlying upward trend since the early 1980s (Bryson and McKay 1997: 27–8). The authors note, moreover, that concern over insecurity is associated with lower levels of commitment to work in general and to the current employer. *British Social Attitudes* also demonstrates a large increase since 1989 in the percentage of workers in unionised establishment who believe that unions should make a priority of job protection (Bryson and McKay 1997: 37; Hedges 1994: 48).

- A heightened perception of insecurity is particularly apparent amongst those in higher-paid occupations (Felstead *et al.* 1998: 183), and cross-sectional evidence for the 1990s indicates that professional and managerial employees are only slightly less likely than those in other occupational classes to express dissatisfaction with job security (Gallie *et al.* 1998: 142). The relative risk of unemployment for professional and managerial workers has not increased over time, but there has been an absolute increase since the early 1980s and this probably accounts for the upward trend in the attitude data. According to Gallie *et al.* (1998: 143), 'It is the fact that, in their everyday experience, professional and managerial employees were more likely to meet unemployed people from their own background, or to hear about them, that would affect their view of whether their jobs were secure in times of organisational change.'

- The changes described above are discernible across the economy, but the emergence of a more insecure workforce has been particularly apparent in certain industries. Examples include: the end of formal tenure and an increase in fixed-term contract, casual and agency employment in higher education (Husbands 1998; Keep and Sisson 1992; Morgan *et al.*, this volume); the growth of freelancing in publishing and television (Saundry 1998; Stanworth and Stanworth 1997); extensive redundancies and the implementation of new performance management systems in banking (Storey 1995); the increase in 'precarious employment' across local and central government services as a result of market testing and competitive tendering (Horton 1996; Morgan *et al.*, this volume; White and Hutchinson 1996); and the restructuring of privatised utilities with associated redundancies and an increase in outsourcing and the use of agency labour (Colling and Ferner 1995; O'Connell Davidson 1990).

In a review of Cappelli *et al.*'s *Change at Work*, Godard (1998) cautions against exaggeration and suggests that the evidence for growing insecurity in the USA is more fragile than the authors admit. Nevertheless, he accepts that their grim vision of economic restructuring at the expense of American workers is broadly accurate and should excite concern. The evidence presented above supports a similar judgement; that caution should be exercised but concern expressed. On a range of indicators there is evidence of greater worker insecurity in Britain, and this trend forms part of a wider current of change within employment which, as in the USA, has embraced greater inequality (Goodman *et al.* 1997) and the intensification of work (Edwards and Whitston 1993; Gallie 1996; Gallie *et al.* 1998).[7] One need not subscribe to the full-blown insecurity thesis to accept that the dismantling of the postwar system of employment relations is underway and that this is creating a rather bleak and less secure future for many British workers.[8]

The key line of division between adherents of the insecurity thesis and advocates of labour market flexibility concerns the effects of job insecurity, with one side regarding these as beneficial and the other as adverse. Adherents, particularly in their more speculative moments, have identified a long list of negative consequences which extend well beyond the employment relationship, but at the heart of most discussion is the claim that reduced security can generate perverse effects within the firm. One way of examining this issue is to see whether *high* levels of job security are associated with favourable outcomes within organisations, and a cursory review of evidence indicates that they are. Case study research on the introduction of quality management suggests that job security can provide the basis for employee acceptance of programmes (Edwards *et al.* 1998), other studies of workplace innovation indicate the same (Kochan and Osterman 1994: 101–3) and there is evidence of companies basing business strategies of product differentiation and quality enhancement on policies of worker retention, even in sectors like contract catering (Rees and Fielder 1992). According to US case study research by Brown *et al.* (1993), employment security is one of three elements (the other two being employee involvement and extensive training) which are mutually supporting and which can engender the emergence of a 'high performance work system'. Survey findings point in the same direction and some of the recent research on human resource management and business performance establishes a link between employment security and a variety of measures of business success (Delery and Doty 1996; Dyer and Reeves 1995). On the basis of this kind of evidence a wide range of writers on contemporary management have suggested that the trust and commitment required for high performance work systems require employment security (Appelbaum and Blatt 1994; Pfeffer 1994; Whitfield and Poole 1997).

Another way of examining the issue is to establish whether reductions in security elicit negative responses from employees, and again there is supporting evidence. Perceptions of insecurity are associated with lower levels of job involvement (Gallie *et al.* 1998: 232) and studies of downsizing and redundancy suggest that not only is it traumatic and costly for those who lose their jobs, but that it can erode the commitment, morale and flexibility of those who remain

(Kinnie *et al.* 1998; Nolan *et al.*, this volume; Thornhill and Saunders 1998). Attempts to compensate for reduced security through promises of 'employability', moreover, can rebound and are likely to be regarded sceptically by employees unless they are backed up with real investment by managers in the development of portable skills (Ebadan and Winstanley 1997; Martin *et al.* 1998).

There is also evidence that reliance on contingent contracts can prove problematic. Husbands (1998) has identified what he describes as a 'Malvolio complex' amongst part-time teaching auxiliaries in higher education: a decline in performance over time as measured by student ratings which is explained by 'a psychological response of lower commitment, lesser morale and greater alienation and a reluctance to over-exert when both long-term and short-term rewards for doing so are niggardly . . .' In similar vein, Saundry (1998) and Saundry and Turnbull (1996) report that the recent rapid growth of casual and freelance labour in port transport and television has been associated with a range of performance and quality problems and that at least some companies in both sectors have begun to return to more stable patterns of employment. In television, moreover, Saundry (1998) stresses that casualisation has damaged skill formation and across the economy it is clear that 'men and women in flexible jobs, but especially women' (Dex and McCulloch 1997: 77) are less likely to receive training than those who are permanent and full-time.

These findings are only indicative, and clearly it would be inaccurate to claim that all effects of job reduction are negative, or that non-standard forms of employment are invariably inferior in terms of the work behaviour and attitudes they elicit from employees (Benson 1998; Gallie *et al.* 1998: 245). Where job loss is effectively managed, where contingent work is preferred by employees and is adequately compensated, and where mechanisms of skill formation exist beyond the individual company, then the disadvantages listed above might be avoided (Crouch 1997: 376). Despite these qualifications, however, we feel there is sufficient evidence, once again, to justify concern and to support the view that an insecure workforce may be neither content nor optimally effective. An extreme statement of the thesis may not be warranted, but it seems that greater insecurity is likely to reinforce low-trust relations in the workplace (Bryson and McKay 1997) and to confirm the already pronounced bias towards cost reduction as the main route to competitive advantage within British business.

The core proposition for those who regard insecurity as an acceptable cost is that worried workers produce less wage inflation. In both Britain and the USA the emergence of insecurity as a labour market theme has been associated with a dampening of inflationary pressure. In Britain at least, however, the 'age of insecurity' has not witnessed a complete resolution of the inflation problem. In the summer of 1998 pay settlements in large companies were in the range of 4 to 4.5 per cent and private sector earnings were rising at an annual rate of 6.2 per cent, when the tax and price index – which measures the increase in gross wages needed to maintain purchasing power after allowing for changes in prices and taxes – stood at 3.8 per cent (*IDS Report* 767, August 1998; *Pay and Benefits Bulletin* 454, August 1998). Concern over wage inflation has elicited the typical deflationary response from the Monetary Committee of the Bank of England in the form of higher interest rates. Notwithstanding greater labour market flexibility, therefore, the UK economy appears still to be inflation-prone and in certain respects the changes which have generated worker insecurity may also have generated inflationary pressure. Saundry's (1998) review of developments in television, for instance, points to the tightening of labour markets as the externalisation of labour supply has reduced investment in training and to upward pressure on costs as those with scarce talent have used the opportunity afforded by the new freelancing regime to maximise their returns. Making workers more insecure, therefore, may not prove a particularly effective way of controlling wage inflation, and to this objection can be added the ethical question of whether it is right to manage the economy through the erosion of employment conditions backed up by recurrent bouts of deflation. In other European states there has been a seemingly effective resurrection of bargained corporatism in recent years (Visser 1998) and we would suggest that an attempt to develop a more coordinated system of wage determination in Britain is a more attractive, and probably more effective, means of managing inflation in the longer term.

Conclusion

While the impact on company and economic performance has emerged as an important theme in the debate over the insecurity thesis, the prime attraction of insecurity as a focus for academic research is that it places the experiences of employees centre stage. Increasingly over the past two decades, academic work on employment has been driven by an employers' agenda, most notably in research on the question of 'flexibility' and the extent to which both the supply and use of labour have become more flexible as a result of trade union decline and labour market reform (Godard 1998; Kelly 1998: 17–18; Legge 1998: 291–4). The issue of insecurity, in contrast, presents a different starting point and necessarily raises the questions of how employee interests at work should be defined and analysed, and how current change within the workplace is affecting those interests. Moreover, to the extent that it is allied to policy prescription, it places the raising of worker utility at the centre and has generated a series of proposals for reversing or mitigating changes which have adverse effects on employees. Like any bold proposition in the social sciences, the insecurity thesis will inevitably be subject to qualification and even rebuttal but, to the extent to which it swings the focus of attention away from the needs of employers and towards a greater engagement with the interests of employees, the debate over insecurity will prove worthwhile.

Notes

1 Perversity arguments have long been the stock-in-trade of conservative intellectuals faced with progressive reforms of which they disapprove, and claim essentially that any attempt at social amelioration will rebound against the very interests which well-meaning reformers are trying to promote (Hirschman 1991). As the right has become an

agent of radical reform itself, however, its favourite style of argument has been adopted by the left, which now routinely argues that attempts to liberate capitalism from 'excessive' regulation will damage capitalist interests in the longer term.

2 According to Gray (1995: 98–9), '[e]ndless "downsizing" and "flattening" of enterprises fosters ubiquitous insecurity and makes loyalty to the company a cruel joke'.

3 An example of the potential tension between insecurity and quality was provided by one of our partners, Janet Heery, whose supermarket clubcard statement started to arrive suddenly under the name of Janet Hairy. On ringing up to get the mistake rectified she was informed, with surprising candour, that the service had been outsourced and the response of those made redundant had been to indulge in a little farewell sabotage.

4 Indeed, this may be a reason for the use of non-standard contracts in the first place as employers use this type of labour in order to avoid both protective legislation and payroll taxes (Cappelli *et al.* 1997: 24–6). The relatively limited use of temporary labour in Britain, compared with several other European Union countries, is sometimes attributed to the generally low level of employment protection, which reduces the incentive for employers to use non-standard forms (Dex and McCulloch 1997: 9).

5 In an otherwise sceptical response to the insecurity thesis, Spencer (1996: 85) notes that indices of employee and consumer confidence tend to change in tandem over time and that the recovery of consumer confidence was delayed after the recession of the early 1990s in a manner that was not apparent after the recession of the early 1980s.

6 According to Allen and Henry (1996, 1997), a related change is the spread of 'precarious' employment. They mean by this an increase of jobs in subcontracting firms, which may be permanent and full-time, but which are subject to repeated episodes of competitive tendering. The latter can lead to job loss, but more typically result in the review of terms and conditions and generate uncertainty about the future employment relationship.

7 In making this observation we do not want to suggest that there is a uniform trend towards 'employment degradation' (Legge 1998). Gallie (1996; see also Cappelli *et al.* 1997), for example, stresses the ambivalence of recent change when viewed from the perspective of employees and that intensification of work has been accompanied by rising skill levels and greater autonomy, particularly for men and full-time workers.

8 A further issue which has divided adherents and sceptics is the relationship between 'objective' and 'subjective' measures of insecurity. Sceptics have either tended to play down the importance of attitudinal measures of insecurity, claiming that they are media-created, or else point to the fact that 'objectively' insecure employees often do not perceive their situation in these terms, while employees with high job tenure often report the highest levels of insecurity (Robinson, this volume). Guest (this volume) has suggested that the lower sense of felt insecurity amongst younger workers and those who have been mobile in the labour market might reflect adaptation and an adjustment of worker expectations to a changed situation. Adherents, in contrast, both expect and have tried to establish correlation between 'objective' and 'subjective' measures (Turnbull and Wass, this volume). It can be noted, in this regard, that older workers who lose their jobs are likely to pay a higher penalty and that international comparisons of worker feelings of insecurity indicate a link with other aspects of the labour market context: reports of insecurity are highest in countries like the USA and Britain, where the unemployment benefit replacement rate, the level of union membership and coverage by collective bargaining are low (OECD 1997: 149–50). The latter associations suggest that feelings of insecurity are strongest where the employment system accentuates employee dependence on the employer.

References

Allen, J. and Henry, N. (1996) 'Fragments of industry and employment: contract service work and the shift towards precarious employment', in R. Crompton, D. Gallie and K. Purcell (eds) *Changing Forms of Employment: Organisations, Skills and Gender*, London: Routledge.

—— (1997) 'Ulrich Beck's *Risk Society* at work: labour and employment in the contract service industries', *Transactions of the Institute of British Geographers*, New Series, 22, 2: 180–96.

Appelbaum. E. (1989) 'The growth in the US contingent labour force', in R. Drago and R. Perlman (eds) *Macroeconomic Issues in Labor Economics: A New Approach*, New York: Harvester Wheatsheaf.

Appelbaum, E. and Blatt, R. (1994) *The New American Workplace*, Ithaca, NY: ILR Press.

Barker, K. and Christensen, K. (1998) *Contingent Work: American Employment Relations in Transition*, Ithaca, NY: Cornell University Press.

Beatson, M. (1995) *Labour Market Flexibility*, London: Employment Department.

Beck, U. (1992) *Risk Society: Towards a New Modernity*, London: Sage.

Benson, J. (1998) 'Dual commitment: contract workers in Australian manufacturing enterprises', *Journal of Management Studies*, 35, 3: 355–75.

Beynon, H. (1997) 'The changing practices of work', in R.K. Brown (ed.) *The Changing Shape of Work*, Basingstoke: Macmillan.

Bootle, R. (1996) *The Death of Inflation*, London: Nicholas Brealey.

Broadbent J., Dietrich, M. and Roberts, J. (1998) 'The end of the professions?', in J. Broadbent, M. Dietrich and J. Roberts (eds) *The End of the Professions? The Restructuring of Professional Work*, London: Routledge.

Brown, C., Reich, M. and Stern, D. (1993) 'Becoming a high-performance work organisation: the role of security, employee involvement and training', *International Journal of Human Resource Management*, 4, 2: 247–75.

Brown, R.K. (1997) 'Flexibility and security: contradictions in the contemporary labour market', in R.K. Brown (ed.) *The Changing Shape of Work*, Basingstoke: Macmillan.

Bryson, A. and McKay, S. (1997) 'What about the workers?', in R. Jowell, J. Curtice, A. Park, L. Brook, K. Thomson and C. Bryson (eds) *British Social Attitudes: The 14th Report*, Aldershot: Ashgate.

Burgess, S. and Rees, H. (1996) 'Job tenure in Britain 1975–92', *The Economic Journal*, 106: 334–44.

Cappelli, P. (1995) 'Rethinking employment', *British Journal of Industrial Relations*, 33, 4: 563–602.

Cappelli, P., Bassi, L., Katz, H., Knoke, D., Osterman, P. and Useem, M. (1997) *Change at Work*, New York: Oxford University Press.

Casey, B., Metcalf, H. and Millward, N. (1997) *Employers' Use of Flexible Labour*, London: Policy Studies Institute.

Colling, T. and Ferner, A. (1995) 'Privatization and marketization', in P. Edwards (ed.) *Industrial Relations: Theory and Practice in Britain*, Oxford: Blackwell.

Crompton, R., Gallie, D. and Purcell, K. (1996) 'Work, economic restructuring and social regulation', in R. Crompton, D. Gallie and K. Purcell (eds) *Changing Forms of Employment: Organisations, Skills and Gender*, London: Routledge.

Crouch, C. (1997) 'Skill-based full employment: the latest philosopher's stone', *British Journal of Industrial Relations*, 35, 3: 367–84.

Cully, M. and Woodland, S. (1998) 'Trade union membership and recognition 1996–97: an analysis of data from the Certification Officer and the LFS', *Labour Market Trends*, July, 353–62.

Delery, J.E. and Doty, D.H. (1996) 'Modes of theorising and strategic human resource management: tests of universalistic, contingent and configurational performance predictions', *Academy of Management Journal*, 39, 4: 802–35.

Dex, S. and McCulloch, A. (1997) *Flexible Employment*, Basingstoke: Macmillan.

Dore, R. (1997) 'Good jobs, bad jobs and no jobs', *Industrial Relations Journal*, 28, 4: 262–8.

DTI (1998) *Fairness at Work*, London: Department of Trade and Industry.

Dyer, L. and Reeves, T. (1995) 'Human resource strategies and firm performance: what do we know and where do we need to go?', *International Journal of Human Resource Management*, 6, 3: 656–70.

Ebadan, G. and Winstanley, D. (1997) 'Downsizing, delayering and careers – the survivors' perspective', *Human Resource Management Journal*, 7, 1: 79–91.

Edwards, P. and Whitston, C. (1993) *Attending to Work: The Management of Attendance and Shopfloor Order*, Oxford: Blackwell.

Edwards, P., Collinson, M. and Rees, C. (1998) 'The determinants of employee responses to total quality management: six case studies', *Organisation Studies*, 19, 3: 449–75.

Elliott, L. and Atkinson, D. (1998) *The Age of Insecurity*, London: Verso.

Engberg, E. (1993) 'Union responses to the contingent work force', in D.S. Cobble (ed.) *Women and Unions: Forging a Partnership*, Ithaca, NY: ILR Press.

Fabian Society (1996) *Changing Work*, London: The Fabian Society.

Farber, H. (1993) 'The incidence and cost of job loss 1982–91', *Brookings Papers on Economic Activity: Microeconomics*: 73–132.

Felstead, A., Burchell, B. and Green, F. (1998) 'Insecurity at work: is job insecurity really much worse now than before?', *New Economy*, 5: 180–4.

Fredman, S. (1997) 'Labour law in flux: the changing composition of the workforce', *Industrial Law Journal*, 26, 4: 337–52.

Gallie, D. (1996) 'Skill, gender and the quality of employment', in R. Crompton, D. Gallie and K. Purcell (eds) *Changing Forms of Employment*, London: Routledge.

Gallie, D., White, M., Cheng, Y. and Tomlinson, M. (1998) *Restructuring the Employment Relationship*, Oxford: Oxford University Press.

Godard, J. (1998) 'Review of *Change at Work* by P. Cappelli, L. Bassi, H. Katz, D. Knoke, P. Osterman and M. Useem', *British Journal of Industrial Relations*, 36, 3: 501–3.

Goodman, A., Johnson, P. and Webb, S. (1997) *Inequality in the UK*, Oxford: Oxford University Press.

Gray, J. (1995) 'The undoing of conservatism' in J. Gray *Enlightenment's Wake: Politics and Culture at the End of the Modern Age*, London: Routledge.

——— (1996) 'Testing market for the middle classes', *The Guardian* 17 April.

Guest, D. (1997) 'Towards jobs and justice in Europe: a research agenda', *Industrial Relations Journal*, 28, 4: 344–52.

Hedges, B. (1994) 'Work in a changing climate', in R. Jowell, J. Custice, L. Brook and D. Ahrendt (eds) *British Social Attitudes: the 11th Report*, Aldershot: Dartmouth.

Heery, E. (1996) 'Risk, representation and the new pay', *Personnel Review*, 25, 6: 54–65.

Hendry, C. and Jenkins, R. (1997) 'Psychological contracts and new deals', *Human Resource Management Journal*, 7, 1: 38–44.

Herriot, P. and Pemberton, C. (1997) 'Facilitating new deals', *Human Resource Management Journal*, 7, 1: 45–56.

Hirschman, A.O. (1991) *The Rhetorics of Reaction: Perversity, Futility, Jeopardy*, Cambridge, MA: Harvard University Press.

Horton, S. (1996) 'The civil service', in D. Farnham and S. Horton (eds) *Managing People in the Public Services*, Basingstoke: Macmillan.

Husbands, C. (1998) 'Job flexibility and variations in performance and motivations of longer-term part-time teaching auxiliaries in the London School of Economics and Political Science', *Work, Employment and Society*, 12, 1: 121–44.

Hutton, W. (1995) *The State We're In*, London: Jonathan Cape.

IER (1996) *The Guide to Working Life: A New Perspective on Labour Law*, London: The Institute of Employment Rights.

IPD (1996) *Statement on Employment Relations*, London: Institute of Personnel and Development.

Keep, E. and Sisson, K. (1992) 'Owning the problem: personnel issues in higher education policy-making in the 1990s', *Oxford Review of Economic Policy*, 8, 2: 67–78.

Kelly, J. (1997) 'Industrial relations: looking to the future', *British Journal of Industrial Relations*, 35, 3: 393–8.

—— (1998) *Rethinking Industrial Relations: Mobilization, Collectivism and Long Waves*, London: Routledge.

Kessler, S. and Bayliss, F. (1995) *Contemporary British Industrial Relations*, second edition, Basingstoke: Macmillan.

Kinnie, N., Hutchinson, S. and Purcell, J. (1998) 'Downsizing: is it always lean and mean?', *Personnel Review*, 27, 4: 296–311.

Kochan, T. and Osterman, P. (1994) *The Mutual Gains Enterprise: Forging a Winning Partnership among Labor, Management and Government*, Cambridge, MA: Harvard Business School Press.

Lane, C. (1990) 'Vocational training, employment training and new production concepts: some lessons for Britain', *Industrial Relations Journal*, 21, 4: 247–59.

Legge, K. (1998) 'Flexibility: the gift-wrapping of employment degradation', in P. Sparrow and M. Marchington (eds) *Human Resource Management: The New Agenda*, London: Pitman Publishing.

Leisink, P. (1997) 'New union constituencies call for differentiated agendas and democratic participation', *Transfer*, 3: 534–50.

Luttwak, E. (1994) 'Why fascism is the wave of the future', *London Review of Books*, 7 April: 3, 6.

Martin, G., Staines, H. and Pate, J. (1998) 'Linking job security and career development in a new psychological contract', *Human Resource Management Journal*, 8, 3: 20–40.

Mayhew, K. (1991) 'The assessment: the UK labour market in the 1980s', *Oxford Review of Economic Policy*, 7, 1: 1–17.

Millward, N., Stevens, M., Smart, D. and Hawes, W.R. (1992) *Workplace Industrial Relations in Transition*, Aldershot: Dartmouth.

Milner, S. (1995) 'The coverage of collective pay-setting institutions in Britain, 1895–1990', *British Journal of Industrial Relations*, 33, 1: 69–92.

Morgan, J. (1998) 'Making jobs more secure', *New Economy*, 5, 1: 44–8.

NACAB (1990) *Hard Labour*, London: National Association of Citizens' Advice Bureaux.

—— (1993) *Job Insecurity*, London: National Association of Citizens' Advice Bureaux.

—— (1997) *Flexibility Abused*, London: National Association of Citizens' Advice Bureaux.

O'Connell Davidson, J. (1990) 'The commercialization of employment relations: the case of the water industry', *Work, Employment and Society*, 4, 4: 531–49.

OECD (1997) *Employment Outlook*, Paris: Organisation for Economic Cooperation and Development.

Pfeffer, J. (1994) *Competitive Advantage through People*, Boston, MA: Harvard Business School Press.

Rainnie, A. (1998) 'The inevitability of flexibility?', *Work, Employment and Society*, 12, 1: 161–7.

Rees, G. and Fielder, S. (1992) 'The services economy, sub-contracting and new employment relations: contract catering and cleaning', *Work, Employment and Society*, 6, 3: 347–68.

Rubery, J. (1996) 'The labour market outlook and the outlook for labour market analysis', in R. Crompton, D. Gallie and K. Purcell (eds) *Changing Forms of Employment: Organisations, Skills and Gender*, London: Routledge.

Saundry, R. (1998) 'The limits of flexibility: the case of UK television?', *British Journal of Management*, 9, 1: 151–62.

Saundry, R. and Turnbull, P. (1996) 'Mêlée on the Mersey: contracts, competition and labour relations on the docks', *Industrial Relations Journal*. 27, 4: 275–88.

Sisson, K. (1995) 'Change and continuity in British industrial relations: "strategic choice" or "muddling through" ', in R. Locke, T. Kochan and M. Piore (eds) *Employment Relations in a Changing World Economy*, Cambridge, MA: The MIT Press.

Smith, D. (1997) *Job Insecurity vs Labour Market Flexibility*, London: The Social Market Foundation.

Spencer, P. (1996) 'Reactions to a flexible labour market', in R. Jowell, J. Curtice, A. Park, L. Brook and K. Thomson (eds) *British Social Attitudes: the 13th Report*, Aldershot: Dartmouth.

Standing, G. (1997) 'Globalization, labour flexibility and insecurity: the era of market regulation', *European Journal of Industrial Relations*, 3, 1: 7–37.

Stanworth, C. and Stanworth, J. (1997) 'Managing an externalised workforce: freelance labour-use in the UK', *Industrial Relations Journal*, 28, 1: 43–55.

Storey, J. (1995) 'Employment policies in the UK clearing banks: an overview', *Human Resource Management Journal*, 5, 4: 24–43.

Streeck, W. (1989) 'Skills and the limits of neo-liberalism: the enterprise of the future as a place of learning', *Work, Employment and Society*, 3, 1: 89–104.

Thornhill, A. and Saunders, M. (1998) 'The meanings, consequences and implications of the management of downsizing and redundancy: a review', *Personnel Review*, 27, 4: 271–95.

TUC (1996) *All in the Mind? Job Insecurity in Britain Today*, London: Trades Union Congress.

Valkenburg, B. and Beukema, L. (1996) 'The organisation of flexibility: atypical jobs as a challenge for the modernization of trade unions', *Transfer*, 4: 738–54.

Visser, J. (1998) 'Two cheers for corporatism, one for the market: industrial relations, wage moderation and job growth in the Netherlands', *British Journal of Industrial Relations*, 36, 2: 269–92.

Voos, P. B. (1997) 'Discussion', *British Journal of Industrial Relations*, 35, 3: 332–6.

Walsh, J. (1993) 'Internalization v. decentralization: an analysis of recent developments in pay bargaining', *British Journal of Industrial Relations*, 31, 3: 409–32.

Warren, R. C. (1996) 'The empty company: morality and job security', *Personnel Review*, 25, 6: 41–53.

Wever, K. (1998) 'International labor revitalization: enlarging the playing field', *Industrial Relations*, 37, 3: 388–407.

White, G. and Hutchinson, B. (1996) 'Local government', in D. Farnham and S. Horton (eds) *Managing People in the Public Services*, Basingstoke: Macmillan.

Whitfield, K. and Poole, M. (1997) 'Organising employment for high performance: theories, evidence and policy', *Organisation Studies*, 18, 5: 745–64.

Wickham, J. (1997) 'Part-time work in Ireland and Europe', *Work, Employment and Society*, 11, 1: 133–51.

Acknowledgements

Thanks to Philip Morgan, Paul Stewart, Peter Turnbull and Victoria Wass for helpful comments on an earlier draft and to Keith Whitfield and Kim Hoque for help with references.

2 Insecurity and the flexible workforce

Measuring the ill-defined

Peter Robinson

Introduction

There was a strong perception that the UK workforce in the mid-1990s was feeling especially 'insecure'. It was believed that 'jobs for life' were a thing of the past. It was also believed that the UK had experienced especially rapid growth in 'non-standard' or 'flexible' forms of work, such as part-time, temporary and self-employment. It has been suggested that these developments may have contributed to the electoral defeat of the incumbent Conservative Government in 1997.

The aim of this chapter is to try and clarify what is meant by the use of such terms as 'insecurity' and 'flexibility'. It looks at some of the empirical evidence which relates to whether and why the workforce felt more insecure in the mid-1990s. This includes evidence with respect to trends in 'flexible' or 'non-standard' forms of employment. By looking at some comparative data it also seeks to test the common perception that 'insecurity' or 'flexibility' are especially prevalent in relatively deregulated Anglo-Saxon labour markets. The chapter mixes and matches material from such sources as the Labour Force Survey with the results from surveys of the attitudes of the workforce.

Such terms as 'workforce insecurity' and 'labour market flexibility' are widely used in the public policy debate, but often without the terms being clearly defined. 'Insecurity' can mean many things. It could refer to the fear of becoming unemployed and/or to the difficulty of finding a new position following job loss. It could also reflect concerns about blocked promotion or pay prospects, or a lack of control over what goes on in the workplace.

The term 'flexibility' is often used in the context of the growth in different forms of 'non-standard' employment, but it is also used in a number of other ways. For example, reference is often made to relative or aggregate wage flexibility in the external labour market. Reference is also made to 'functional' flexibility, that is the ability to redeploy labour within firms. Without clear definitions of the terms being used, the debate can become diffuse and confused.

Given the wide range of topics which could be covered under the headings of workforce insecurity or labour market flexibility, this chapter concentrates on two core issues. First, by looking at the likelihood of, and the costs of, job loss, and changes in employment regulation, it tries to assess the evidence as to why the workforce might feel significantly more insecure in the mid-1990s, when compared with some earlier point in time. Secondly, defining the flexible workforce as people not employed as full-time permanent employees, the chapter looks at trends in the employment structure in the UK. For both of these topics, comparisons are made between the UK and other OECD countries.

Evidence on workforce insecurity

Many researchers have a shared framework for looking at the issue of workforce insecurity. They also have shared sources of data. However, different interpretations can be drawn from these data. The shared framework focuses on three questions:

1   Is there evidence to suggest that workers face a higher risk of redundancy and unemployment, or that there is more churning going on in the labour market?
2   For people who do lose their jobs, are the costs of job loss higher than in the past, with the unemployed facing a harsher benefits regime, or having a lower probability of finding a new job, or with replacement jobs being of declining quality?
3   What impact have changes in the legislative and institutional framework had on workforce insecurity?

One of the most difficult problems in any analysis is to find the right reference point for comparison with the mid-1990s. A statement to the effect that 'the workforce is feeling more insecure' implies that this is held to be true when compared with some date in the recent past. When compared with the 'golden age' of full employment before 1973–4, it seems obvious why there might be more insecurity in the 1990s. However, when comparing the mid-1990s with the mid-1980s, it is less obvious.

One might think that the level of unemployment would be the most important determinant of the level of workforce insecurity. However, unemployment (as measured by either the claimant count or the Labour Force Survey) was clearly much lower over the period 1994–7 when compared with the period 1984–7. Yet in 1987 a Conservative Government won a secure majority, while in 1997 they were heavily defeated.

In fact it is by no means obvious that the workforce *was* feeling more insecure in 1997 than in the mid-1980s. Felstead *et al.* (1998) reported the results of a comparison of the answers of samples of employees to identical questions on two surveys carried out in 1986 and 1997. They showed that in aggregate, *job* insecurity, defined as the likelihood of losing your job or becoming unemployed in the next 12 months, had not risen significantly between these two dates. When combined with a second measure which looked at the ease with which someone who had been displaced could obtain another job as good as the current one, what the authors defined as *employment* insecurity had actually fallen significantly between

1986 and 1997. This seems to contrast with other findings using, for example, the British Household Panel Survey, which suggested a significant decline in the proportion of employees satisfied with their job security over the period 1992–6 (OECD 1997).

This last paragraph has already hinted at one of the problems in this debate. Comparisons across time are frequently limited by the availability of data. However, it is also the case that the choice of reference point can lead to different conclusions, which in itself counsels caution about how far the evidence can support the thesis that the workforce feels more insecure.

Insecurity and job tenure: an imperfect proxy

One of the main proxies which has been used to 'measure' the extent of workforce insecurity is the length of time people have been in their jobs. Short tenure is assumed to equate with insecurity, while a lengthy sojourn in a job is seen to signal greater security. Unfortunately, it is not clear that job tenure is a good proxy.

The major difficulty in assessing what job tenure data can tell us is that it reflects the impact of both quits and redundancies. Quits are more common during upturns in the labour market. Redundancies are obviously more common during recessions. Because there are always more people quitting their job than being made redundant, there is *more* turnover in the labour market during upturns than during recessions. So we observe that aggregate job tenure lengthens in recessions and falls during recoveries. In order to understand whether job tenure might be in secular decline, we need to compare two years which represent similar points in the economic cycle.

Data on tenure are discussed in more detail by Gregg *et al.* in this volume, using the Labour Force Survey. They show that over the period between 1975 and 1984 there was a decline in median job tenure for men. Although the absence of data prevents us from being certain, this most probably occurred in the early 1980s, and was associated with the traumatic haemorrhage of jobs from manufacturing at this time. However, if we compare the labour market in the mid-1990s with a similar point in the mid-1980s, the trends are less clear. Median job tenure has risen for women, though this is confined largely to women with dependent children who appear to be making more frequent use of maternity rights to maintain continuity of employment during periods of family formation.

A judgement about what has happened to male tenure is more dependent on the choice of years for comparison. A comparison of 1985 and 1995 would tend to suggest a modest fall in average tenure for men; a comparison of 1994 with 1987 (when male unemployment rates were very similar, at just over 11 per cent and falling modestly) would suggest a modest rise in average tenure. However, these aggregate changes may hide the trends for different age groups. There is clear evidence that average job tenure for older men, and indeed older women, continued to decline after 1984 and this finding is not sensitive to the choice of years for comparison.

The different trends for men and women throw an interesting light on the public debate. When people talk about the 'end of jobs for life', they appear to have in mind a golden age in the 1950s and 1960s when it seemed that many men had access to jobs with long tenure. However, women generally never had access to such lifetime employment and it would even be an exaggeration to say that more than a minority of men really had lifetime jobs, in the sense that the jobs they entered soon after leaving full-time education were the jobs they remained in for the rest of their lives. Most individuals today do not have access to lifetime jobs, but then most individuals never had access to lifetime jobs even during the 'golden' age of full employment.

There are major problems in using job tenure to proxy job insecurity. Felstead *et al.* (1998) found that job insecurity was higher amongst workers with shorter job tenure of less than two years, but was also quite high amongst workers with very long job tenure of over twenty years. International survey data in the mid-1990s seemed to suggest that job insecurity was especially pronounced in the UK, the USA and Japan, itself a puzzle as these countries had relatively low and/or declining unemployment rates (OECD 1997). However, there was no significant correlation between measures of job tenure across countries and perceptions of job insecurity. So Japan, for example, with its relatively high average job tenure (and low unemployment), nevertheless appeared to have an especially worried workforce.

The likelihood of job loss – the chances of experiencing unemployment

Given that most job moves are voluntary, that is they reflect quits, interpreting data on job tenure to throw light on insecurity is always going to be problematic. Of more direct relevance might be data on the likelihood of becoming unemployed (see Table 2.1). Consistent evidence here only goes back to the mid-1980s, and clearly shows that the proportion of the working age population experiencing at least one spell of claimant unemployment was no different in the early to mid-1990s from the mid- to late 1980s. Over time a fairly constant proportion of just over a quarter of the working age population had experienced claimant unemployment over any given five-year period. These data from claimant records are supported by data from the British Household Panel Survey, which show that between 1991 and 1994, 71 per cent of all men were in continuous employment, while 29 per cent experienced at least one spell out of work (in unemployment or inactivity), with 9 per cent out of work over all four years (Gosling *et al.* 1997).

A consistent time series on redundancies is not available, but a comparison of data from the Labour Force Survey available since 1989, with the administrative series on confirmed redundancies which ran up to 1992, suggests that redundancies in 1994–6 were running at a similar rate to 1987–8 and well below levels experienced in the early 1980s.

Although the proportion of the total working age population experiencing unemployment does not appear to have increased, there is evidence that unemployment was more evenly distributed in the early to mid-1990s than was

Table 2.1 Number of people making at least one claim for unemployment-related benefits

Five year period	Millions	Percentage of working age population
1985–89	10.5	30
1986–90	10.2	29
1987–91	10.3	29
1988–92	10.3	29
1989–93	10.4	29
1990–94	10.5	29
1991–95	10.6	29
1992–96	10.4	29

Source: Teasdale (1998)

the case in the mid-1980s. The dispersion in regional unemployment rates has narrowed dramatically, with unemployment in London in the mid-1990s running at a higher rate than in Scotland. The experience of unemployment seems to have been more evenly distributed across all industries and occupations in the early 1990s, when compared with the mid-1980s.

Fortunately this portrait of a more even distribution of unemployment by the mid-1990s matches well with the survey findings reported by Felstead *et al.* (1998). They found that the fall in the overall level of employment insecurity masked significant rises in job insecurity (that is the perceived risk of becoming unemployed) for those with higher education and for non-manual and professional workers. Job insecurity had fallen for workers in manufacturing, but had risen for those in finance and construction.

The perception of greater insecurity in the labour market in the mid-1990s then could be a function of more advantaged and more articulate groups having witnessed a relatively harsher labour (and housing) market in the early 1990s, when compared with the early 1980s' recession, which was much more concentrated by region and by industry. Put bluntly, *Guardian* readers faced the kind of harsh labour market in the early 1990s which *Mirror* readers had already faced to a much greater degree in the early 1980s.

One irony here is that economists generally welcomed evidence of a more even distribution of unemployment in the mid-1990s, because it suggested fewer structural barriers to a reduction in unemployment. Indeed, the steady fall in aggregate unemployment from 1993 through to 1997 without the emergence of any significant wage inflation, could have been in part the result of a more even distribution of unemployment and fewer imbalances in the labour market, by region, by industry and occupation and by educational group.

The costs of job loss

Although the labour market in the mid-1990s is not necessarily more turbulent than it was in the mid-1980s, it is possible that the costs of job loss have risen.

Certainly, the unemployment benefits system was less generous and provided a less adequate safety net by the mid-1990s. Unemployment benefits had been linked to prices rather than earnings since 1980, so that average replacement ratios (the amount of income in work replaced by benefits when out of work) had fallen significantly. Since 1986 the Employment Service had steadily increased the pressure on the unemployed to actively search for work and to be more 'flexible' in the kinds of work they should be prepared to accept, culminating in the introduction of the Jobseeker's Allowance in 1996, which reduced the insurance element of benefit payments from twelve to six months. At the same time, people on income support now had to wait nine months before full mortgage interest payments were covered.

It is also of interest that international comparisons find a strong correlation between perceptions of workforce insecurity and the generosity of unemployment benefits (OECD 1997). Countries with less generous benefits, including the USA, the UK and Japan, have higher levels of insecurity. So a less generous safety net for those who do lose their jobs may play a significant role in explaining insecurity.

The probability of the unemployed leaving claimant unemployment did not, however, appear to change significantly when comparing the mid-1990s with the mid-1980s. The Labour Force Survey also showed that the flows out of ILO unemployment in the mid-1990s looked very similar to those observed in the 1980s (Gregg and Wadsworth 1996a). That is, the unemployed did not seem to be any less likely to find work again.

Around half of all those who leave claimant unemployment return to the claimant count within a year, which is an indication of the degree of recurrent unemployment apparent at the bottom end of the labour market. However, this proportion had not changed significantly when comparing the mid-1990s with the mid-1980s. Typically, a high proportion of people who leave unemployment find less good jobs on their immediate return to the labour market, often facing a cut in their wages of 20 per cent or more compared with their previous job (Gosling *et al.* 1997). This lost ground is often made up subsequently if the job is maintained or a better one found. However, what is not clear is whether this wage penalty associated with job loss was greater in the mid-1990s when compared with the mid-1980s.

Interestingly, the main reason why the surveys reported in Felstead *et al.* (1998) showed an overall decline in employment insecurity was because workers thought it much more likely in the labour market circumstances of 1997 that they would be able to find an acceptable alternative job if they lost their own, when compared with the labour market of 1986. In other words the perceived cost of job loss had fallen significantly between 1986 and 1997. Employment insecurity was significantly higher for workers aged over fifty and for those with over twenty years in their current job. It is these workers who have the most to lose if their current employment comes to an end.

It has been observed that a far higher proportion of the ILO unemployed enter into part-time and temporary jobs than would be suggested by the representation of those jobs in the total stock of employment. Table 2.2 shows the changing composition of the types of jobs which are entered into by people moving from ILO unemployment (and can be contrasted with Table 2.3 showing the overall stock of employment). A much higher proportion of the jobs taken by ILO unemployed people are part-time and temporary. This is the flip-side of the observation that part-time and temporary jobs last for a shorter period of time and are therefore over-represented in the flow of vacancies to which the ILO unemployed have access. The proportion of all 'entry jobs' which are for full-time permanent employees has declined since 1979, though in fact more slowly than their representation amongst the stock of all jobs (see Table 2.3). The slack has been taken up primarily by a greater proportion of the unemployed entering self-employment, with these changes occurring largely in the 1980s rather than the 1990s. The proportion of the unemployed entering part-time and temporary jobs has altered little over the period since 1988.

Changes in the legislative and institutional framework

In the period after 1979 there was only one major change in the legislative frame-work which restricted individual employment rights, that is the extension from six months to two years in the length of time an employee had to have been in continuous employment before gaining access to rights against unfair dismissal and to redundancy payments. These restrictions were in place by 1985. On the other hand, as a result of a House of Lords decision in 1995, part-timers gained access to the same employment rights as full-timers. This decision built on a continuing stream of enhancements to individual employment rights which have been the result of European Union directives and court interpretations of the Treaty of Rome. It would be wrong therefore to refer, as some authors do, to the 'vestiges' of employment protection in the UK, or to imply that 'deregulation' has led to greater workforce insecurity. In the field of individual employment rights

Table 2.2 The changing composition of jobs entered by people formally ILO unemployed

	1979	1985	1988	1994
Full-time employees	53.4	49.2	47.0	47.0
permanent		38.4	35.8	35.1
temporary		7.9	7.6	9.1
schemes		1.8	2.9	2.4
Part-time employees	41.2	40.7	43.0	40.9
permanent		26.1	26.2	26.7
temporary		10.6	10.6	8.7
schemes		3.6	5.7	5.0
Self-employed				
full-time	2.5	6.2	6.0	7.9
part-time	1.2	3.6	3.3	4.2

Sources: Labour Force Survey, spring; Gregg and Wadsworth (1996a)

Table 2.3 The changing composition of all employment, 1979–97

	Percentage of all in employment			
	1979	*1984*	*1990*	*1997*
Full-time employees	76.7	69.7	67.1	65.2
permanent		67.4	64.8	61.7
temporary		2.3	2.3	3.5
Part-time employees	16.1	18.8	19.4	22.2
permanent		16.5	17.2	19.2
temporary		2.3	2.2	3.0
Full-time self-employed	6.5	9.4	11.3	9.9
Part-time self-employed	0.7	1.9	2.1	2.6

Source: Labour Force Survey, spring

Note: Excluding those on government schemes and unpaid family workers

there was no net deregulation in the period after 1979 in Britain. Looking across countries, there appears to be no significant correlation between perceptions of job insecurity and measures of the extent of legal protection offered by employment protection legislation (OECD 1997).

Union membership and union power in the UK have been in steady decline since 1979. This may have had an impact on workers' sense of job security. The main changes in union coverage and in industrial relations legislation took place in the 1980s, rather than the 1990s, so any impact on insecurity seems to have been delayed. However, international comparisons reveal a correlation between the extent of coverage of collective bargaining and the degree of job insecurity (OECD 1997). Countries with relatively lower levels of collective bargaining coverage, including the UK by the mid-1990s, appeared to have a more insecure workforce.

In 1993 the Wages Councils were abolished, their coverage having been restricted during the 1980s. This may have increased insecurity at the lower end of the labour market in those sectors that the Councils covered. But it is unclear why the average worker would have felt any effects from the abolition of minimum wage protection. As we have already noted it appears that any increase in actual workforce insecurity when comparing the mid-1990s to the mid-1980s was confined to the highly qualified and professional workers, who of course were never covered by minimum wage regulation.

The growth of 'flexible' forms of employment

Another significant strand in the portrait of 'increased workforce insecurity' is the growth in 'non-standard' forms of employment, which are perceived to be inherently inferior and less secure than full-time, permanent jobs for employees. Felstead *et al.* (1998) found that part-timers and especially temporary employees *did* feel less secure than their full-time and permanent colleagues. On the other hand, the self-employed did *not* register higher levels of insecurity, when compared with employees. This suggests that lumping together all forms of non-standard employment may be a mistake.

The pattern of growth in the share of 'flexible' or 'non-standard' forms of employment suggests that the sharpest fall in the share of employment of full-time permanent employees took place in the early 1980s, since when the pace of change has slackened considerably (see Table 2.3). Between 1979 and 1984 the share of full-time employees as a proportion of the total workforce fell by seven percentage points. Between 1990 and 1997 the share of full-time permanent employees fell by just three percentage points.

It is important to distinguish carefully between the trends in part-time, temporary and self-employment, another reason for not lumping them all together. Part-time employment has been growing steadily over the whole postwar period, largely reflecting the growth in female labour force participation. The fastest rate of growth in part-time employment occurred in the 1960s, when its share of total employment rose by seven percentage points, from 9 per cent of the total employed workforce in 1961 to 16 per cent by 1971. By contrast, between 1984 and 1997 the share of part-time employment rose by just four percentage points, and the share of all forms of 'flexible' employment rose by just under six percentage points, less than the growth in the share of part-time employment alone in the 1960s. The incidence of part-time employment has risen significantly in most industries since 1984, with one exception being manufacturing, which has one of the lowest overall incidences of part-time employment.

The only significant post-1979 break in the growth of different forms of 'flexible' employment was the sharp growth in the share of self-employment, which was heavily concentrated in the early 1980s (see Table 2.3). However, since 1990 this growth in self-employment appears to have ground to a halt. In the 1980s the incidence of self-employment grew within all industries (except distribution), and more than 90 per cent of the growth in self-employment occurred due to an increased incidence *within* industries, rather than a shift in employment away from sectors (mainly manufacturing) with a low incidence of self-employment. Since 1990 the rise in the share of self-employment has come to a halt across most industries, which seems to confirm that 1990 represents another break in trend.

The growth in temporary employment in the UK is a very recent phenomenon. Between 1984 and 1990 there was no increase in the proportion of the workforce who were temporary employees (see Table 2.3). Between 1990 and 1997 there was an increase in the proportion of the workforce who were temporary employees from 4.5 to 6.5 per cent of the total workforce. Since 1991 the incidence of temporary employment has grown in all industries (except distribution). One of the highest incidences of temporary employment is in public administration, education and health, the sector which has also seen the fastest rate of growth in absolute terms. Manufacturing has the lowest incidence of temporary employment.

In terms of occupations, the highest incidence of temporary working is for professional workers and this occupational group has also seen the fastest growth in absolute terms. This suggests some parallels with the findings of Felstead *et al.* (1998), who reported that it was amongst professional workers only that they could detect a significant increase in job insecurity. Structural changes such as the introduction of health service trusts and local management of schools, combined with budget restrictions in the mid-1990s, appeared to contribute to a sharp increase in the recruitment of professional workers on fixed-term contracts, and this in turn may have contributed to the increasing sense of insecurity amongst this section of the workforce.

In terms of the growth in different forms of 'flexible' employment, one sector – manufacturing – stands out in terms of having one of the lowest incidences of part-time employment, with no significant increase since 1984; having one of the lowest incidences of self-employment with no growth since 1990; and the lowest incidence of temporary employment. If one wished to study the phenomenon of the growth in different forms of 'flexible' employment, manufacturing would not be a good sector to pick.

When compared with both the immediate past and the experience of previous decades, the UK labour market in the 1990s has not seen shifts into forms of flexible employment which are dramatically out of line with historical experience. The growth in the share of all forms of 'non-standard' employment since 1984 has been lower than the growth in the share of part-time employment alone in the 1960s. The growth in the share of 'flexible' forms of employment in the first half of the 1990s was equal to only a third of the rate experienced in the early 1980s.

In a comparative context, the sharp growth in self-employment in Britain in the 1980s was out of line with the experience of most other OECD countries. The incidence of self-employment by 1995 was higher in Britain than in some other comparable countries (see Figure 2.1).

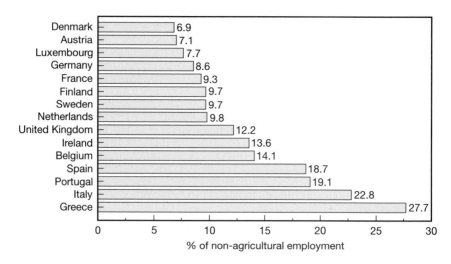

Figure 2.1 Incidence of self-employment in the EU countries, 1995

Source: Eurostat

The incidence of part-time employment is higher in the UK than in most other countries (see Figure 2.2). However, this was already the case in 1979 and the rate of growth since 1979 has not been out of line with the experience of a number of other countries. There is a strong positive correlation internationally between the incidence of part-time employment and female labour force participation rates, and between the growth in part-time employment and the growth in female labour force participation rates. Britain has both an above average incidence of part-time employment and an above average female labour force participation rate.

The incidence of temporary employment is significantly lower in the UK than in most other countries (see Figure 2.3) and shows a lower rate of increase than in some other countries. The OECD country with the lowest incidence of temporary employment is the USA. Countries with less regulated labour markets – the UK and the USA – have a *lower* incidence of temporary employment when compared with countries with more tightly regulated labour markets such as France or Spain.

A higher incidence of self-employment is also associated with higher levels of employment regulation, especially in the southern European economies. On the other hand, less regulated labour markets tend to have higher levels of female labour force participation and therefore a higher incidence of part-time employment.

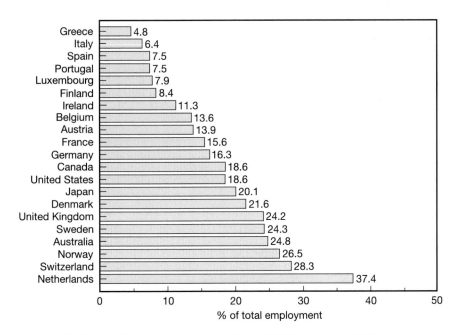

Figure 2.2 Incidence of part-time employment in the OECD countries, 1995

Source: OECD Employment Outlook 1996, Table E
Note: Ireland 1994

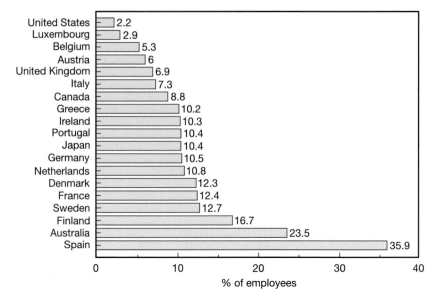

Figure 2.3 Incidence of temporary employment in the OECD countries, 1995

Source: OECD/Eurostat
Note: Luxembourg, Canada, Japan, Australia 1994

It is not true then that the UK and the USA, with their relatively less regulated labour markets, have a higher proportion of their workforces in 'flexible' forms of employment, when compared with other countries with more regulated labour markets. This is because the regulation of 'standard' forms of employment is relatively modest in Anglo-Saxon labour markets, and always has been, so that employers have generally not had the incentive to switch to forms of employment which allow them to avoid regulation.

Conclusion

The terms 'deregulation' and 'flexibility' are not readily interchangeable. Neither can these terms be simply equated with 'insecurity'. The UK has always had a relatively less regulated labour market. Since 1979, in the field of individual employment rights there has been no net deregulation. The weakening of employment protection legislation has been offset by several legislative changes in the field of equal opportunities. Non-standard forms of employment have generally not grown more rapidly in the UK than in other countries and any such growth cannot be put down to a general trend to greater deregulation.

Part-timers (especially men) and temporary workers in the UK do report less job security than their full-time and permanent counterparts. However, looking across countries there is no significant correlation between reported job insecurity and the incidence of temporary employment (OECD 1997). The USA has an average proportion of its workforce in part-time employment, a low proportion in self-employment and the lowest proportion in temporary employment. Put another way, the USA has a higher proportion of its workforce in full-time permanent jobs as employees than most other OECD countries, but also a higher reported level of concern about job security.

In the UK, legislative changes in the 1980s and 1990s which might be relevant to the issue of workforce insecurity were most extensive in the areas of industrial relations and minimum wage regulation. The decline in coverage of the unions and of collective bargaining may be associated with greater workforce insecurity. However, deregulation since 1979 seems to have played little role in explaining changes in the structure of employment, and with the exception of professional workers employed on fixed-term contracts in the public sector, there is little obvious link with job insecurity.

There is no clear convincing evidence which provides backing for the notion that workers *were* feeling more insecure in the 1990s when compared with the mid-1980s. Rather, greater job insecurity seems to be confined to certain articulate groups such as well-qualified professionals. Moreover, in understanding the phenomenon of workforce insecurity it might be a mistake to concentrate on those in 'flexible' forms of employment. Three-fifths of the workforce in the mid-1990s were still full-time permanent employees. This proportion tends to fall most sharply in recessions, making the point that it is this most 'standard' form of employment which appears to be most vulnerable during downturns. Recessions typically eliminate full-time permanent jobs, and those older workers with the longest tenure in their current job have the most to lose.

There is an ironic twist to the debate on workforce insecurity. Whether it is a real phenomenon or not, many observers in both the USA and the UK have suggested that insecurity may be one reason why wage inflation remained relatively subdued in the mid-1990s, despite significant falls in aggregate unemployment. If this is true then it suggests that those of us who are not sure whether or why this insecurity exists should probably keep their mouths shut. If the phenomenon – real or imagined – was helping to deliver a much improved trade-off between unemployment and inflation, then arguably its existence could be a very positive feature of the labour market. The overall evening out of unemployment in the mid-1990s, by region, highest qualification held, occupation and industry, represented the kind of structural change which should have made it easier to run the economy at lower levels of aggregate unemployment without an acceleration of inflation. If the flipside of this improvement in overall labour market performance was a higher level of insecurity amongst *Guardian* readers, then arguably this could have been a price worth paying.

References

Felstead, A., Burchell, B. and Green, F. (1998) 'Insecurity at work. Is job insecurity really much worse now than before?', *New Economy*, 5, 3: 180–4.

Gosling, A., Johnson, P., McCrae J. and Paull, G. (1997) *The Dynamics of Low Pay and Unemployment in Early 1990s Britain*, London: Institute for Fiscal Studies Working Paper.

Gregg, P. and Wadsworth, J. (1996a) 'Feeling insecure?', *Employment Audit*, Autumn, Employment Policy Institute.

—— (1996b) *Mind the Gap, Please? The Changing Nature of Entry Jobs in Britain*, Working Paper No. 796, London: Centre for Economic Performance, London School of Economics.

OECD (1997) 'Is job insecurity on the increase in OECD countries?', *Employment Outlook*, Paris: Organisation for Economic Cooperation and Development.

Teasdale, P. (1998) 'Incidence and repeat spells of unemployment: an analysis using claimant data', *Labour Market Trends*, 106, 11: 555–62.

3 Heaven knows I'm miserable now

Job insecurity in the British labour market

Paul Gregg, Genevieve Knight and
Jonathan Wadsworth

I was looking for a job and then I found a job
and heaven knows I'm miserable now.
Morrisey, 1983

Introduction

There is a public perception, magnified in some sections of the media, that job security has deteriorated in Britain over recent years. The OECD (1997) reports the results of an international survey for 1996, in which two-thirds of British workers said that they felt that their job was not secure. However, some commentators have suggested that feelings of insecurity are misplaced. They claim that policies aimed at the creation of a flexible labour market had improved the workings of the labour market with no such nasty side-effects. In their opinion, greater employment flexibility was not leading to more hires and fires, or job insecurity and that most new jobs were good jobs.[1]

Are the public really subject to a mass neurosis? Feelings of insecurity are hard to quantify. Insecurity is about risk assessment and is likely to depend on some combination of the legal protection workers enjoy, the workplace environment, the likelihood of job loss and any costs that arise as a consequence of job loss. The responses to opinion polls may be influenced by a variety of underlying factors, many of which would be personal or difficult to measure. We can, however, analyse data from the British labour market to help determine whether there have been developments which may have led to greater cause to fear job loss. We focus on two main issues: the length of job tenure, and the earnings loss associated with job displacement.

The most widely cited measure of employment stability is median job tenure, the length of time the typical worker has spent in their current job.[2] Insecurity is also, however, concerned with future prospects, whereas this measure is firmly rooted in the past. A more appropriate measure may be the chance of losing the current job involuntarily and of securing a new job. Furthermore, public concern with job security could arise not only from a belief that a long-term employment relationship is now less likely, but also that the replacement job is likely to be of lower quality, paying lower wages and with a higher chance of breaking up. This then may be an additional reason to feel insecure which could be measured by the pay loss associated with job displacement. Farber (1993; 1997) highlights a rise in job displacement rates despite sustained recovery in the USA, together with wage losses of the order of 10 per cent in the event of job displacement. There appears to be no increase in this wage penalty over time, however.

In what follows, we draw on the Labour Force Survey (LFS), General Household Surveys (GHS) and British Household Panel Survey (BHPS), to detail the evidence on elements of job protection, job stability and the costs of job loss. We highlight which groups have been affected most and offer some explanation as to which factors are responsible. We argue that small changes in stability patterns at the aggregate level are masking more obvious declines for around three-quarters of the workforce. Median job tenure has not changed much over the past twenty years, although there is some dispute between data sources about the picture prior to 1985. For men there is a small fall, but for women an equally clear rise. Yet, as we show below, there may be reasons to believe that even this aggregate impression is misleading. The employed labour force has been ageing since 1984 and older people have longer tenure. Age-specific tenure changes show a very different pattern to the aggregate numbers in terms of the extent of change. The gender differences are age specific with women aged between 25 and 49 showing marked rises in tenure. Yet even here the change is only for women with dependent children. It appears plausible that increased use of a remaining vestige of job protection, namely the provision of maternity leave, may explain much of the increase in female job tenure. Women are increasingly returning to the same employer after childbirth and having no break in tenure. Women without children are experiencing the same trends as men.

As the wage returns to experience rise within any occupation or skill group, then the job currently held is likely to pay more than any new job gained after a displacement. The longer a worker has been in the job, the greater will be this penalty if some or all of the returns to accumulated on-the-job experience are lost in the next job. So the costs of job loss may be higher among older and more experienced workers or wherever job loss is a relatively rare event. As yet there is little evidence for Britain on this issue. Gregory and Jukes (1997) use New Earnings Survey data to analyse the effect of claimant unemployment on the subsequent earnings of British men. Here we broaden the scope of inquiry by including all unemployment spells (claimant or otherwise) and spells of economic inactivity (allowing for discouraged job seekers), together with information for women and/or part-time working. The evidence suggests that job loss results in wage losses of 10 per cent on average. This loss is much larger for older and more experienced workers and the less educated.

The next section describes the data used in our study. Evidence on job tenure is then outlined, followed by evidence on the cost of job loss. The chapter concludes by bringing these two strands together in order to assess whether fears about increased job insecurity are well founded.

Data

In order to measure changes in the distribution of job duration over time we use the information contained in the LFS in the spring of each year. The responses in the LFS have always been to the same question, namely 'How long have you been continuously employed by your current employer/continuously self-employed?' Data on job tenure appeared in banded form in 1975 and from 1984 until 1991. Information on tenure among the self-employed was not collected in 1984. However, since 1992, tenure data have been collected in a continuous form. In order to undertake a consistent analysis over a longer time period, we match the continuous data for the later years to the tenure bands of the earlier years. Information on children, a key variable, as shown below, is only available in the LFS from 1981 onward.

The GHS covers 4,000 households sampled throughout a twelve-month period and has asked questions on job tenure every year since 1974. Again the information is recorded in discrete tenure bands, but the bands are not consistent over time. The only way of obtaining consistent grouping across the whole GHS sample period is to categorise responses into three tenure bands; less than one year, one to five years and more than five years. However, after 1984 most years allow further decomposition of the more than five years category, and we use this to calculate a median tenure value whenever the fiftieth percentile is over five years.

The discrete nature of the data therefore influences much of our estimation work. For instance, the estimation of mean tenure requires assumptions about the open upper band of the tenure groups.[3] Estimation of the median and other quantiles of the distribution is possible if we are prepared to assume a uniform distribution within the tenure band in which the quantile lies.

Estimation of the cost of job loss utilises the information contained within the labour market histories embedded in the BHPS. The BHPS has been carried out annually since 1991 and currently runs for six waves. Information on labour market status, together with gross monthly pay, hours and other job characteristics, if in work, is recorded normally between September and December of each year.[4] Job characteristics focus around the three main dates of the interview, 1 September of that survey year and 1 September the previous year. Details of any changes in employment status in the period beginning in the September of the previous year are recorded in a series of job history spell data. Responses are then matched to data for the same individual from the earlier wave.[5]

Our basic strategy is to compare earnings data in the current job with earnings in the previous job, with or without an intervening spell of worklessness. We are unable to determine whether this cost of job loss has changed over time because of the relatively small time period covered by the BHPS. Individuals are only included in our sample if they have at least two wage observations over the six waves. Hours data are only recorded in the current spell. So if this differs from that in September we have no hours data for this observation. This means we have far fewer observations for hourly wage changes but there is more information on part or full-time job basis and we present this wherever possible.

Students in full-time education and those on maternity leave are removed from the sample. We focus on the earnings changes of three groups: those reporting no change in employer (stayers), those who lost their job either through redundancy, dismissal, or the termination of a temporary contract (displaced), and those that left their last employment for family, health reasons or retirement (leavers). Most of our analysis is confined to those displaced workers and job leavers who are observed in taking a replacement job (movers). Missing data on several variables, notably previous job tenure, reduce the final sample to 27,666 person years, of which 816 are displaced workers. Missing data on hours worked reduce the respective samples to 20,892 and 346. Earnings are deflated by the retail price index into September 1995 prices.

Changes in job duration, 1975–97

Changes in job stability may arise from either a change in the incidence of new job creation or a change in the pattern of job separations, which can occur anywhere in the tenure distribution. We therefore draw on the information on the entire job tenure distribution to analyse changes in job stability. Tables 3.1 to 3.3 and Figures 3.1 and 3.2 highlight changes in the distribution of job tenure over the past twenty years. Figure 3.1 shows that job tenure is highly counter-cyclical. Quits dominate lay-offs in tenure formation and the stock of those in new jobs rises in tight labour markets. As Table 3.3 shows, this counter-cyclical behaviour is more pronounced amongst workers with tenure of less than one year than for those with tenure greater than ten years. Figure 3.1 also shows how the LFS and GHS data sources differ little from 1985 onwards but sharply disagree on the picture in 1975. As the LFS has no data from 1977 to 1984, for the LFS we focus on the post-1985 period and do not rely on the 1975 estimates. Tenure is very counter-cyclical and it is important for valid comparisons to choose specific years which reflect similar points in the relevant cycle. This then removes the confounding cyclical changes, isolating any other changes more clearly. As job tenure is driven by job arrival rather than job loss, it is the vacancy cycle and not the unemployment cycle which should be used to assess tenure development. As such, based on the vacancy cycle, we compare the year 1995 with 1985.

Median tenure rose by 5 per cent between 1985 and 1995 (see Table 3.1). For men, there was a fall of 4 per cent, whilst for women it grew by 17 per cent. The strong rise in tenure for women since 1985 has been largely confined to those with dependent children.[6] Work undertaken at the Policy Studies Institute has shown that the proportion returning to the same employer after childbirth rose from 24 per cent in 1979 to 65 per cent in 1988,[7] amongst women who worked full-time prior to pregnancy. For women working part-time, the proportion returning rose from 37 per cent to 64 per cent. Women are increasingly utilising one of the few major pieces of employment legislation – maternity leave rights – to maintain continuous employment.

Table 3.1 Distribution of job tenure by sex and dependent children

	Year	25th percentile	50th percentile	75th percentile	% tenure < 1 year	% tenure > = 10 years
All	1985	1y 7m	5y 2m	12y 5m	18.7	29.7
	1990	1y 4m	4y 4m	12y	21.5	28.8
	1995	1y 8m	5y 6m	11y 10m	17.8	28.4
% change	1985–95	−6.3	4.8	−12.1	2.0	−4.3
Men	1985	2y 1m	6y 8m	15y 1m	15.5	36.2
	1990	1y 7m	5y 5m	14y 10m	18.2	35.2
	1995	1y 11m	6y 6m	14y 6m	16.2	34.0
% change	1985–95	−15.9	−3.7	−8.4	11.1	−6.9
Women (all)	1985	1y 2m	3y 11m	8y 11m	23.1	20.3
	1990	1y	2y 2m	8y 6m	25.9	20.2
	1995	1y 4m	4y 7m	8y 10m	21.3	20.5
% change	1985–95	8.7	17.0	0.1	−8.0	0.9
Women with no	1985	1y 8m	5y 1m	10y 1m	17.3	27.6
dependent children	1990	1y 4m	4y 1m	10y 10m	21.4	26.7
	1995	1y 9m	5y 5m	10y 10m	17.2	26.6
% change	1985–95	5.0	6.6	7.4	−0.6	0.0
Women with dependent	1985	10m	2y 8m	6y 8m	29.8	11.9
children	1990	10m	2y 4m	5y 7m	31.7	11.8
	1995	1y 2m	− 3y 9m	7y 11m	23.0	14.4
% change	1985–95	40.0	40.6	18.6	−27.4	21.9

Failure to control for the changing age composition of the workforce may lead to incorrect inference about these aggregate tenure patterns. The average age of the employed workforce has risen by around two years since 1984.[8] So because there are now more older workers in the workforce who, on average, have longer tenure, this will raise aggregate tenure estimates. This shifting age pattern produces a veil of unwarranted stability in job tenure patterns since 1985, which is lifted when tenure patterns are disaggregated by age. Table 3.2 confirms that changing tenure patterns differ across age groups.

Cyclical variation in median job tenure declines noticeably with age, as shown in Figure 3.2. However, there appear to be trends within age groups on top of these cyclical movements. Younger and older workers in particular have experienced large falls. Median tenure fell by 11 per cent for young workers under 25 between 1985 and 1995. Median tenure for older workers (49–55/64) fell by 20 per cent over the same period. Among prime age workers only modest falls are registered. Yet it is here that there are clear differences across gender and between women with and without dependent children. Median tenure has risen most, by around 60 per cent since 1985, amongst women in the 25–34-year-old age group with dependent children. Tenure patterns amongst women without dependent children are very similar to those of men and have seen falls of around 10 per cent since 1985.

Table 3.2 Median job tenure by age

	Age			
	16–24	*25–34*	*35–49*	*50+*
Total				
1985	1y 7m	4y 6m	7y 8m	13y 1m
1995	1y 5m	4y 4m	7y 4m	10y 7m
% change 1985–95	−10.5%	−3.7%	−4.3%	−19.1%
Men				
1985	1y 8m	5y 5m	10y 1m	15y 10m
1995	1y 6m	4y 11m	9y 2m	12y 10m
% change 1985–95	−10%	−9.2%	−9.1%	−18.9%
Women				
1985	1y 5m	3y 3m	5y 1m	10y 1m
1995	1y 5m	3y 8m	5y 7m	9y
% change 1985–95	0%	12.8%	9.8%	−10.7%
Women with dep. children				
1985	0y 11m	1y 11m	4y 2m	7y 11m
1995	1y	3y 1m	4y 7m	7y 1m
% change 1985–95	9.1%	60.9%	10%	−10.5%
Women – no children				
1985	1y 10m	4y 10m	7y 11m	10y 8m
1995	1y 7m	4y 2m	7y 6m	9y 3m
% change 1985–95	−13.6%	−13.8%	−5.3%	−13.3%

As a way of summarising this information we follow Farber (1996) in comparing specific points in the tenure distribution, looking at the fraction of jobs
with (a) tenure less than one year, (b) tenure in excess of five years, using GHS
data for the period 1975–95, and (c) the fraction with tenure in excess of ten
years, using LFS data for 1985–97. If job turnover has risen over time, then
the fraction of the workforce with tenure less than one year should have risen
and the fraction with tenure more than ten years should have fallen. We
present in Table 3.3 separate estimates from regressions of the probability of
belonging to one of the three tenure categories for the entire employed population, for men and women with and without children. We give two sets of
estimates, one the raw yearly differences in the probability of belonging to the
relevant category, the second controlling for differences in age, education and
region over time. The coefficients are all measured relative to 1975 for GHS
and 1985 for LFS.

The results shown in Table 3.3 confirm the earlier impression that changes in
tenure patterns differ substantially across age group. There is a small rise in short-
term jobs at the aggregate level which disguises a larger rise for men and neutral-
ity for women, which is in turn the result of offsetting trends between women with
and without dependent children. Columns 1 and 2 for each group show the
estimated differences in the proportions over time, with and without demographic

Table 3.3a Changes in the probability of job with tenure under one year – GHS, 1975 = base

Variable	Total		Men		Women no children		Women with children	
1977	−.019	−.019	−.017	−.019	−.027	−.028	−.011	−.010
	(.004)	(.004)	(.005)	(.005)	(.009)	(.009)	(.012)	(.012)
1980	−.017	−.021	−.020	−.024	−.006	−.012	−.026	−.027
	(.004)	(.004)	(.005)	(.005)	(.010)	(.009)	(.012)	(.011)
1983	−.032	−.025	−.029	−.024	−.019	−.018	−.056	−.038
	(.004)	(.005)	(.005)	(.005)	(.010)	(.010)	(.012)	(.013)
1986	.009	.008	.012	.009	.006	−.007	.013	.025
	(.005)	(.005)	(.006)	(.006)	(.010)	(.010)	(.013)	(.014)
1989	.025	.031	.027	.028	.031	.030	.010	.027
	(.005)	(.005)	(.006)	(.006)	(.011)	(.010)	(.013)	(.014)
1992	−.025	−.013	−.016	−.008	−.013	−.006	−.068	−.050
	(.005)	(.005)	(.006)	(.006)	(.010)	(.010)	(.013)	(.013)
1995	−.001	.019	.011	.025	.007	.027	−.049	−.023
	(.005)	(.005)	(.006)	(.007)	(.010)	(.011)	(.012)	(.014)
Controls	No	Yes	No	Yes	No	Yes	No	Yes
Sample mean	.178	.178	.150	.150	.174	.174	.271	.271
Pseudo R^2	.003	.115	.004	.123	.003	.113	.005	.075
N	230,289	230,289	127,919	127,919	61,669	44,909	43,433	43,433

Notes: Standard errors in brackets.
Controls: age, qualifications, region, marriage, sex (total only), children (total and men only)

controls. Unadjusted, the proportion of short-term jobs is broadly unchanged, allowing for the economic cycle. However, when allowance is made for the differing demographic make-up of the workforce, then a small upward trend in the proportion of short-tenure jobs begins to emerge (compare 1983 and 1992, or 1986 and 1995). The chances of men being in short-term jobs is around 2.5 percentage points up (column 4), a chance 20 per cent higher in 1995 than in 1975. Again, women without dependent children look very much like men. Amongst women with children, however, the proportion of short-term jobs has fallen by around 2 percentage points, or by 15 per cent since 1975 (column 8). Looking at the proportion in jobs over ten years in Table 3.3c,[9] the outcome is the opposite, as expected, and with less cyclical variation. Men and women without dependent children show declining shares in these long-tenure jobs once age and other characteristics are controlled for. By contrast, women with children in the home have seen marked increases in these long-tenure jobs in recent years.

Table 3.3b Changes in probability of job with tenure over five years – GHS, 1975 = base

Variable	Total		Men		Women no children		Women with children	
1977	.009	.009	−.001	.004	.023	.018	.022	.021
	(.007)	(.007)	(.008)	(.009)	(.014)	(.015)	(.016)	(.016)
1980	.051	.051	.027	.033	.064	.064	.081	.111
	(.007)	(.007)	(.008)	(.008)	(.014)	(.014)	(.016)	(.016)
1983	.067	.069	.035	.040	.079	.072	.161	.164
	(.007)	(.007)	(.009)	(.009)	(.015)	(.015)	(.018)	(.018)
1986	.036	.047	.010	.020	.064	.083	.093	.104
	(.007)	(.007)	(.009)	(.009)	(.014)	(.014)	(.018)	(.018)
1989	−.006	−.002	−.031	−.026	.014	.030	.065	.062
	(.007)	(.007)	(.009)	(.009)	(.015)	(.015)	(.017)	(.017)
1992	.001	.005	−.026	−.020	−.003	.005	.121	.112
	(.007)	(.007)	(.009)	(.009)	(.015)	(.015)	(.017)	(.018)
1995	.033	.036	−.011	.001	.020	.025	.093	.188
	(.007)	(.007)	(.009)	(.010)	(.015)	(.015)	(.018)	(.018)
Controls	No	Yes	No	Yes	No	Yes	No	Yes
Sample mean	.585	.585	.656	.656	.605	.605	.340	.340
Pseudo R^2	.002	.088	.002	.065	.004	.044	.008	.052
N	187,852	187,852	106,309	106,309	44,790	44,790	36,753	36,753

Cost of job loss

We now examine the second potential source of insecurity fears, namely the potential for a worker to suffer a drop in earnings if displaced from a job. Several authors (Topel 1991; Jacobson *et al.* 1993; Huff Stevens 1995; Farber 1993; 1997) have provided evidence from the USA to the effect that job displacement involves reductions in wages. The reasons advanced for this are loss of firm-specific human capital, loss of good job match capital or loss of wage premia. Gregg and Wadsworth (1996), for Britain, have shown that the wages of jobs taken by those who were out of work have fallen relative to others in work. In part this decline is due to higher job-specific returns, rewards to seniority and experience at the firm, which cannot be transferred.

US evidence suggests that the costs of job displacement rise with age, tenure in previous job and with loss of a union job. Moreover, earnings appear to fall within the job prior to displacement. Earnings do recover after a new job is secured, but not all these losses are recouped after re-entry. Ruhm (1991), Jacobson *et al.* (1993) and Huff Stevens (1995) all provide evidence of a large persistent negative earnings effect. Huff Stevens suggests that this largely occurs because of subsequent, repeated job loss.

Table 3.3c Changes in probability of job with tenure over ten years – LFS, 1985 = base

Variable	Total		Men		Women no children		Women with children	
1986	.007	.012	.013	.016	.014	.010	−.005	−.004
	(.004)	(.004)	(.005)	(.005)	(.008)	(.007)	(.007)	(.007)
1989	−.007	−.005	−.006	−.004	−.002	−.004	−.010	−.010
	(.004)	(.007)	(.005)	(.005)	(.008)	(.006)	(.006)	(.007)
1992	−.008	−.015	−.003	−.012	−.016	−.025	.003	−.005
	(.003)	(.003)	(.005)	(.005)	(.008)	(.006)	(.007)	(.007)
1995	−.017	−.026	−.017	−.028	−.013	−.029	.010	−.005
	(.004)	(.003)	(.005)	(.005)	(.008)	(.006)	(.007)	(.007)
1997	−.010	−.017	−.023	−.034	−.001	−.019	.049	.042
	(.004)	(.003)	(.005)	(.005)	(.008)	(.006)	(.008)	(.008)
Controls	No	Yes	No	Yes	No	Yes	No	Yes
Sample mean	.297	.297	.364	.364	.276	.276	.132	.132
Pseudo R^2	.001	.182	.001	.157	.001	.195	.003	.056
N	363,061	363,061	203,590	203,590	89,291	89,291	70,180	70,180

Note: Standard errors in brackets.
Controls: age, qualifications, region, marriage, sex (total only), children (total and men only)

Using BHPS data for the period 1991–6 we calculate the change in real earnings between jobs experienced by displaced workers. We then compare these earnings changes with those of workers who were not displaced, showing the differences in pay growth for these different groups of workers. Table 3.4 summarises these earnings changes. The numbers are in logs and so can be read as approximate percentage changes in pay. Monthly wages of the average displaced worker are around 10 per cent lower in the new job than in the job lost. Where the person moves from one full-time job to another the direct penalty is 8 per cent.[10] Monthly and hourly earnings of those who remain with their employer rise by around 5 per cent over the year. So displaced workers not only experience wage losses relative to their previous job but they also forgo general increases in wage levels. T tests on the equality of the means of the stayer and displaced groups confirm that the monthly and hourly mean pay changes are significantly different in the two groups. The estimate is for a total pay penalty of 15 per cent in monthly earnings with a 12 per cent total pay penalty for those working full-time both before and after displacement. For the small sample where hours are observed, the monthly penalty is 7 per cent and 5 per cent for hourly wages. Thus some of the observed fall is due to shorter hours after displacement. For those who leave for family or health reasons, the penalties are evident but are smaller.

There is considerable variation around these averages. Comparison of earnings

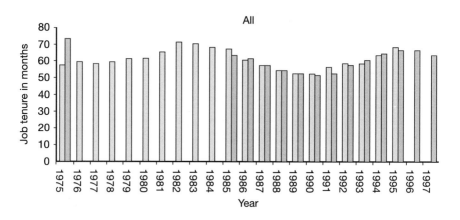

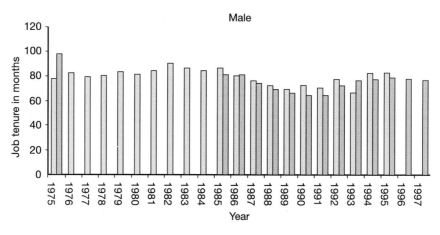

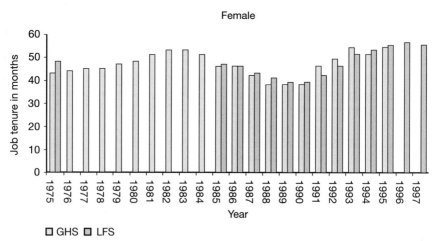

☐ GHS ☐ LFS

Figure 3.1 Median job tenure, 1975–1997

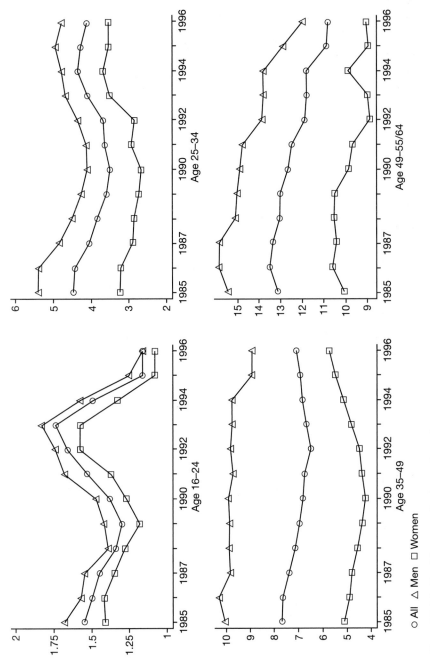

Figure 3.2 Median job tenure, by age and gender

Table 3.4 Log real pay change

		Mean	Std. Dev.	Number
Total	m	.048	.39	27,666
	ftftm	.043	.32	
	ptptm	.048	.39	
	ftptm	−.563	.77	
	h	.040	.28	20,892
	mh	.039	.28	20,892
Stayers	m	.055	.37	26,100
	ftftm	.047	.31	
	ptptm	.049	.38	
	ftptm	−.536	.77	
	h	.041	.26	20,179
	mh	.041	.26	20,179
Movers	m	−.070**	.67	1,566
	ftftm	−.032	.54	
	ptptm	.038	.65	
	ftptm	−.616	.77	
	h	.022	.57	713
	mh	.005	.59	713
of these				
Displaced	m	−.102**	.64	816
	ftftm	−.075	.55	
	ptptm	−.023	.68	
	ftptm	−.601	.77	
	h	−.007**	.60	346
	mh	−.030*	.57	346
Leavers	m	−.036**	.71	750
	h	.050	.53	367
	mh	.039**	.30	367

Notes:
m = gross monthly
h = monthly/hours
mh = monthly if hourly data present
ftftm = full-time before and full-time after, gross monthly
ptptm = part-time before and part-time after, gross monthly
ftptm = full-time before and part-time after, gross monthly
total = the annual log real pay change
leavers: reason for leaving is children/homecare, care of other person, illness, retirement, other.
** = 1% * = 5%, statistical significance at the 1%, 5% level of significance in t test of means between the mean of each group and the mean of the stayer group.

changes of displaced workers and stayers by individual characteristics are reported in Table 3.5. Women experience larger wage losses than men. Older workers and the least qualified also face higher monthly pay cuts than the average. Length of time out is also positively correlated with the size of earnings loss. Displaced workers out of work for more than six months experience average wage change losses that are twice those experienced by those out of work for under one

Table 3.5 Average log real monthly gross pay change by worker characteristics

	Displaced	Leavers	Stayers	Leaver-stayer gap	Displaced-stayer gap
Sex					
female	−.161 (.69)	−.167 (.73)	.063 (.36)	−.230**	−.224**
male	−.065 (.62)	−.042 (.68)	.047 (.37)	−.089*	−.122**
Age group					
youths < 25	.013 (.68)	.068 (.66)	.141 (.37)	−.073	−.128
prime 25–49	−.129 (.61)	−.198 (.74)	.054 (.35)	−.252**	−.183
mature 50+	−.227 (.69)	−.218 (.62)	.014 (.38)	−.232**	−.241**
Marital status					
single	−.017 (.66)	−.053 (.71)	.082 (.37)	−.135**	−.099**
married	−.198 (.63)	−.169 (.70)	.040 (.36)	−.209**	−.238**
Qualifications					
O level/below	−.140 (.57)	−.085 (.73)	.051 (.36)	−.136**	−.191**
Intermediate	−.103 (.71)	−.153 (.67)	.057 (.37)	−.210**	−.160**
Degree/futher ed.	.067 (.68)	−.071 (.72)	.058 (.37)	−.129	.009
Tenure in previous job					
0–1 years	−.067 (.65)	−.047 (.70)	.182 (.54)	−.229**	−.249**
1–2 years	−.053 (.57)	−.107 (.63)	.076 (.37)	−.183**	−.129**
2–5 years	−.144 (.63)	−.073 (.82)	.062 (.34)	−.135	−.206**
5+ years	−.300 (.67)	−.383 (.66)	.028 (.35)	−.411**	−.328**
Length of time out					
0–1 mth	−.066 (.63)	−.059 (.69)	n.a.	—	—
1–3 mth	−.083 (.67)	−.018 (.71)	n.a.	—	—
3–6 mth	−.133 (.64)	−.252 (.63)	n.a.	—	—
6+ mth	−.136 (.64)	−.141 (.75)	n.a.	—	—

Notes: ** = 1%, * = 5%, statistical significance at the 1%, 5% level of significance in t test of means between the mean of each group and the mean of the stayer group.

month. Being married more than doubles the loss in wage change for displaced workers, although this may be related to age. The biggest variation is by length of tenure in the previous job, with those displaced having more than five years' job tenure suffering very large losses, around 30 per cent. Displacement tends to be rarer as jobs lengthen, but the cost of losing those jobs rises greatly.

An interesting question is whether these losses occur because people are being displaced from high-paying but perhaps declining industries, and then being re-employed in expanding but lower-paying sectors. Likewise we can think of these shocks in terms of occupational or firm size displacement. Table 3.6 reports the implied change in wages that would occur if the displaced worker received the average wage for all individuals, both in the industry before the change and in the industry after displacement. A similar exercise is undertaken for occupation and firm size. As stayers do not generally change industry (some job to job moves are included, however), they get the returns of pay growth within that industry. Industry changes after displacement would actually result in no monthly pay

Table 3.6 Industry and occupation effects on displaced workers

		Monthly mean	Hourly mean
given occupation & industry move	Stayers	.023	.010*
	Movers	.016***	.006*
given occupation move only	Stayers	.020	.009***
	Movers	−.015***	−.001***
given industry move only	Stayers	.016	.010***
	Movers	.012	.019***
given firm size	Stayers	.018	.010
	Movers	.040***	.009
Reason for leaving old job Displaced	*given occ. & ind.*	−.003***	−.003*
	given occ.	−.020**	.007***
	given ind.	−.004*	−.009*
	given firm size	.029*	.011
Leavers	*given occ. & ind.*	.004	.014
	given occ.	−.009**	−.005
	given ind.	.030	.020**
	given firm size	.052***	.019

Note: *** = 1%, ** = 5%, * = 10%, statistical significance at the 1%, 5% or 10% level of significance in t test of means between the mean of the stayer group and each other category

losses if wages reflected the average industry wages before and after displacement. Occupation downgrading would produce 4 per cent wage falls for displaced workers (stayers receive 2 per cent (0.02 row 3 column 1) and the displaced lose another 2 per cent (−0.02 row 10, column 1), thus 4 per cent), but firm size has little negative effect on wage growth, instead providing growth in line with pay growth of stayers. Thus, industry displacement would predict 0.4 per cent lower wage growth (−0.004 row 11, column 1), occupational downgrading gives 2 per cent lower wage growth but with firm size giving no measurable negative effect. Occupation and industry considered together imply a wage loss of 2.6 per cent from displacement (stayers receive 2.3 per cent (0.023 row 1, column 1) while displaced lose an additional 0.3 per cent (−0.003 row 9, column1)). Hence only a small fraction of the observed wage losses for the displaced can be discounted as being sourced from changing industry or occupation status, with the wage penalty to involuntary job loss still imposing a significant effect on the later earnings of the worker.

Finally we explore the size of these wage changes controlling for all observed differences in worker characteristics using a regression. Table 3.7 explores these variations of cost of job loss relative to stayers conditional on these different characteristics. The estimate in Table 3.7 is then the difference in wage growth between job stayers and displaced workers. We present the regressions as a base

Table 3.7 Regressions results

Log real pay change*	Displaced-Stayers difference		
	monthly	*monthly with full-part-time controls*	*hourly*
Base	−.106	−.097	−.093
male, prime age 25–49, no qualifications, 2–5 years in previous job, 0–1 month out of job.			
Changing to	*becomes*	*becomes*	*becomes*
Sex			
female	−.162	−.138	−.036
Age group			
youths < 25	−.028	.009	−.18
mature worker 49+	−.126	−.098	−.193
Qualification			
intermediate	−.087	−.101	−.065
degree	.071	.071	.085
Time in previous			
0–1 year	−.161	−.13	−.084
1–2 years	−.075	−.038	−.249
5+	−.247	−.23	−.321
Length of time out			
1–3 mth	−.151	−.125	−.037
3–6 mth	−.192	−.164	−.081
6+	−.193	−.170	−.169

Notes: Included, but not reported variables in the regression are data missing dummies, ethnicity. Intermediate qualification = A levels, GCSE, O levels, apprentice, teaching/nursing/other non-degree higher non qualification = CSE, commercial, none, still studying.

Entries are the calculated difference between the coefficients for regressions run on each sample, but the length of time out calculation is difference from zero as stayers have no time out. The F test on each regression was statistically significant indicating good fit.

* When conditions as for Table 3.4.

case and then explore deviations from this base. The base is a prime age (25–49) male, with no formal qualifications, with two to five years' experience in the job observed prior to displacement and who experiences less than one month of joblessness. We present estimates for monthly, monthly with full and part-time controls before and after job loss, and hourly earnings changes. The base case worker sees differences in monthly wages between displaced workers and stayers of 11 per cent. Women with otherwise similar characteristics to the base suffer larger falls, of the order of 16 per cent. More educated workers have smaller falls and the highly educated can see wage gains. Those with longer job tenure see very large falls, as do those out for three months or more. An example of the accumulation of these effects is the case of a man of more than fifty years, with no formal qualifications, more than five years in his job before displacement and who then goes without a job for more than six months before returning to a job. Such a man suffers a 35 per cent loss in real wage growth, while an equivalent woman suffers a 41 per cent loss. In the best-case scenario a male youth, with 1–2 years in his previous job, with degree qualifications, and who is jobless for less than one month, might receive a pay gain. As we noted before, older men have had particularly large changes in tenure. The hourly differences across categories are a little smaller and the small sample size means a lack of statistical precision, but apart from gender and youth coefficients, the patterns confirm the wage growth penalty observed in gross monthly earnings.[11]

Conclusions

We set out to examine whether the public perception of increased job insecurity could be confirmed by labour market data. Our analysis indicates that there may be some reason to think that job insecurity is justified for some sections of the workforce, if job security can be measured by the chances of leaving a job and the likely earnings loss associated with involuntary job change. For nearly three-quarters of the workforce, job instability as measured by job tenure has increased in the last ten years or so. The largest rise has been amongst men, for whom median job tenure has fallen by around 12 per cent over the last ten years, but childless women have also experienced more instability. It seems that increased use of one of the remaining aspects of job regulation, provision of maternity leave, may well be responsible for rising tenure for women with dependent children. In addition, it appears that displaced workers who experience a spell out of work will enter jobs that pay monthly wages, on average, around 10 percentage points less than those they left behind. Compared with those who remain continuously in the same post, the wage gap is around 15 per cent. However, far larger costs are experienced by older experienced displaced workers and the less educated. It is also older people who have seen the largest falls in job tenure. Older workers are a group for whom voluntary job changes are very rare, and so the involuntary wage losses represented by displaced workers which we observe are more likely for job changes in this group. It is not certain that these changes justify feelings of insecurity for these sections of the workforce, but they are not inconsistent with them. This rather bleak picture for older less educated workers may lie behind the dramatic increases in the incidence of economic inactivity among this group.

Notes

1 For examples of two opposing media views see: 'But as many employees will attest, job insecurity is not only real, but also unlikely to disappear' (Ian Wylie *The Guardian*, 5 April 1997) and 'There have been plenty of examples of mass hysteria in our history. Belief in witchcraft, the fear that little green men are about to descend from outer

space are all examples. Insecurity may fall into the same irrational category' (David Smith *Sunday Times*, 9 February 1997).

2 See Burgess and Rees (1996), Gregg and Wadsworth (1995) and Farber (1996) for the USA.

3 The upper tenure band is twenty years and above in the LFS.

4 Wage data are also collected for every new spell in the twelve months following the September previous year measure, but a few crucial details about the job are not recorded so we do not use this information here.

5 Attempts to match the current spell in the last wave to a particular spell in the job history data in the following wave proved fraught with errors. The September data across the waves matches better. This is because the 1 September information is requested in every wave. The spell histories then count forward from this point until the date of interview and backwards to 1 September of the previous year. Matching the current job from the previous wave is hampered both because the interview date floats between September and April of the following year and then due to recall error in dating events between last September and the previous interview date. See Halpin (1997) or Paull (1997) on problems in spell data and recall error across waves in the BHPS.

6 Information on dependent children and qualifications is not available for 1975.

7 The figures are taken from McRae (1991: 195): 45 per cent returned to work and 20 per cent were seeking work after childbirth, thus 65 per cent.

8 Median age of the employed workforce was 39 years 1 month in 1975, 37 years and 3 months in 1985 and 38 years 9 months in 1995.

9 We do not use GHS as the LFS is the only available source for these data.

10 There is only a very small hourly wage penalty, on average, for being displaced but this is mainly a selection effect, as the monthly wage gap is much smaller for those where hourly wages are defined.

11 Given that these penalties are for gross real monthly wage growth, a regressive tax regime with heavy impact on lower earners might multiply these effects.

References

Burgess, S. and Rees, H. (1996) 'Job tenure in Britain 1975–92', *The Economic Journal*, 106, 1: 334–44.

Farber, H. (1993) 'The incidence and cost of job loss: 1982–91', *Brookings Papers on Economic Activity: Microeconomics*, 73–132.

—— (1996) *Are Lifetime Jobs Disappearing? Job Duration in the United States*, Industrial Relations Working Paper No. 341, Princeton, NJ: Princeton University.

—— (1997) *The Changing Face of Job Loss in the United States 1981–95*, Industrial Relations Working Paper No. 360, Princeton, NJ: Princeton University.

Gregg, P. and Wadsworth, J. (1995) 'A short history of labour turnover, job tenure and job security, 1975–93', *Oxford Review of Economic Policy*, 11, 1: 73–90.

—— (1996) *Mind the Gap: The Changing Distribution of Entry Wages in Great Britain*, Centre for Economic Performance Discussion Paper No. 303, London: London School of Economics and Political Science.

Gregory, M. and Jukes, R. (1997) *The Effects of Unemployment on Subsequent Earnings: A study of British Men, 1984–94*, Department of Education and Employment Working Paper.

Hall, R. (1982) 'The importance of lifetime jobs in the US economy', *American Economic Review*, 72, 4: 716–24.

Halpin, B. (1997) *Unified BHPS Work-life Histories: Combining Multiple Sources into a User-friendly*

Format, Colchester: ESRC Research Centre on Micro-social Change Technical, Paper No. 13.

Huff-Stevens, A. (1997) 'Persistent effects of job displacement', in J. Addison (ed.) *Job Displacement: Consequences and Implications for Policy*, Detroit, IL: Wayne State University.

Jacobson, L., LaLonde, R. and Sullivan, D. (1993) 'Earnings losses of displaced workers', *American Economic Review*, 83, 3: 685–709.

McRae, S. (1991), *Maternity Rights in Britain*, London: Policy Studies Institute.

OECD (1997), 'Is job insecurity on the increase in OECD countries?', *Employment Outlook*, Paris: Organisation for Economic Cooperation and Development.

Paull, G. (1997) *Dynamic Labour Market Behaviour in the BHPS: The Effects of Recall Bias and Panel Attrition*, London: Centre for Economic Performance and Institute of Economics and Statistics Programme into Labour Market Consequences of Technical and Structural Change, Discussion Paper No. 10.

Ruhm, C. (1991) 'Are workers permanently scarred by job displacements?', *American Economic Review*, 81, 1: 319–24.

Topel, R., (1991) 'Specific capital, mobility and wages', *Journal of Political Economy*, 99: 145–75.

Acknowledgements

Big thanks to Julian Steer and Kirstine Hansen for help with the LFS and GHS data tables. LFS and BHPS data were supplied by the ESRC Data Archive at Essex University with permission from OPCS.

4 Redundancy and the paradox of job insecurity

Peter Turnbull and Victoria Wass

Introduction

When asked about the security of their employment, the majority of British workers report fears of impending job loss and feelings of insecurity.[1] The Industrial Relations Services/MORI index of insecurity rose steadily during the early 1990s and the annual survey of employee satisfaction conducted by International Survey Research found that by the mid-1990s, feelings of employment security were in 'free fall' (ISR 1996: 15–17). These data prompted the media to lament the end of 'jobs for life', especially among the 'middle classes' of 'middle England'.[2] In contrast, however, David Smith of the think tank SMF has argued that 'the notion of generalised job insecurity is a will o' the wisp, unsupported by the evidence' (*Guardian*, 10 February 1997). In fact, standard statistical measures of job security, job tenure and labour turnover indicate only very modest change and, according to Burgess and Rees (1996: 344), 'emphatically do not support the view that the dramatic changes in the labour market, technology and competition have spelt the end of "jobs for life"'.

This is the paradox of insecurity in the 1990s: while attitude surveys report a growing sense of insecurity among the workforce, academic research on job tenure and turnover indicate that very little has changed. Discounting the possibility of mass neurosis, Gregg *et al.* (1997) suggest a number of factors to explain the apparent inconsistency between the rise in reported job insecurity and the absence of any marked decline in job tenure. Statistically, any fall in average job tenure has been partially offset by the demographic ageing of the workforce, because age and tenure are positively correlated, and the marginal fall in aggregate (median) job tenure disguises more substantial falls among particular groups, most notably men and the less skilled. More importantly, insecurity is influenced by the cost of job loss, as well as the risk, and these costs have increased in recent years as a result of unemployment and occupational downgrading among those who find themselves out of work. During the recession of 1991, for example, the proportion of redundant men who experienced a significant spell of unemployment was 62 per cent. More recently, according to unpublished data from the Labour Force Survey, during the spring quarter of 1996 around 50 per cent of all men who reported having been made redundant within the previous three months were unemployed at the time of their interview. Over the period 1992–96, one in three men of working age experienced at least one spell of unemployment (Blyton and Turnbull 1998: 56–7). For many workers there is not only a high risk of unemployment, but the prospect of inferior terms and conditions of employment if they do find work (see, *inter alia*, Anderton 1997; Elias, 1997; Gregg and Wadsworth 1995; Gregg *et al.* 1997; Harris 1988; MacKay and Jones 1989; Turnbull and Wass 1994; Westergaard *et al.* 1988; and Withington 1989).

Workers' (subjective) perception of insecurity (i.e. their appraisal of the risks and consequences of future job loss) is therefore determined, in large part, by their fear of redundancy and deteriorating conditions in the labour market (Roskies and Louis-Guerin 1990). In this chapter we demonstrate that workers' fear of redundancy is well founded for two principal reasons. First, over the past twenty years the labour market has witnessed a secular increase in the number of involuntary job losses, in both absolute terms and as a proportion of all job losses. The significance of this rise is that involuntary job separations are not only an important source of job insecurity but the key to resolving the paradox between the observed stability of job tenure and the rise in reported job insecurity. Job tenure is in fact a rather poor measure of job security as it is the product of two separate decisions, namely involuntary and voluntary exits from the firm, taken by different actors for very different reasons: involuntary exits (redundancies) are initiated by firms seeking to reduce labour costs while voluntary exits (quits) are initiated by workers, typically in order to take up a better job. During a recession, those in employment fear the consequences of unemployment and hold onto their jobs. The impact on average job tenure is therefore positive because exits and recruitment decline (the proportion of long-tenure employees increases and the proportion of short-tenure employees declines), but the impact on job security is negative because firms seek to compensate for the decline in voluntary separations by implementing involuntary quits, in the form of redundancy. The majority of involuntary job separations in Britain are in fact the result of redundancy (see Taylor and Booth 1996: 17).

The second reason why workers' fear of redundancy is well founded is that both statutory and non-statutory redundancy arrangements in Britain undermine employment protection. The law confers the right of management to declare redundancies and, provided the employer can demonstrate that any redundancies meet the 'needs of the business', they are unlikely to be challenged by industrial tribunals. The employer also determines the scale of any job losses. Of course, the risk of losing one's job is not simply determined by scale (how many jobs go?), but also selection (who goes?), and if redundancy is in the offing but selection criteria are agreed, then the impact on workers' feelings of insecurity may be partly mitigated. For example, if long-tenure employees are secure in the knowledge that it will always be their junior/short-service colleagues who are made redundant first (on the principle of last-in, first-out), then generalised feelings of insecurity will only become manifest during the most severe recessions. In practice, however, selection is typically based on managerial definitions of employee performance, with last-in, first-out usually considered only as a 'last resort' (see Turnbull 1988:

208–9). Even under so-called 'voluntary' severance arrangements, employers can still control selection by targeting particular groups or categories of employee and by structuring compensation payments in such a way that the 'right' people 'volunteer' (see Wass 1996).

In the following section, cyclical and secular trends in the labour market over the past twenty years are examined, illustrating the growing scale of redundancy. Crucially, the data suggest a 'ratchet effect' is at work, whereby redundancies never quite return to their pre-recession level. Thus, even when the economy picks up, workers are still concerned about their job security. We then examine the impact of statutory and non-statutory redundancy arrangements on job security, demonstrating that without adequate legislative support, and in the absence of effective institutional arrangements such as jointly agreed procedures, workers in Britain feel particularly vulnerable to redundancy. Increasingly, this applies not only during recessionary periods but to more profitable years also, as redundancy is no longer simply 'demand led'. In fact, a premise of 'downsizing' – one of the most corrosive (Anglo-Saxon) managerial preoccupations of recent years – is that reductions in employment are not accompanied by lower levels of output (Cappelli 1995: 577).

The deleterious effects of redundancy on those who lose their job are well documented, and there is now growing concern about the effects on 'survivors' who retain their jobs. Post-redundancy, organisational competitiveness can be undermined by low morale, declining commitment and productivity, and growing mistrust towards management among retained employees (see, *inter alia*, Cameron 1994: 190; Cappelli 1995: 587–7; Guest and Peccei 1992: 37; Hartley *et al.* 1991; IPD 1996: 11; and Kets de Vries and Balazs 1997). The concluding section therefore considers alternative redundancy arrangements that might go some way towards alleviating insecurity and reversing what many commentators, including Tony Blair (speaking at the CBI Conference in November 1995), perceive to be 'permanent corporate anorexia', a situation where:

> Below the chief executive and his [*sic*] cheerleading human resources department . . . companies resemble nothing so much as buildings blasted by a neutron bomb. The processes and structures are all there, but no human life to make them productive.
>
> (Caulkin 1995: 29; see also ACAS 1994: 9)

Job insecurity and the 'redundancy ratchet'

Redundancy both reflects and shapes the history of the labour market. Over the twenty-year period from 1977 there were two major economic recessions, a secular shift away from industrial and manufacturing production towards distribution and services and, from 1980 onwards, a wholesale onslaught on employees' rights and conditions of work (see Blyton and Turnbull 1998: 37–66, 158–66). These general trends are reflected in both the scale and distribution of redundancies. Redundancies peaked during the 'Thatcher' recession of 1980–1 and again

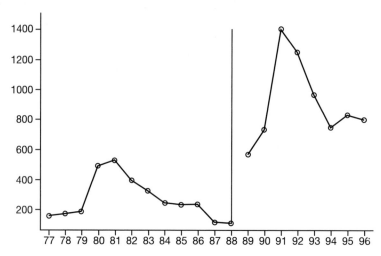

Figure 4.1 Redundancies (thousands) in Britain 1977–1996

Source: Labour Market Trends, unpublished Labour Force Survey
Notes: 1977–1988 annual confirmed redundancies based on statutory returns (ES955) to
Department of Employment. Redundancy figures for 1987 and 1988 are affected by
under-reporting. 1989–1996 annual estimates from individual reports of having been
made redundant in last three months collected in the Labour Force Survey.

during the 'Major' recession of 1991–2, as illustrated in Figure 4.1. Unfortunately
the data series for exits and redundancies are not consistent over the whole period
(see the Data Appendix for details). In particular, the series for 1977 to 1988 are
based on statutory returns and these data understate the level of redundancies
due to under-reporting. The problem of under-reporting was exacerbated after
1986 when rebates for statutory redundancy payments from the Redundancy
Fund were effectively abolished.[3] From 1989, government statisticians have preferred to rely on data collected from individual returns in the Labour Force
Survey (LFS).

Although data inconsistencies make any comparison between the two redundancy peaks (1980–1 and 1991–2) somewhat hazardous, a complete economic
cycle is captured by each series and it is interesting to note that the level of post-
recession redundancies remained *above* the pre-recession level. During 1989,
568,000 employees were made redundant – 25.6 per thousand employees (*Labour
Market Trends* 1991: 461). The number of redundancies in 1996 was 799,000 –
36.3 per thousand employees (calculated from unpublished Labour Force Survey
data). This suggests that a 'ratchet' effect is at work, evidence perhaps of 'downsizing' as opposed to straightforward redundancy, but certainly indicative of an
increase in involuntary separations over time. The 'ratchet effect' is more difficult
to observe over the earlier economic cycle where redundancy figures are based on
statutory returns, because there is a sharp drop in the redundancy rate after 1986.

However, the likelihood is that this was the result of the withdrawal of rebates from the Redundancy Fund, rather than any genuine decline in the number of redundancies (see *Employment Gazette* 1990: 452–3 and note 3; further details can be found in the Data Appendix). If the levels of redundancies are compared between 1977 and 1986, the longest series for which the redundancy figures are consistent (even if they are not reliable), then the ratchet effect is also observed over the earlier cycle. The annual redundancy rate increased from 7.2 per thousand (158,000 employees) in 1977 to 11.4 per thousand (238,000 employees) in 1986 (*Employment Gazette* 1985: 203 and 1988: s42).

Peaks in employment tend to coincide with peaks in production, as illustrated in Figure 4.2. However, the recovery in employment tends to lag behind the recovery in production by around two years, the so-called 'employment lag'. In the downturn of the economic cycle, the relationship between employment and production is mediated by job separations that lead to non-employment (either unemployment or non-participation). This is clearly demonstrated by the counter-cyclical nature of the unemployment rate depicted in Figure 4.3. Figure 4.3 also illustrates the dramatic fall in separation rates during the downswing and subsequent rise in a period of recovery.[4] Voluntary exits dominate job separations and voluntary exits decline as the prospects of post-separation unemployment increases. In the internal labour market workers seek to hang onto their jobs in the face of falling demand in the external labour market. In a situation where firms require a greater number of exits but where fewer exits are initiated by workers, the impasse is broken by involuntary separations. Put differently, firms initiate any exits they require via redundancy.

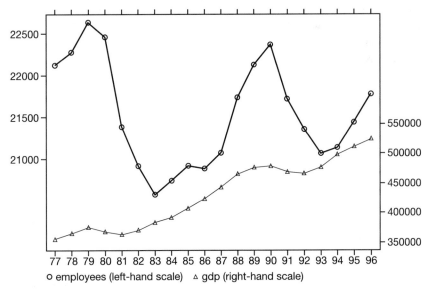

Figure 4.2 Production (£ million) and employment (thousands) in Britain, 1977–1996

Source: Economic Trends Table 1.2; *Employment Gazette* Historical Abstract Table 1.2

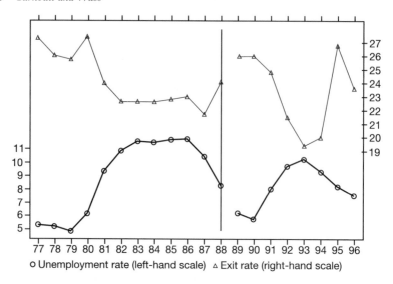

Figure 4.3 Percentage unemployment and exit rates in Britain, 1977–1996

Source: Economic Trends Table 1.2; Labour Market Trends and unpublished Labour Force
Survey, 1992–6

Notes: 1977–1988 exit rates were collected by Department of Employment from firms and refer
to the manufacturing sector
1989–1996 exit rates were collected from individuals in the Labour Force Survey and
include all industries.

Figure 4.4 illustrates how redundancy compensates for the decline in voluntary
turnover during the downswing. As non-redundancy separations, most of which
will be voluntary, fell between 1977–82 and 1991–3, the redundancy rate
increased before falling back again as voluntary turnover increased during the
upswing. This inverse relationship between voluntary and involuntary exits is
clearly demonstrated in Figure 4.5, where redundancies are measured as a proportion of all separations. In the years of deepest recession, 1981 and 1991,
around 30 per cent of all exits were enforced. The ratchet effect is clearly evident
over the 1990s' cycle, as the trend in redundancies as a proportion of separations
never quite returns to the pre-recession level. The same effect can be inferred
over the recession of the 1980s, when account is taken of substantial downward
bias in the redundancy figures in 1987 and 1988. The secular increase in redundancy and other forms of dismissal such as non-renewal of (fixed-term) contracts, are corroborated by data from the British Household Panel Survey.
Redundancies measured as a proportion of all job separations for employees
who experienced a subsequent spell of unemployment increased from 29.3 per
cent during the 1980s to 45.6 per cent in the period 1990–6 (Taylor and Booth
1996: 17).

Notwithstanding the inconsistencies in the data series, the evidence suggests a
clear increase in involuntary separations in the form of redundancy over the last

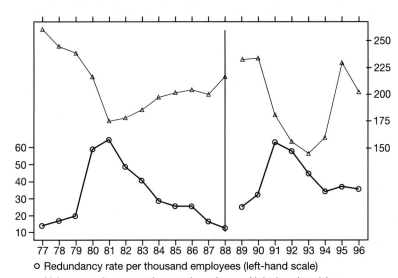

o Redundancy rate per thousand employees (left-hand scale)

△ Voluntary exit rate per thousand employees (right-hand scale)

Figure 4.4 Redundancy and voluntary exit rates in Britain, 1977–1996

Source: Labour Market Trends; unpublished Labour Force Survey, 1992–6

Notes: 1977–1988 redundancy and exit rates were collected by Department of Employment from firms and refer to the manufacturing sector

1989–1996 redundancy and exit rates were collected from individuals in the Labour Force Survey and include all industries.

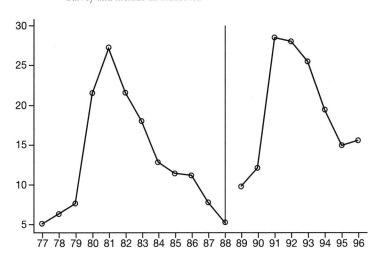

Figure 4.5 Redundancies as a percentage of exits in Britain, 1977–1996

Source: Labour Market Trends; unpublished Labour Force Survey, 1992–6

Notes: 1977–1988 redundancy and exit rates were collected by Department of Employment from firms and refer to the manufacturing sector

1989–1996 redundancy and exit rates were collected from individuals in the Labour Force Survey and include all industries.

twenty years. The sheer scale of redundancy in Britain, when allied to ever greater recourse to redundancy during upturns (the ratchet effect), suggests that workers' fear of job loss is well founded. To be sure, average job tenure declined by only 4 per cent between 1975 and 1996 (Gregg *et al.* 1997), but these statistics are of little comfort to those who have experienced redundancy and subsequent 'downward mobility', or indeed to the survivors who know the firm will cut jobs again. It is the experience and expectation of *in*voluntary separation that determine workers' perception of job insecurity. In the absence of protection from the law or from those bastions of employment security in days gone by, namely seniority and service, it is increasingly difficult for workers to expunge their feelings of insecurity.

Job insecurity and the management of redundancy

Although the Redundancy Payments Act (RPA) 1965 was enacted on the grounds of economic efficiency (promoting labour mobility in the external labour market and the acceptance of technological change and restructuring in the internal labour market) as well as social protection (compensating workers for the loss of 'job property rights'), there was also a very clear managerial agenda behind the Act (see Turnbull and Wass 1997: 30–1). As Clegg (1965: 10) pointed out at the time,

> To a group of workers, the likelihood that redundancy will bring serious hardship to a few is enough to justify resistance since no one knows beforehand on whom the hardship will fall, and whose turn it will be to go next . . . this means insecurity for all.

Prior to 1965 most unions vehemently opposed redundancies and argued strongly for selection to be based on the principle of last-in, first-out (LIFO) in the event of any unavoidable job losses (see, for example, Eldridge 1968: 32; Fryer 1973b: 5; Mukherjee 1973: 107; and Wedderburn 1968: 68). The RPA was therefore designed to 'formalise' the process of job losses among long-serving employees and 'institutionalise' the inevitable conflicts that ensued between management and labour. The latter invariably revolved around management's desire to impose technological, economic or business criteria in the selection of employees for redundancy, thereby forcing workers to surrender hard-won job controls and the principle of LIFO (see Bulmer 1971: 12; Fryer 1973a: 241–2 and 1973b: 5; Grunfeld 1980: 6; and Parker *et al.* 1971: 10).

The principal features of the RPA 1965 and subsequent legislation such as the Employment Protection Act 1975 and the Employment Protection (Consolidation) Act 1978, were the provision of statutory redundancy payments for workers based on age and length of service (see note 3), advance notice of any impending redundancies (currently at least 30 days for 20–99 redundancies, and at least 90 days for 100 or more redundancies), and written information to recognised trade unions, or from 1995 elected employee representatives, specifying the reason(s) for any redundancies, the numbers involved, the categories of employees affected, method(s) of selection to apply, and procedures to be implemented. This process is depicted in Figure 4.6 which emphasises the fact that the need to declare redundancies, the scale of any job losses, and the selection of workers for redundancy are essentially determined by managerial prerogative. First and foremost, the RPA confirms the unilateral right of management, in law, to declare workers redundant. The only statutory requirement is that the employer must experience 'a reduction or cessation of work of a particular kind', but the legal test is simply whether, *in the employer's opinion*, fewer workers are required to perform the particular work in question (see Lewis 1985: 26). The most prevalent, and indeed most straightforward, form of redundancy is where the employer simply declares a particular job redundant, along with the job holder (see Casey 1992: 324–5; Millward *et al.*, 1993: 325; and Turnbull 1988: 203).

As Figure 4.6 indicates, individual workers or their trade union representatives may challenge management's 'need' to declare redundancies, *post hoc*, but judicial interpretation has favoured the employer at every turn – a 'reduction or cessation of work' may arise from a lack of demand, the introduction of new machinery, new working methods, reorganisation or relocation, and 'work of a particular kind' is defined by reference to the contract of employment rather than the job that the employee was actually performing, which enables considerable flexibility to be read into the employment contract by the judiciary (see Lewis 1993: 72). This has resulted in very explicit support for managerial definitions of efficiency and the (financial) 'needs of the business' (Turnbull 1988: 209–10), not only with respect to who goes but also who stays: workers can be declared redundant because of new working methods and new techniques, and those who remain must adapt to higher work rates and improved standards of quality and efficiency.

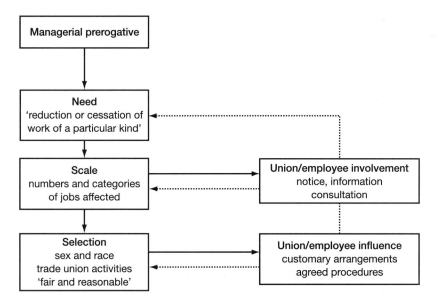

Figure 4.6 The process of redundancy

Workers who fail to meet these new standards may also be dismissed and some may not even qualify for redundancy pay (see Anderman 1986: 436–7).

Other statutory 'restrictions' on managerial prerogative in redundancy situations can be equally ineffectual. Prior notice involves 'consultation' rather than 'negotiation', typically to explore alternatives to redundancy such as early retirement or redeployment (Turnbull 1988: 208), but many companies fail to use the full consultation period, preferring instead to make additional payments in lieu of notice to expedite the process (IDS 1982). Thus, provisions for union and/or employee involvement typically constitute only a 'minor hindrance' on managerial autonomy (White 1983: 35; see also Lewis 1993: 102–6). This is not to imply that consultation is merely nugatory, rather to emphasise that the decision to declare redundancies has already been taken *before* consultation takes place, and that subsequent discussion tends to focus on facilitating the process of redundancy (see Edwards *et al.*, 1998). The same applies to statutory 'restrictions' on selection. Beyond the regulations preventing discriminatory selection based on sex, race or trade union activities, employers have been able to impose criteria based on corporate performance and managerial definitions of a worker's efficiency (see ACAS 1987; Casey 1992: 430; Lewis 1993: 100; Spilsbury *et al.* 1993: 320; and Turnbull 1988: 209–11).

If there are 'customary arrangements' or 'agreed procedures' negotiated with trade unions, then these must be followed. But the former must pass a 'frequency test' and the latter are in fact surprisingly rare (ACAS 1987: 7; Daniel and Stilgoe 1978: 21; Spilsbury *et al.* 1993: 313–14; and White 1983: 35). As already noted, trade unions and many employees favour LIFO and seek to apply this criterion in any agreed procedure, but LIFO is typically considered only after other criteria have been exhausted (Turnbull 1988: 209–11). As ACAS found, 'over the 1980s it became rarer for managers to agree to, or to observe, pre-determined redundancy arrangements emphasising the principle of "last in – first out"' (1992: 16). In the early 1990s, 'more managers [were] looking to other criteria related to efficiency and potential contribution to the business, sometimes overturning long-standing agreements' (*ibid.*; see also ACAS 1993: 12). Not surprisingly, employers report that statutory redundancy arrangements actually *facilitate* the process of shedding labour (see ACAS 1987: 19; IMS 1981; and Parker *et al.* 1971: 29).

Of course, the consequences for workers of greater resort to redundancy by employers are greater uncertainty and insecurity of employment. This is compounded by the fact that whenever statutory obligations restrict, or trade unions oppose, managerial autonomy over questions of redundancy, employers can simply operate 'outside' the law and target specific individuals by using 'voluntary' severance arrangements and offering enhanced severance payments (see, *inter alia*, Casey 1992: 331–5; Daniel and Stilgoe 1978: 15–16; Gordon 1984; Millward *et al.* 1992: 324; Parker *et al.* 1971; and Spilsbury *et al.* 1993: 313–14).[5] This process is illustrated in Figure 4.7, where management factors set the 'organisational context' in which redundancies take place. For example, management might concoct overly pessimistic manpower plans involving large-scale redundancies in order to generate an atmosphere of despondency and resignation towards

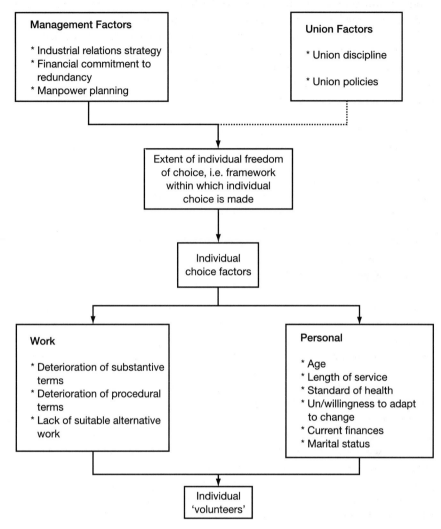

Figure 4.7 The process of 'voluntary' redundancy
Source: Adapted from Lewis (1993: 33)

impending redundancy (Lewis 1993: 34), and as part of the firm's industrial relations strategy might seek to communicate the news of upcoming job losses directly to individual employees rather than through trade union representatives. Unions might well contest the firm's manpower plans and seek to persuade individuals not to sign up for severance payments, but most unions do not oppose job losses if they are 'voluntary' and very few unions have the necessary discipline over their members to prevent them opting for severance (see Clegg 1972: 288; and Hardy 1985).

Typically, then, it is management rather than union factors that determine the extent of individual 'freedom of choice', as illustrated in Figure 4.7. Whether particular individuals will 'volunteer' for redundancy will depend on a range of work and personal factors, but employee 'self-selection' for redundancy is still within the influence, if not the control, of management, giving rise to what many employees perceive to be 'forced voluntary' redundancy (see Turnbull and Wass 1994 and 1997). Some employees are more than willing to accept extrastatutory redundancy pay but, strictly speaking, the term 'voluntary redundancy' is a misnomer, as management will invariably announce a restructuring of work as part of, if not the occasion for, redundancy, knowing full well that this will 'persuade' certain individuals to 'volunteer'. How many university lecturers, for example, would 'volunteer' for redundancy if their employer proposed teaching-only contracts with over 30 hours' contact time each week? Whether particular individuals 'volunteer' will also depend on their personal circumstances (e.g. health and financial status), but yet again management can influence the outcome by offering extrastatutory severance payments to particular groups based on their age, length of service, job category and the like (see Wass 1996). In some industries management have even been able to target union activists, contrary to the provisions of the legislation, and ultimately derecognise the trade union through 'voluntary' severance arrangements (see Turnbull and Wass 1994). As a final pillar to managerial prerogative, if the 'wrong' employees 'volunteer' – for example those with important skills, knowledge or capabilities deemed essential to the organisation – then management will typically refuse the application (see Gordon 1984: 48). The *Mobility Incentive Scheme 1997/98* operated by the University of Leeds (1997), for example, states that applications for voluntary severance 'will only be approved when they are judged to be in the University's managerial interest . . . Final decisions on whether any particular application is in the University's managerial interest and the terms of any offer will be made by the University.'

In sum, redundancy arrangements in Britain compound rather than alleviate job insecurity. Not only is there greater recourse to involuntary separation, the so-called 'redundancy ratchet', but workers are often unsure of their status and security in relation to the 'interests of the business' or managerial definitions of 'performance'. What most employees are all too well aware of, however, is that the 'interests of the business' are invariably equated with those of the shareholders (see Kelly 1998: 46–7), and the key 'performance' measure is profitability. When organisations downsize, by definition, they sacrifice the interests of employees (security) in favour of shareholders (profits), as the following, not untypical, report from *The Financial Times* (20 December 1993) bears witness:

> Fisons, the troubled pharmaceuticals and scientific equipment group, is planning plant closures and large scale redundancies *in a bid to restore confidence in the company*.
>
> (Quoted by Beaumont 1995: 103, emphasis added.)

More recently, as economic growth slowed and inflation rose, the Chartered Institute of Purchasing and Supply reported that Britain's manufacturers were once again sacking workers to protect profits, with the 'rot' beginning to spread to services (*Guardian*, 4 July 1998).

Conclusions – rebuilding security in the labour market

The UK now has some of the least restrictive employment protection laws in Europe, especially for individual dismissal and redundancy (Grubb and Wells 1993: 13–16; see also CEC 1986; Emerson 1988: 789–90; Nickell 1997: 59–61; and OECD 1994: 72–3). Whereas employers in France, Germany, Italy, the Netherlands, Portugal and Spain regard obstacles to the termination of employment contracts to be 'fundamental', UK employers regard any such obstacles to be 'insignificant' (IOE, 1985).[6] Moreover, the costs of statutory severance in Britain are paltry.[7] Neo-classical economic theory predicts that maximising the ease of dismissal and minimising the costs will improve both allocative efficiency in the external labour market and organisational efficiency in the internal labour market. But the evidence suggests otherwise (see Dore 1988).

Under current redundancy provisions where firms control selection, those who are least likely to find alternative employment as a result of their age, experience, skills, mobility and the like are most likely to be made redundant (see Daniel 1985: 85; Turnbull and Wass 1997). Moreover, if the employer decides who goes, the market infers that any workers made redundant must be of low quality or ability. Firms are therefore reluctant to hire redundant workers, especially when there is a surplus of unemployed labour in the market (Gibbons and Katz 1991: 375). As a result, redundancy procedures are more likely to add to long-term unemployment and structural rigidities than to encourage job matching in the external labour market (see MacKay and Jones 1989: 44; and Turnbull and Wass 1997). As for organisational performance and the internal labour market, at best current redundancy arrangements in Britain provide a short-term fillip to performance (Turnbull 1988: 210) and possibly share prices, but in the long term, productivity tends to stagnate after downsizing (Henkoff 1990). More importantly, statutory redundancy arrangements and corporate redundancy policies facilitate, if not encourage, what Lazonick (1991) describes as 'adaptive' rather than 'innovative' behaviour, a situation where companies seek to minimise competitive uncertainty by minimising fixed commitments (including labour), rather than invest in new productive capacity or develop new products. Put differently, the organisation 'reaps' instead of 'sows', perpetuating outmoded techniques and promoting work intensification. As Lazonick (1991: 57) argues, it is essential that adaptive behaviour be constrained if firms and economies are to remain competitive. If private enterprise cannot itself create the organisational conditions for innovation, then state intervention is warranted.

Recognising the adverse effects of redundancy on morale, motivation and productivity, the Institute of Personnel and Development (IPD) recently published a new *Guide on Redundancy* to promote the more effective management of involuntary job separations. The policies advocated by the IPD (1996: 2) included:

- a management attitude or organisational culture which sees redundancy as a last resort and gives a high priority to preventative strategies and processes;
- creative use of a variety of employment arrangements (such as annualised hours, flexitime, and job-sharing) and adopting flexible conditions of employment (including variable retirement provisions, career breaks and multi-skilling);
- retraining to enable employees threatened with redundancy to acquire new skills, and continuous development to create an adaptable and highly skilled workforce;
- buying in non-core functions or using external resources to cover peaks in work;
- developing training and development strategies to encourage employees to improve their employability; and
- negotiating redundancy agreements and/or developing policies which set out the procedures to be followed when redundancies occur.

While each of these policies may be perfectly laudable and in many respects appropriate in terms of minimising the number of redundancies required (through preventative strategies and promoting alternative employment arrangements), helping the redundant find alternative employment (through retraining and employability), and allaying fears of insecurity among existing staff (though 'core/periphery' employment, employability and redundancy agreements/procedures), their widespread adoption seems unlikely in a 'deregulated' labour market.

Most employers recognise the advantages of employing a stable and committed workforce, and advocates of modern-day 'human resource management' extol the virtues of employment security, but many firms are unable to develop appropriate employment policies, because of financial and organisational constraints (see Rubery 1994: 56). In a free market environment, employers know that other firms will always cut their expenditure on 'good employee relations' in order to secure a competitive (cost) advantage, such that any voluntary guarantee of employment security would tend to be the exception from a predominant pattern of 'flexible' and insecure employment (Streeck 1992: 21). Thus, flexible employment has more often been driven by a desire to cut costs than to benefit employees, employer-led training provision has failed to provide the skills workers need in a modern economy and, as already indicated, there has been a move away from predetermined redundancy arrangements under the deregulated labour market policies of the 1980s and 1990s (see Blyton and Turnbull 1998: 37–66). Employment security is therefore more likely to be created, and to be effective, as a matter of (statutory) obligation rather than corporate self-interest.

The principal objectives of any statutory redundancy policy must be twofold: first, to provide employment protection for existing staff in the internal labour market and, secondly, to ensure that displaced workers are able to find jobs in the external labour market. Thus, the first issue that any revised statutory redundancy arrangements must address is the question of qualification for statutory protection. Put differently, when do workers acquire 'job property rights'? One effect of raising the qualification period for unfair dismissal from six months to one year in 1979, and then to two years in 1985, has been to increase the number of employees who are routinely dismissed a matter of weeks or even days before they qualify for statutory employment protection or redundancy pay (see Blyton and Turnbull 1998: 156–7). Less than half of all employees made redundant in Britain receive any redundancy pay (either statutory or non-statutory) (*Employment Gazette*, 1991: 398), which suggests that a relatively simple way to enhance job security would be to shorten the qualification period for statutory employment rights to one year or even six months.[8] Employers and free market economists would no doubt object to such a change, but this would force organisations to consider their human resource planning more carefully. Moreover, it must be remembered that, for most firms, statutory redundancy payments are not excessive (see note 7).

The next question to address is whether employers should enjoy the unilateral right to declare redundancies – or, more accurately, to what extent employers' prerogative should be constrained by third parties such as trade unions, works councils, government agencies or the courts. As Wedderburn (1965: 97) pointed out many years ago, 'We have to decide to whom in a modern society jobs really belong.' In Britain, jobs belong to employers, whereas in Europe there is much greater third party intervention and influence (see Emerson 1988: 787–90). No doubt British employers would deplore such restrictions on managerial prerogatives, but it is important to note that, in a European context, employer 'complaints' about employment regulation or third party involvement do not correlate perfectly with the 'strictness' of employment regulation. As Grubb and Wells (1993: 30) demonstrate, third party involvement through advance notification and consultation is helpful to all parties and can serve to promote greater trust and more considered human resource planning by employers (see also Nickell 1997; Streeck 1988: 420). Surely employers should not be allowed to 'buy out' statutory notice periods, as this is supposed to be a time when alternatives to redundancy such as retraining, relocation, short-time working, or early retirement are considered and implemented in order to minimise the number of job losses required. In other countries there is far greater emphasis on the avoidance of, and alternatives to, redundancy than is the case in Britain (Lewis 1993: 165).

Employment security would be further enhanced by greater third party involvement and influence over selection. In Germany, for example, selection must be made with due regard for social considerations, and not simply 'business needs' (Casey 1992: 428–9; see also Bosch 1990), and in most industrialised countries economic difficulties alone do not legally entitle the employer to unilaterally terminate the employment contract (see Turnbull and Wass 1997: 42). At present, redundancy in Britain is seen as an exogenous policy instrument that imposes a private cost on employers and on redundant workers. MacKay and Jones (1989: 61–2) argue convincingly that redundancy is not independent of the labour market impacts generated as a result of enforced job losses. Rather, redundancy is part of a self-perpetuating cycle in which redundancy is exacerbated by high rates of unemployment: because those most likely to be made redundant are least likely to find alternative employment, current selection procedures not only compound high rates of unemployment but also deter voluntary turnover. In this way redundancy is a source, as well as an outcome, of inflexibility in the labour market.

Neither are the costs of redundancy confined to those directly affected. Redundancy imposes external costs that are borne by society as a whole, through structural unemployment and social security payments. If redundant workers are to find alternative employment they must be offered training and assistance with job search, but most employers accept little, if any, responsibility for what happens in the external labour market as a consequence of the restructuring of their internal labour market. This situation could be reversed by changing the structure of statutory redundancy payments, from a one-off lump-sum to ongoing weekly payments until the redundant worker finds suitable alternative employment. Especially in the event of large-scale redundancies, but possibly more widely, employers should be required to offer appropriate retraining before or immediately after redundancy, preferably in conjunction with state (re)training provision. As Bosch (1990: 116) argues, 'by changing purely compensatory budgets (redundancy pay, unemployment benefit) into active employment policy measures, it makes it possible to operate in a way that is managerially more efficient, possibly cheaper, but in any event socially and economically more effective'. Instead of a Redundancy Fund to cross-subsidise job losses, employers could contribute to a Reconversion Fund to provide training and enhance employability in the external labour market (*ibid.*).

In combination, these changes will have a significant effect in slowing down the dynamic adjustment of labour demand as employers can no longer hire and fire at will (employment will grow less rapidly in the boom, and decline more slowly in recession). But evidence suggests that firing restrictions have a minimal or even positive effect on the long-run level of labour demand (Bosch 1985: 194; and Morgan 1997). Enhancing statutory employment security will send a clear signal to employers that workers have a legitimate stake in their organisation. At present, statutory redundancy arrangements render workers the most easily varied and disposable factor of production. As a result workers are denied basic employment rights in the workplace which are vital to human dignity, self-esteem and productive endeavour. (In)security is determined by commitment as well as risk, but in Britain's deregulated labour market, spontaneous commitment on the part of employers towards their employees is all too often in short supply. The law can 'underwrite' such commitment, promoting the social and economic benefits of secure employment to the advantage of workers, firms and the wider society.

DATA APPENDIX

The data series for exits and redundancies are not consistent over the period 1977 to 1996. The break occurs in 1989 and involves a complete change in the way each variable is collected and measured. Between 1977 and 1988, redundancy figures were compiled from the number of confirmed redundancies reported by firms to the Department of Employment each year in the form of a statutory return (ES955). For a number of reasons, this measure understates the level of redundancies. First, despite the nomenclature, there was in fact no statutory obligation on firms to report redundancies. Secondly, firms were not required to report redundancies of ten or less and redundant workers who did not qualify for statutory severance pay (because they were aged 18 years or less and had less than two years continuous service) and these figures were invariably excluded from the data (see Turnbull 1988: 204–5). Prior to 1986, however, there was an incentive for firms to report statutory redundancies because they could claim a rebate from the Redundancy Fund (see note 3). Under-reporting became a serious problem after 1986 when the rebate was abolished for all firms with more than ten employees (see *Employment Gazette* 1990: 454–3). Thus, prior to 1989, not only are the redundancy figures unreliable (biased downwards) due to under-reporting, the data collected after 1986 are inconsistent with the earlier period because under-reporting was exacerbated by the abolition of the Redundancy Fund. Exit rates were compiled in a similar way, relying on returns completed by the employer. Exit figures are published only for manufacturing industries before 1989 and, where comparisons are made between exit rates and redundancy rates (Figures 4.3–4.5), both rates refer to the manufacturing sector.

From 1989 onwards both redundancy and labour turnover statistics are based on individual self-reports collected in the Labour Force Survey (LFS) covering all industry groups. Each respondent to the LFS is asked if s/he left a job in the last three months, and if the answer is 'yes', whether or not this was a result of redundancy. The data are annualised using a formula reported by the Office for National Statistics (ONS) (see *Labour Market Trends* 1996: 329–32). Although the wording of the question has changed over the period, the content has remained the same (see *Labour Market Trends* 1997: 142).

The two data sources on redundancy ran in parallel between 1989 and 1991 and the extent of downward bias in the statistics compiled from the statutory redundancy return is revealed in a comparison between the two series. In 1989, according to the statutory return the redundancy rate per thousand employees was 5.3, compared to 25.6 according to the LFS. In 1990 the figures were 7.0 and 32.7 per thousand, respectively, and in 1991 the figures were 11.1 and 63.8 per thousand, respectively (*Employment Gazette* 1992: s40; and *Labour Market Trends* 1994: 16).

It is not possible to reconcile the data for the two periods and thus draw any inferences concerning secular trends in redundancies from a simple time series review of these data. For example, the size of the peaks in Figure 4.1 does not indicate that redundancies were higher during the recession of the early 1990s than during the early 1980s. The lower peak in 1981 is more likely to reflect the level of under-reporting under the system of statutory returns. For this reason the time series analysis that we present and the inferences drawn concerning a secular increase are based on trends *within* each cycle and not *across* cycles.

Notes

1 See, (e.g. *The Financial Times*, 5 July 1993 and *The Independent on Sunday*, 14 May 1995).
2 See, (e.g. *The Independent on Sunday*, 16 June 1996).
3 The cost of statutory redundancy payments was previously shared by employers via a contribution to National Insurance payments, regardless of whether the firm made any workers redundant. Originally, under the Redundancy Payments Act 1965, firms could claim a rebate of 70 per cent against any statutory redundancy payment (calculated on the basis of half a week's pay for workers aged 18–21 years with at least two years' continuous service, one week's pay for workers aged 22–40 years, and one and a half week's pay for workers aged 41–65 years, up to a maximum of twenty years' service and subject to a weekly ceiling). The rebate was reduced to 50 per cent in 1969, 41 per cent in 1977, and 35 per cent from 1985. The Wages Act 1986 abolished rebates for all firms except those with fewer than ten employees. Rebates were finally abolished for all firms in 1992.
4 The data for exit rates are not consistent across the two cycles. Prior to 1989 exit rates were collected by firms and cover only manufacturing industries. After 1989 data have been collected from individuals and are available for all industries.
5 In the early 1980s around 40 per cent of workers eligible for statutory redundancy pay also received extrastatutory redundancy payments (ESRP). By the early 1990s the proportion had increased to around 60 per cent.
6 Employers in Austria, Belgium, Ireland, Norway and Sweden claimed obstacles to the termination of employment contracts to be 'serious', while employers in Denmark and Finland regard such obstacles to be 'minor' (IOE 1985).
7 The maximum statutory redundancy payment is currently just £6,600 (twenty years' service times one and a half weeks' pay up to the weekly maximum of £220), a sum which hardly reflects the real costs of job loss to an employee or household (see Beck 1997; Emerson 1988: 790; and Turnbull 1988: 212). Employers can offset some of their ESRP against tax liabilities.
8 The new White Paper, *Fairness at Work* (DTI 1998) proposes to reduce the qualifying period for unfair dismissal to one year, but the two-year qualification period for statutory redundancy pay remains unchanged. Moreover, whereas the law governing fixed-term contracts will in future prohibit 'waivers' under which employees sign away their rights to unfair dismissal protection, the government intends to allow waivers for statutory redundancy payments. Increasingly, however, successive fixed-term contracts are a substitute for permanent employment (for example, in higher education), and waiver clauses for redundancy pay should therefore be outlawed

References

ACAS (1987) *Redundancy Arrangements: The 1986 ACAS Survey*, Occasional Paper 37, London: Advisory, Conciliation & Arbitration Service.
——— (1992) *Annual Report 1991*, London: Advisory, Conciliation & Arbitration Service.
——— (1993) *Annual Report 1992*, London: Advisory, Conciliation & Arbitration Service.
——— (1994) *Annual Report 1993*, London: Advisory, Conciliation & Arbitration Service.
Anderman, S. (1986) 'Unfair Dismissal and Redundancy', in R. Lewis (ed.) *Labour Law in Britain*, Oxford: Blackwell, 415–47.
Anderton, R. (1997) *UK Labour Market Reforms and Sectoral Wage Formation*, Discussion Paper No. 121, London: *National Institute of Economic & Social Research*.
Beaumont, P.B. (1995) *The Future of Employment Relations*, London: Sage.
Beck, M.P. (1997) 'Employment Insecurity and the Law', paper presented at Employment Research Unit Annual Conference, Cardiff Business School, Cardiff University.

Blyton, P. and Turnbull, P. (1998) *The Dynamics of Employee Relations* (second edition), Houndmills: Macmillan.

Bosch, G. (1985) 'West Germany', in M. Cross (ed.) *Managing Workforce Reduction: An International Survey*, London: Croom Helm, 164–98.

—— (1990) *Retraining – Not Redundancy: Innovative Approaches to Industrial Restructuring in Germany and France*, Geneva: International Institute for Labour Studies.

Bulmer, M.A. (1971) 'Mining Redundancy: A Case Study of the Workings of the Redundancy Payments Act in the Durham Coalfield', *Industrial Relations Journal*, 2, 4: 3–21.

Burgess, S. and Rees, H. (1996) 'Job Tenure in Britain 1975–92', *Economic Journal*, 106, 435: 334–44.

Cameron, K.S. (1994) 'Strategies for Successful Organisational Downsizing', *Human Resource Management*, 33, 2: 189–211.

Cappelli, P. (1995) 'Rethinking Employment', *British Journal of Industrial Relations*, 33, 4: 563–602.

Casey, B. (1992) 'Redundancy and Early Retirement: The Interaction of Public and Private Policy in Britain, Germany and the USA', *British Journal of Industrial Relations*, 30, 3: 425–43.

Caulkin, S. (1995) 'Take Your Partners', *Management Today*, February: 26–30.

CEC (1986) *Results of a Survey of Labour Market Flexibility, Commission of the European Community*, European Economy No. 27, Brussels: Commission of the European Community.

Clegg, H.A. (1965) 'Mobility of Labour', *National Provincial Bank Review*, 70: 9–13.

—— (1972) *The System of Industrial Relations in Great Britain*, Oxford: Blackwell.

Daniel, W.W. (1985) 'The United Kingdom', in M. Cross (ed.) *Managing Workforce Reduction: An International Survey*, London: Croom Helm, 67–90.

Daniel, W.W. and Stilgoe, E. (1978) *The Impact of Employment Protection Laws*, London: Policy Studies Institute.

Dore, R. (1988) 'Rigidities in the Labour Market', *Government & Opposition*, 23, 4: 393–412.

DTI (1998) *Fairness and Work*, London: Department of Trade and Industry.

Edwards, P., Hall, M. and Smith, J. (1998) *Redundancy Consultation: Contemporary Practice and the Role of Regulation*, Employment Relations Series, London; Department of Trade & Industry.

Eldridge, J.E.T. (1968) *Industrial Disputes*, Oxford: Blackwell.

Elias, P. (1997) *Restructuring, Reskilling and Redundancy: A Study of the Dynamics of the UK Labour Market*, Working Paper No. 97–20, Colchester: ESRC Research Centre on Micro-Social Change in Britain, University of Essex.

Emerson, M. (1988) 'Regulation or Deregulation of the Labour Market: Policy Regimes for the Recruitment and Dismissal of Employees in the Industrialised Countries', *European Economic Review*, 23: 775–817.

Fryer, R.H. (1973a) 'Redundancy and Public Policy', in R. Martin and R.H. Fryer (eds) *Redundancy and Paternalist Capitalism*, London: Allen & Unwin, 216–60.

—— (1973b) 'Redundancy, Values and Public Policy', *Industrial Relations Journal*, 4, 2: 2–19.

Gibbons, R. and Katz, L.F. (1991) 'Layoffs and Lemons', *Journal of Labor Economics*, 9, 4: 351–80.

Gordon, A. (1984) *Redundancy in the 1980s*, Aldershot: Gower.

Gregg, P., Knight, G. and Wadsworth, J. (1997) 'Heaven Knows I'm Miserable Now: Job Insecurity in the British Labour Market', Working Paper No. 892, London: Centre for Economic Performance, London School of Economics.

Gregg, P. and Wadsworth, J. (1995) 'A Short History of Labour Turnover, Job Tenure and Job Security. 1975–93', *Oxford Review of Economic Policy*, 11, 1: 73–90.

Grubb, D. and Wells, W. (1993) 'Employment Regulation and Patterns of Work in EC Countries', *OECD Economic Studies*, 21, Paris: Organisation for Economic Cooperation and Development.

Grunfeld, C. (1980) *The Law of Redundancy*, London: Sweet & Maxwell.

Guest, D. and Peccei, R. (1992) 'Employee Involvement: Redundancy as a Critical Case', *Human Resource Management Journal*, 2, 3: 34–59.

Hardy, C. (1985) 'Responses to Industrial Closure', *Industrial Relations Journal*, 16, 1: 16–24.

Harris, C. (1988) *Redundancy and Recession in South Wales*, Oxford: Blackwell.

Hartley, J., Jacobson, D., Klandermans, B., Van Vuuren, T., Greenhalgh, L. and Sutton, R. (1991) *Job Insecurity: Coping With Jobs at Risk*, London: Sage.

Henkoff, R. (1990) 'Cost Cutting: How to do it Right', *Fortune*, 121, 8: 40–9.

IDS (1982) *IDS Study*, No. 280, London: Income Data Services.

IMS (1981) *Redundancy Provisions Surveys, Part 1*, IMS Manpower Commentary No. 13, Brighton: Institute of Manpower Studies.

IOE (1985) *Adapting the Labour Market*, Geneva: International Organisation of Employers.

IPD (1996) *The IPD Guide on Redundancy*, London: Institute of Personnel & Development.

ISR (1996) *Employee Satisfaction: Tracking European Trends*, London: International Survey Research.

Kelly, J. (1998) *Rethinking Industrial Relations: Mobilization, Collectivism and Long Waves*, London: Routledge.

Kets de Vries, M.F.R. and Balazs, K. (1997) 'The Downside of Downsizing', *Human Relations*, 50, 1: 11–50.

Lazonick, W. (1991) *Business Organization and the Myth of the Market Economy*, Cambridge: Cambridge University Press.

Lewis, P. (1985) *Twenty Years of Statutory Redundancy Payments in Great Britain*, Occasional Papers in Industrial Relations, No. 8, Leeds: Universities of Leeds and Nottingham.

—— (1993) *The Successful Management of Redundancy*, Oxford: Blackwell.

MacKay, R. and Jones, D. (1989) *Labour Markets in Distress*, Aldershot: Avebury.

Millward, N., Stevens, M., Smart, D. and Hawes, W.R. (1992) *Workplace Industrial Relations in Transition*, Aldershot: Dartmouth.

Morgan, J. (1997) *Employment Protection and Labour Demand in Europe*, London: National Institute of Economic & Social Research.

Mukherjee, S. (1973) *Through No Fault of Their Own: Systems for Handling Redundancies in Britain, France and Germany*, London: Macdonald.

Nickell, S. (1997) 'Unemployment and labour market rigidities', *Journal of Economic Perspectives*, 11, 3: 55–79.

OECD (1994) *The OECD Jobs Study: Evidence and Explanations*, Paris: Organisation for Economic Cooperation and Development.

Parker, S.R., Thomas, C.G., Ellis, N.D. and McCarthy, W.E.J. (1971) *Effects of the Redundancy Payments Act*, London: HMSO.

Roskies, E. and Louis-Guerin, C. (1990) 'Job Insecurity in Managers: Antecedents and Consequences', *Journal of Organisational Behaviour*, 11, 5: 345–59.

Rubery, J. (1994) 'Internal and External Labour Markets: Towards and Integrated Analysis', in J. Rubery and F. Wilkinson (eds) *Employer Strategy and the Labour Market*, Oxford: Oxford University Press, 37–68.

Spilsbury, D., McIntosh, A. and Banerji, J. (1993) 'Redundancies and the Statutory Redundancy Payments Scheme: Results from a Survey of Employers', *Employment Gazette*, July: 313–24.

Streeck, W. (1988) 'Comment on Ronald Dore, "Rigidities in the Labour Market"', *Government & Opposition*, 23, 4: 413–23.

—— (1992) *Social Institutions and Economic Performance*, London: Sage.

Taylor, M. and Booth, A. (1996) *The Changing Picture of Male Unemployment in Britain*, Working Paper No. 96–18, Colchester: ESRC Research Centre in Micro-Social Change in Britain, University of Essex.

Turnbull, P. (1988) 'Leaner and Possibly Fitter: The Management of Redundancy in Britain', *Industrial Relations Journal*, 19, 3: 201–13.

Turnbull, P. and Wass, V. (1994) 'The Greatest Game No More – Redundant Dockers and the Demise of "Dock Work"', *Work, Employment & Society*, 8, 4: 487–506.

—— (1997) 'Job Insecurity and Labour Market Lemons: The (Mis)management of Redundancy in Steel Making, Coal Mining and Port Transport', *Journal of Management Studies*, 34, 1: 27–51.

University of Leeds (1997) *Premature Retirement and Mobility Incentive Schemes, 1997/98*, August, Leeds: University of Leeds.

Wass, V. (1996) 'Who Controls Selection Under "Voluntary" Redundancy? The Case of the Redundant Mineworkers Payment Scheme', *British Journal of Industrial Relations*, 34, 2: 249–65.

Wedderburn, D. (1968) 'Redundancy', in D. Pym (ed.) *Industrial Society: Social Sciences in Management*, London: Penguin, 65–81.

Wedderburn, K.W. (1965) *The Worker and the Law*, London: Pelican.

Westergaard, J., Noble, I. and Walker, A. (1988) 'After Redundancy: Economic Experience and Political Outlook Among Former Steel Employees in Sheffield', in D. Rose (ed.) *Social Stratification and Economic Change*, London: Hutchinson, 153–73.

White, P.J. (1983) 'The Management of Redundancy', *Industrial Relations Journal*, 14, 1: 32–40.

Withington, J. (1989) *Shutdown: The Anatomy of a Shipyard Closure*, London: Bedford Square Press.

5 Employment insecurity in the public services

Philip Morgan, Nigel Allington and Edmund Heery

Introduction

Job security, until recently, has been seen as a defining characteristic of traditional public sector employment, and the 'risk-averse', time-serving bureaucrat is a common, negative stereotype of the public sector worker. As the restructuring of the public sector has gathered pace over the last twenty years, however, the security of employees has come under threat. The primary purpose of this chapter is to review the extent to which public service workers have become more insecure. Using the broad framework for analysing employment security suggested by Heery and Salmon (this volume), we use a range of secondary and official sources to examine 'objective' changes in the structure of public service jobs, changes in the institutional and economic environment surrounding those jobs and the 'subjective' perceptions of insecurity of public service workers. Along each of these paths our aim is to measure the extent of change in order to reach an overall assessment of the degree and manner in which the employment security of public service workers has been eroded over the past two decades.

In providing an estimate of the degree to which employment insecurity now characterises public service, our aim is to contribute to the wider debate which is current over the extent and nature of change in public sector employment relations. Simplifying somewhat, there are two main positions in this debate. The first holds that exposure of public services to commercial pressure and the spread of new management techniques have led to a break with the traditional model of public sector employment, and the emergence of a new pattern, sometimes described as 'neo-Taylorist' (Pollitt 1993; Sinclair *et al.* 1996). It is further suggested that this change has led to the degradation of public sector employment and, while this may have generated short-term efficiency benefits, it jeopardises the effectiveness of the public services in the longer term, principally through the erosion of the peculiar commitment and motivation of public sector workers – what is known as the 'public service ethos' (Pratchett and Wingfield 1996). In the light of this claim our review is concerned, not just with the extent of change, but with a consideration of some of its consequences and, in particular, with the degree to which greater insecurity has had a negative effect on worker attitudes.

The second position is more diffuse and is occupied by those who emphasise a degree of continuity in public service employment relations and the limited extent to which the behaviour and motivations of public sector workers have been affected negatively by recent change (Bach and Winchester 1994; Heery 1998; Kessler 1991; Pratchett and Wingfield 1996). A key line of argument is that the distinctiveness of public sector employment remains and that convergence with patterns of employment in the private sector, much of which does have a history of job insecurity, has not really taken place (Boyne *et al.* 1999). We also want to examine this claim and in what follows we seek to measure the relative security of public sector and private sector workers whenever data are available.

The primary focus of our review is on the core and traditionally non-traded public services, such as the civil service, local government, education and the National Health Service (NHS) and is structured as follows. First, we examine the changing context of public sector employment and the factors which are likely to have generated any erosion of worker security. These include pressures to cut costs and reduce public sector employment, the exposure of services to competitive and commercial pressures and the spread of new management thinking and techniques garnered from the private sector – frequently described as the 'new public management' (Ferlie *et al.* 1997). Second, we examine changes in public sector jobs with a particular focus on the emergence of 'precarious' employment (Allen and Henry 1996) as a result of competitive tendering, the spread of non-standard and contingent employment and the increased use of performance-related pay. Third, we review institutional developments which may serve to exacerbate insecurity with a particular focus on changes in employment law and trade union density and coverage by collective bargaining. Finally, we focus on public sector workers themselves and the extent to which they evince a growing perception of, and concern with, job insecurity.

The restructuring of the public sector

Change in employment relations in the public services over the past two decades has formed part of a wider restructuring of the public sector (Farnham and Horton 1996a; White 1996). The purpose of this section therefore is to review the main themes within this process. Four separate but interlocking changes can be identified, each of which has impacted upon public service employment and arguably served to erode the security of public sector workers. These changes are: pressure to reduce public expenditure by holding down the cost of service provision; the exposure of public services to market competition through privatization, tendering and the introduction of internal markets; organisational changes which have resulted in the break up of large bureaucracies in a process analogous to the divisionalisation of large private sector firms (Purcell and Ahlstrand 1994); and the strengthening of a general management function within services which has been accompanied by the diffusion of new management techniques.

Control of expenditure

Since the oil crisis of the early 1970s there has been pressure on successive British governments to control public expenditure. With the election of the Conservative administration of Margaret Thatcher in 1979, the reduction in the extent and cost of public service provision became a central objective of state policy. An 'excessively' large public sector was seen variously as a constraint on entre-preneurial vigour, a bastion of inefficiency and poor industrial relations, a cause of high taxation and a stimulant to inflationary pressure. Accordingly, through the 1980s and 1990s governments have pursued a range of policies to control public expenditure. In the civil service these have taken the form of across-the-board staff reduction targets, the replacement of volume-planning with cash limits, a cash limit assumption about pay increases, the funding of pay increases by job losses and productivity improvement, a new system of devolved budgeting and financial control (the Financial Management Initiative), the transfer of agencies to private ownership and the use of market testing to enforce cost reduction and productivity growth (Corby 1998; Horton 1996). Equivalent developments occurred in other branches of public service and many of these policies remain in place under the New Labour government of Tony Blair, which accepted the Conservatives' public expenditure plans for 1996–98 and continued the tight control of public sector pay.

The results of these policies have been mixed, but government expenditure dropped from a peak of 47.25 per cent of gross domestic product in 1982–3 to 37.75 per cent in 1988–9, then rose steadily to 43.25 per cent in 1993–4, as a consequence of growing unemployment, before falling again in the period of economic recovery. The primary impact on public service employment of policies of expenditure control has been a reduction in the number of jobs (see Table 5.1). Public sector employment peaked in 1979 at 7.5 million and declined as a result of privatisation, competitive tendering and efficiency savings to 5.8 million in 1991 and 5.1 million in 1996, a total fall of 31 per cent. During the same period private sector employment grew to a total of 20.6 million, an increase of 14 per cent on the 1979 figure. The decline has not been uniform across all public services or occupations, however, and the public corporations and the civil service have been most heavily cut. Other services, such as the police, health and social services provided by local authorities and the NHS, have experienced stability or growth in employment and a marked feature of several services has been an absolute and disproportionate increase in the number of managerial employees (Kessler and Bayliss 1995; Winchester and Bach 1995).

Exposure to markets

While policy has focused on reducing the size and cost of the public sector, it has sought also to make it more efficient and effective, so that the level of service can be maintained in a context of stable or declining resources. The primary means by which these goals have been pursued is through the exposure of

Table 5.1 Public sector employment, 1961–96 (at mid-year)

Year	Total Employed ('000)								Percentage Change			
	1961	1964	1974	1979	1984	1989	1994	1996	1964–74	1974–84	1984–96	1979–96
Total workforce	24,183	24,950	25,148	25,507	24,426	26,957	25,511	25,881	0.8	-2.95	5.62	1.5
Private sector	18,598	18,989	18,266	18,057	17,351	20,409	20,283	20,570	-3.8	-5.27	15.62	13.9
Public sector	5,859	5,961	6,882	7,450	6,900	6,086	5,232	5,130	15.5	0.26	-34.5	-31.1
Breakdown of public sector												
Central government	1,790	1,794	2,115	2,388	2,359	2,314	1,185	981	17.9	10.34	-140.47	-59
Local authority	1,821	2,088	2,782	2,997	2,942	2,940	2,642	2,637	33.2	-84.64	-11.57	-12
Public corporations	2,200	2,079	1,985	2,065	1,599	832	1,467	1,512	-4.5	-24.14	-5.75	-26.8
NHS Trusts	0	0	0	0	0	0	1,000	1,102	N/A	N/A	N/A	N/A
NHS (non-Trusts)	575	627	911	1,152	1,223	1,226	177	84	45	25.51	-1,355.95	-92.7
Total NHS	575	627	911	1,152	1,223	1,226	1,177	1,186	45	25.51	-3.12	3

Source: Economic trends annual supplement HMSO, 1997.

public services to market competition. Central to this programme of reform has been the belief that markets provide the best mechanism for determining pricing and output issues within public services. The 'marketisation' of the public sector has assumed a variety of different forms, with full privatisation or the transfer of services to private, profit-seeking owners representing the extreme case. For services which have been retained in public ownership, such as health, education and central and local government, two reforms have proved particularly significant. The first is compulsory competitive tendering (CCT) or market testing, in which services which were previously provided in-house are put out to tender and as a consequence may be delivered on behalf of a public service organisation by a private sector firm (Walsh 1995). In the NHS, competitive tendering for ancillary services has been mandatory since 1983 (Bach 1989), while in local government the number of services exposed to CCT increased in stages through the 1980s and 1990s and now embraces a wide range of both manual and professional work (Escott and Whitfield 1995; Walsh and Davis 1993).

The second key reform has been the establishment of 'internal markets' in which service providers, such as NHS Trust Hospitals, contract with grant-funded purchasers, such as district health authorities and fund-holding general practitioners, to provide a given level of service at an agreed cost. This quasi-market mechanism is designed to promote competition amongst service providers and has been associated with attempts to measure the performance of agencies involved in service delivery and to rank them in performance league tables. Markets have implied measurement as those purchasing services have sought information which can allow the monitoring of the discharge of contracts and inform the decision whether to recontract or seek a better deal elsewhere.

New Labour has proposed some reform of these arrangements and is committed to ending the internal market in the NHS as it is presently constituted and replacing CCT in local government with a new policy known as 'Best Value'. This seeks to broaden the performance criteria used to evaluate local government services and will end the legal requirement to put them out to tender. The emphasis on competition, performance rating and benchmarking will be retained, however, and according to the Local Government Management Board, 'it is very likely that tendering of contracts will continue in the long term for what are currently described as blue and white collar services and perhaps in other areas as well' (LGMB 1997b: 86). The retention of competition as a form of external discipline on public sector organisations seems likely to remain a feature of state policy for all public services notwithstanding the change of government.

Organisational change

The creation of markets and exposure to competition have, in turn, required sweeping organisational changes within public services. On the one hand, there has been the formal separation of provider and purchaser roles which can be seen in the division between Whitehall ministries and civil service Executive Agencies, between the purchasing arm of local authorities and direct service organisations (DSOs) and in the division between NHS trusts and district health authorities. On the other hand, there has been a process of organisational decentralisation as centrally coordinated bureaucracies have been broken up into constituent units which have been endowed with greater operational autonomy in order to permit competition and allow individual service providers to respond to market signals (Blundell and Murdock 1997). Across the public services, operational units have been allowed greater freedom to manage their internal operations within the context of competition for financial resources. This process is analogous to that of divisionalisation within large firms, in which product-based divisions and business units compete internally for funding on the basis of success at meeting exacting financial targets. In all of the public services, operational units have therefore acquired greater autonomy in managing and remunerating their staff. Civil service Executive Agencies, local authority DSOs, NHS trusts and locally managed schools, colleges and universities have all acquired greater discretion in the management of human resources in recent years (Corby 1996, 1998; Farnham and Giles 1996; Horton 1996; Walsh and Davis 1993; White and Hutchinson 1996; Winchester and Bach 1995). Again, this development will not be substantially reversed by the Blair government which, in certain services such as education, is committed to a further devolution of management responsibility to operational units.

Managerialism

Exposure to competition and organisational devolution have implied a further change, the strengthening of the management function within public services, a development which is variously labelled 'new managerialism' or 'new public management' (NPM). According to Michael Heseltine (1980), the then Secretary of State for the Environment, 'Efficient management is a key to the national revival ... And the management ethos must run through our national life – private and public companies, civil service, nationalised industries, local government, the National Health Service' (quoted in Farnham and Horton 1996a: 320). The pursuit of efficient management has occurred in a number of ways. Governments have called upon senior executives from the private sector and management consultants to review and reform the management of public services (examples include the Griffiths report on the NHS, the Ibbs report and Rayner review of the civil service and the Sheehy report on the police). They have also appointed or seconded private sector managers to key positions within the public services, a notable example being the appointment of Len Peach, erstwhile director of personal and corporate affairs at IBM, to the NHS Executive Board where he was instrumental in introducing performance management and performance pay to the health service (Farnham and Horton 1996b).

The influx of private sector expertise and ideology has been supplemented by structural changes designed either to create or strengthen a line management hierarchy within public services. At its apex, this has been attempted through a reform of corporate governance arrangements and the adoption in the NHS and other services of a private sector, board of directors model which has in turn been linked with the marginalisation of elected staff and consumer representatives. The position of chief executive has been established or bolstered across services and supported by the creation of a new cadre of general managers, as in the NHS, and the development of a more formalised management hierarchy within the public service professions. Head teachers, clinical directors, university vice-chancellors, deans and professors have all acquired new functions within a more explicit managerial hierarchy.

The strengthening of management has gone hand-in-hand with the diffusion of new management techniques, and the public services have provided fertile ground in recent years for experiment with the full panoply of modern management methods from TQM to business process re-engineering (Farnham and Horton 1996b; Kirkpatrick and Martinez Lucio 1995). Two linked trends arguably have been particularly important, both of which imply closer management control of public service professionals (Morgan and Potter 1995; Potter and Morgan 1997). The first has been the spread or reform of performance appraisal and other performance management techniques, which have served to translate the new disciplines of competition down to the individual employment relationship (see Davies and Kirkpatrick 1995; Healy 1997; Townley 1990/91). The second has been the spread of individual performance-related pay, which for many groups of public servants has partly replaced the traditional reliance on time, seniority and fair comparison as principles of public service pay determination (see Burchill and Casey 1996; Heery 1998; IDS Public Sector Unit 1989). Once again, these initiatives have been confirmed rather than reversed by New Labour, which has maintained a tough stance towards public service professions and is committed to the further extension of performance-related pay, most notably to school teachers.

Changing jobs

While there has undoubtedly been an extensive reform and restructuring of the public sector, the extent and manner in which this has resulted in a decline in employee security remain uncertain. In this section we begin our review of this question by examining change in the structure of public service jobs. Our concern is with four issues: the extent to which the risk of losing one's job has risen in public services; the degree to which employment has become more precarious through exposure to competitive tendering; the extent to which use of temporary work and other non-standard employment contracts has grown within the public sector; and the degree to which changes in pay determination have placed the earnings of public service workers at significant risk. For each issue we wish to examine both the extent of change since the early 1980s, when restructuring began, and the degree to which there has been a 'levelling down' of employment security in the public sector, such that the relative security of public service workers *vis-à-vis* the private sector has come to an end. In carrying out this review we have attempted to draw evenly on evidence from the civil service, local government, NHS and education. However, the uneven quantity of published material has meant that this has not always been possible.

Risk of job loss

The risk of losing one's job can most obviously be measured by the incidence of workforce reduction and redundancy. It is perhaps most acute where employers resort to compulsory redundancy, such that employees are selected for job loss potentially against their will, though there may also be an element of compulsion where job loss occurs through voluntary redundancy and early retirement (Turnbull and Wass, this volume). Case study and survey evidence from a number of public services suggest that restructuring has led to increased resort to redundancy by managers and that occupational groups which previously were immune to this experience have begun to be affected. Lloyd and Seifert (1995) report redundancies amongst NHS professionals as a direct consequence of the internal market; Ironside and Seifert (1995; see also Sinclair *et al.* 1996) also claim that local management of schools has increased redundancy amongst teachers; and Walsh and Davis's (1993) survey of the impact of CCT in local government indicates that workforce reduction has led to redundancy in at least some local authorities. Table 5.2, moreover, indicates that the period of restructuring in the civil service in the wake of the Next Steps initiative has led to a sharp increase in 'early departures' from the service. The latter consist primarily of early retirements and redundancies and the figures show that these have become relatively more frequent forms of job loss in the 1990s 'reflecting the growing pressure to increase efficiency and reduce staff costs' (GSS 1998: 12).

Some parts of the public service, therefore, provide evidence of an increased risk of job loss through redundancy, but public service employment in general carries less of a risk of this kind than private sector employment. Since 1993 *Labour Market Trends* has carried figures for the rate of redundancy (redundancies per 1,000 employees) by industry in such a way that allows comparison of public services with the private sector. In spring 1998 the rate for 'public administration, education and health' stood at two redundancies per thousand workers, the lowest across the economy. The redundancy rates for other industries were as follows: manufacturing 15, construction 11, distribution, hotels and restaurants 9, transport 10 and banking, finance and insurance 9 (*Labour Market Trends*, August: S55). This broad pattern has remained unchanged over the five-year period for which data are available, albeit with some annual and seasonal variations.

Further evidence of a continuing 'security gap' between the public and private sector is shown in Table 5.3 which presents information on workforce reduction and redundancy from the 1990 Workplace Industrial Relations Survey (WIRS). It indicates that in the survey year the incidence of workforce reduction in all three main sectors of the economy was broadly the same, but that the public sector was distinctive in its avoidance of compulsory redundancy and reliance on early retirement. Figures for individual branches of the public service, moreover,

Table 5.2 Early departures from the Civil Service, 1989–97 (percentage of total leavers)

	1989–90	1990–1	1991–2	1992–3	1993–4	1994–5	1995–6	1996–7
All early leavers from service	3.9	7.8	11.2	22.8	19.2	24.3	30.9	24.8
Of which:								
Early retirements	3.1	4.4	5.7	14.0	12.7	16.6	20.8	15.8
Early severance	0.8	3.4	5.5	8.9	6.5	7.7	10.0	9.0

Source: Civil Service Statistics, 1996, 1997

Note: Statistics not collected on this basis before 1989

Table 5.3 Workforce reduction and redundancy in the public and private sectors, 1990 (percentages)

	All establishments	Private manufacturing	Private services	Public sector
Reductions in any section or sections of the workforce in last year	32	39	28	34
Methods used to reduce a section or sections of the workforce				
Natural wastage	67	64	68	70
Redeployment within workplace	45	53	42	40
Early retirement	26	20	18	41
Voluntary redundancies	21	26	16	23
Compulsory redundancies	30	52	35	4
Other methods	7	7	5	11
None	9	10	11	5

Source: Millward *et al.* (1992)

confirm this pattern: in central government 32 per cent of workplaces reported workforce reduction but fewer than 0.5 per cent of establishments reported compulsory redundancies, while equivalent figures for local government and 'medical services' were 44 and 4 per cent and 24 and 2 per cent, respectively (Millward *et al.* 1992: 345).

The period since 1990 may have witnessed some erosion of the difference between public and private sectors in their management of job loss, but it is unlikely that full convergence has occurred. Moreover, a survey of members of the Institute of Management, reported by Boyne *et al.* (1999), suggests that public sector attachment to security of employment remained higher than in the private sector in 1995. Survey respondents were asked whether their organisation had a policy of providing 'lifetime job security'; this was denied by 36 per cent of private sector managers, compared with only 27 per cent of public sector managers (the difference in mean response between the two groups was statistically significant at the .001 level). While the evidence is patchy and incomplete, therefore, it suggests that the restructuring of public services has increased the risk of job loss for public sector workers and in some quarters there has been increased resort to redundancy as a means of workforce reduction. The public sector remains distinctive when compared with the private sector, however, and employer preparedness to avoid redundancy and mitigate the adverse consequences for the workforce is still apparent.

Precarious employment

The concept of 'precarious employment' has recently been advanced by Allen and Henry (1996) in a discussion of the employment relation of private sector contract workers in three low-skilled, labour-intensive contract industries: cleaning, catering and security. They use the term to refer to three main forms of insecurity to which employees in these industries are exposed. First, employment is only guaranteed for the duration of a particular cleaning, catering or security contract, which in most cases is three to four years. Second, when contracts are renewed they are frequently renegotiated and this, in turn, may result in the reformulation of the employment contract and the imposition of inferior rates of pay and conditions of employment. Third, when contracts are lost, employees may retain their jobs through transfer to a new employer, but this change may also result in changed conditions and uncertainty as to the future employment relationship, notwithstanding the Transfer of Undertaking (Protection of Employment) (TUPE) Regulations. Even for employees with continuous and regular employment over a series of contracts the contracting regime can engender insecurity.

At the core of public sector restructuring has been the emergence of the 'contract state' (Kirkpatrick and Martinez Lucio 1996) and the extension of competitive tendering and contracting throughout the public services. In this section we shall consider the extent to which this transition has led to more precarious employment for public service workers and the pattern of insecurity and uncertainty described in Allen and Henry's case studies of the private sector.

Exposure to tendering and market testing has affected a large proportion of the public service workforce over the past two decades. In the health service, contracting of catering, laundry and domestic services has been obligatory since 1983 (Cousins 1988) and in local government CCT has been extended in a series of stages to embrace a wide range of manual and professional services (see Table 5.4). The National Health Service and Community Care Act 1990, moreover, furnished a similar regime of market testing and tendering for local authority social services and parallel initiatives have affected other branches of public service. According to Escott and Whitfield (1995: 4), the extension of CCT to white-collar services in local government is affecting approximately 200,000 employees.

One way of assessing whether contracting is making work 'precarious' is to examine its association with workforce reduction. It is difficult to disentangle the effects of CCT from other pressures to reduce staff numbers, but Colling and Ferner (1995: 497) report an estimate of 110,000 health service jobs lost since the

Table 5.4 Services exposed to compulsory competitive tendering in local government

---

Local Government Planning and Land Act 1980

　Building repair and maintenance
　Highways work

Local Government Act 1988

　Building cleaning
　Refuse collection
　Street cleansing
　Catering (civic, school, welfare)
　Grounds maintenance
　Vehicle maintenance
　Sports and leisure

Competing for Quality 1991

　Home to school transport
　Vehicle fleet management
　Security services for buildings
　Parking services
　Management of theatre and arts facilities
　Library support services
　Housing management (95%)
　Architectural services (65%)
　Engineering services (65%)
　Property management services (65%)
　Legal services (45%)
　Computing services (70%)
　Financial services (35%)
　Personnel services (35%)

Source: Escott and Whitfield (1995)

introduction of CCT in 1983, equivalent to 40 per cent of the manual workforce. In local government, Walsh and Davis (1993: 159) report that there had been a 12.2 per cent reduction in staffing levels across the manual services exposed to competition by the Local Government Act 1988, with a particularly sharp drop in refuse collection, building cleaning and grounds maintenance. Escott and Whitfield (1995: 147), on the basis of later findings, produce a higher estimate of 21 per cent, though again identify building cleaning and refuse collection as services which have been particularly hard hit, and report a 13 per cent reduction in manual social services jobs as a result of community care. They also predict 40,000 job losses as a result of white-collar CCT, almost a quarter of those affected.

A second way of assessing the impact of contracts is to examine contract length and gauge the extent to which previously open-ended employment has been replaced by what is effectively a fixed-term contract. In local government, legislation stipulates contracts of between three and ten years, depending on the service. Research on contracts for manual services indicates that most run for approximately four years and are towards the lower end of the statutory range (LGMB 1997b: 15; Walsh and Davis 1993: 49). When framing contracts, therefore, local authorities appear to have prioritised flexibility, and their own ability to review and modify contracts, over the reduction of uncertainty for the workforce. In a small proportion of cases, moreover, contracts have been terminated before their full span as a result of performance failure on the part of the contractor. Walsh and Davis's survey (1993: 116) provides an estimate for contract failure of 3.3 per cent.

There is also considerable evidence that exposure to tendering has led to the erosion of terms and conditions of employment, at least for manual workers. Case studies of contracting of services in both the NHS and local government report cuts in pay, hours and employment benefits and the withdrawal of bonus schemes and incentives at the same time that work was undergoing intensification (Bach 1989; Colling 1993; Cousins 1988). Walsh and Davis's (1993: 156) survey of local authority responses to CCT reports that 15 per cent of authorities had withdrawn bonus schemes, 7 per cent had cut basic wages, 18 per cent had altered their approach to sick pay and 12 per cent had changed holiday entitlement. The primary response, apart from workforce reduction, however, had been to rearrange hours of work, reported by 51 per cent of authorities. Walsh and Davis also note that, while the major change in employment conditions had occurred at the point of initial exposure to competition, a significant proportion of authorities had continued to make changes after contracts had been awarded. Escott and Whitfield's (1995) survey reveals a broadly similar pattern, with contracting leading, in a minority of authorities, to the erosion of national pay rates, the reduction or withdrawal of overtime, bonus and sick pay and the weakening of maternity support. The adverse effect on employment conditions, they also note, has been borne primarily by part-time women workers.

Allen and Henry's final measure of precariousness is the risk of transfer of employees from one employer to another and in health and local government this is best measured by the percentage of contracts awarded to private firms. In both services the majority of contracts have been won by in-house bids (Winchester and Bach 1995). In 1997 local government DSOs were successful in winning 56.5 per cent contracts and 71 per cent of work tendered by value (LGMB 1997b: 12; see also Escott and Whitfield 1995; Walsh and Davis 1993). The lowest levels of in-house success were recorded in building cleaning (43.8 per cent) and grounds maintenance (53.1 per cent), and the highest levels in sports and leisure (74.2 per cent), education and welfare catering (70.3 per cent) and vehicle maintenance (69.9 per cent). It is sometimes suggested that the retention of work in-house represents a pyrrhic victory for public service workers, as the cost of success is the erosion of terms and conditions. The latter has occurred, as has been demonstrated, but evidence suggests that rates of pay and conditions of employment continue to be better in local authority DSOs than in private contractor firms (Escott and Whitfield 1995). Given this, it is significant that over time there appears not to have been an increase in the proportion of contracts being lost to the private sector. However, Escott and Whitfield (*ibid.*: 179) report management perceptions of increased competition and pressure to reduce labour costs further as they entered the second round of tendering for manual services.

In summary, it appears that the spread of contracting and market testing in public services has made employment more precarious for large numbers of public sector workers. It has led to a significant increase in the risk of job loss and reduction in employment standards and, in the manner suggested by Allen and Henry, has instituted a regime of ongoing uncertainty as contracts are relet and service managers seek periodic renegotiation of the employment relationship. Despite deterioration over time, however, it seems that employment conditions remain more favourable in public service than they do in private sector contracting firms, even for manual workers in hard-pressed local authority DSOs.

Casualisation

A third broad indicator of rising worker insecurity is an increase in the proportion of jobs which are non-permanent, and the purpose of this section is to review the trend in the use of temporary employment contracts in public services. The available evidence indicates an unambiguous increase in the use of contingent contracts in public services and on this dimension, for at least some indicators, the incidence of worker insecurity appears to be greater in public services than it is in the private sector.

With regard to increases in the use of temporary labour over time in public services, two primary sources are available, the annual Labour Force Survey (LFS) and the periodic WIRS. According to Casey *et al.* (1997: 33), evidence from the former for the period 1984–94 indicates an increase of 66.6 per cent in the use of temporary work in public administration, of 57.1 per cent in education and 66.4 per cent in health and social work. In these three core areas of public service employment temporary work constituted 5.8, 15.8 and 7.3 per cent of total employment, respectively, in 1994. The evidence from WIRS allows a comparison of 1984 and 1990 and points to a substantial increase in the use of short-term contract workers in the public sector between these two points in time (Casey *et al.* 1997: 69). In 1984, 17 per cent of establishments in the non-trading public services could be classified as high users of contract staff (i.e. 5 per cent or more of the workforce were on this kind of contract). By 1990 this had risen to 26 per cent. Services with a particularly high level of contract staff included schools, further education, health and local authority construction, all of which increased their use between the two surveys.

Other evidence points in the same direction. In the civil service, the NHS and local authorities there has been an increase in the use of fixed-term contracts for senior managers, which in some cases has been used to justify increases in salaries and access to performance pay (Corby 1996; Cousins 1988; Horton 1996; LACSAB 1990b). Amongst professional groups similar developments have been recorded, including increased use of nursing banks in health and the emergence of a significant body of agency labour in schools and further education (Corby 1996; Lloyd and Seifert 1995). At the base of the occupational hierarchy, moreover, amongst local authority manual workers, there is evidence of an increase in the number of those on shorter hours, who can be classed as insecure by virtue of their limited access to social protection (LGMB 1997a). In addition, Escott and Whitfield (1995: 159–60) report that CCT has stimulated increased use by local authority DSOs of temporary contracts, registers of casual staff, term-time only and fixed-term contracts and agency labour.

Particularly heavy use of temporary work can be seen in universities, where increased reliance on fixed-term contracts has been a primary response of employers to apply pressure on budgets. Table 5.5 indicates that more than a fifth of teaching academics in traditional universities are now employed on this basis, suggesting that this form of contract is now spreading from academic research work, where it has long been dominant and is used for virtually all university employees. The table also demonstrates that female academics are more likely to be employed on a temporary, fixed-term basis than their male colleagues.

Table 5.5 Fixed-term contracts in UK universities (percentages)

	1995–6	*1996–7*
Teaching staff (including staff engaged on teaching plus research)		
Total fixed-term	21.9	22.8
Males	18.0	18.3
Females	34.4	34.9
Research staff		
Total fixed-term	95.7	95.6
Males	95.2	95.0
Females	96.4	96.5

Source: HESA Services Ltd.

Not only has there been an increase in the use of temporary work in public services over the past two decades, but there is also evidence that the incidence of at least some forms of temporary work is higher in parts of the public service than it is in the private sector. According to LFS data (Casey *et al.* 1997: 15), the highest user of temporary labour in 1994 was education, while health and social work (but not public administration) also recorded a figure above the national average (6.5 per cent) (see also Gallie *et al.* 1998: 173–4). A later analysis of LFS data for spring 1996, which compared the incidence of temporary working in local government with that in the wider economy, found that 293,000 local authority workers – 13 per cent of the total – were on temporary contracts, compared with 7 per cent of all employees, 5 per cent of employees in manufacturing and 8 per cent in other service industries (LGMB 1997a: 95). The higher use of temporary work in local government, moreover, is apparent whether one considers full-time or part-time employees: 7 per cent of local government full-timers were temporary, compared with 5 per cent in the wider economy, and the equivalent figures for part-timers were 22 and 13 per cent.

Table 5.6, which presents material from the 1990 WIRS, indicates more strongly that the public services are distinctive in their use of temporary contracts. High use of short-term contracts, those of twelve months' duration or less, appears to be concentrated in the non-trading public sector and education, again, stands out as being particularly reliant on this form of employment contract. The public sector is not a distinctive user of all forms of non-standard contract, however, and the WIRS data indicate that use of freelances is a largely private sector

Table 5.6 The incidence of short-term contract workers, 1990 (percentages)

	Proportion of workplaces where number of short-term contract workers, as a proportion of the whole, was:		
	High (5%+)	*Low (1–4%)*	*Zero*
All workplaces	10	9	80
Broad sector			
Public services (non-trading)	26	19	53
Trading sector	4	5	91
Manufacturing	4	3	93
Private services	4	6	90
Public services			
Construction	39	—	61
Higher education	8	20	69
Schools	44	29	26
Other education	41	—	59
Medical services	13	40	42
Miscellaneous services	21	17	60

Source: Casey *et al.* (1997)

phenomenon (Casey *et al.* 1997: 54). The only branches of the public service which appear to make extensive use of this form are higher and further education, where freelance lecturing staff are employed in significant numbers.

In summary, therefore, our third indicator of a shift towards insecure work, the growth of temporary work, also provides evidence of substantial change in the public services where there has been a particularly marked growth in the use of fixed-term contracts in recent years. Many public sector managers and professionals, such as teachers, lecturers, social workers and nurses, now work under this kind of employment contract and, according to the LGMB (1997a: 97) a fifth of education professionals are now engaged in temporary work. On this dimension, moreover, there is evidence that insecure work is more characteristic of public service than it is of the private sector, which perhaps lends credence to the belief that the 'flexible firm' is a theoretical model which has most relevance to public sector experience (Pollert 1988; Pollitt 1993).

Performance-related pay

While insecurity at work is usually understood in terms of a threat to continuity of tenure, it can also be defined in terms of systems of payment which expose employee earnings to risk and uncertainty. Accordingly, the final dimension of public service jobs that we want to consider is the changing form of remuneration and the degree to which pay for performance has displaced other, traditional principles of pay determination for public service workers. The latter have comprised the payment of a standard rate (or scale) for the job across an entire branch of public service, reliance on the principle of comparability with the private sector in determining wage and salary increases and, for white-collar workers, progression through fixed incremental scales on the basis of seniority. From the perspective of the individual employee these principles afforded a secure and predictable, if often relatively modest, wage or salary, and our aim is to gauge whether this degree of security and predictability has been weakened.

The key development which seems to represent a threat to the security of public service incomes is the spread of systems of individual performance-related pay (IPRP), which tie earnings to the results of an individual appraisal or performance review. Payment systems of this kind were virtually unknown within public services at the start of the 1980s but have since been adopted, for at least a proportion of non-manual employees, across most branches of public service. In the civil service, IPRP was first introduced for senior grades in 1985 and has since been extended to the full range of staff; in the NHS, performance pay has been applied to senior and middle managers from the late 1980s and has been extended to a small number of other grades in individual NHS trusts; and in local government about a quarter of authorities have applied IPRP, largely to management grades, though in a small number of cases to all white-collar workers (Dawson *et al.* 1995; Heery 1998; LACSAB 1990b; White 1996, 1999). Schemes have also been applied to senior staff in other services, including universities, colleges of education and schools, but to date pressure from successive governments has yet to result in the introduction of a national IPRP scheme for teachers or lecturers (Farnham and Giles 1996).

The spread of IPRP has imported the principle of pay for performance for a substantial number of white-collar workers in public services since the mid-1980s, but since the late 1960s productivity bonus and incentive schemes have been widely applied to public service manual workers. In many cases, however, these traditional pay-for-performance systems had ceased to operate as effective incentives, and functioned as a routinely awarded supplement to basic pay, particularly for male manual workers. The restructuring of public services and exposure to competition have led to two kinds of change with regard to these 'decayed' bonus schemes. In some cases they have been withdrawn, as a means of reducing labour costs, and in others, and particularly in refuse collection, they have been overhauled in order to re-establish the connection between performance and payment and force up productivity (Escott and Whitfield 1995; Walsh and Davis 1993).

Across much of the public sector and across a range of occupational groups, therefore, there has been an attempt to alter principles of pay determination and to link pay to performance. This suggests that the earnings of public service workers have become more contingent and less secure, but this view requires qualification, at least as far as white-collar IPRP schemes are concerned. Public service IPRP schemes have tended to assume a non-radical form in which only a modest proportion of pay is at risk in any one performance year and which operate alongside collectively bargained cost of living awards. Their primary purpose in some services has been to raise the level of pay for managers and professionals in order to solve recruitment and retention problems and evidence on the application of schemes points to only limited differentiation of employees through performance rating, so that the majority continue to earn a standard, predictable rate of pay (Dowling and Richardson 1997; Heery 1998; LACSAB 1990a, 1990b; Marsden and Richardson 1994; White 1996). The introduction of performance pay, therefore, may represent a step towards worker insecurity, but the form and operation of public service schemes are such that the degree of risk imposed appears limited.

It is also the case that public service workers remain less likely to be exposed to contingent systems of reward than their private sector counterparts. WIRS 1990 indicated that public service establishments were less likely to use payment by results (IPRP, individual and group incentive schemes) than private sector workplaces (Millward *et al.* 1992: 261), a finding which is probably due in part to the intense opposition to performance pay of public service white-collar trade unions (Heery and Warhurst 1994). Boyne *et al.*'s (1999) analysis of survey responses from members of the Institute of Management confirms this pattern: public sector managers were less likely to report policies of rewarding merit, productivity gains, customer service or the sharing of risks and rewards with the workforce and were more likely to report a policy of equal pay for equal work, that is the established public service tradition of paying the rate for the job. It is also the case that more radical systems of performance pay, which impose a higher degree of risk on employees, tend to be reported in private sector organisations. There is evidence of a shift in the private sector in the 1990s towards 'merit only' IPRP schemes, which abandon a separate 'cost of living' element, and the adoption of 'variable pay', in which the value of base salary and fringe benefits are reduced or held constant while the proportion of 'at risk' pay is increased (Heery 1996). With the possible exception of a number of civil service agencies (Corby 1998), this shift towards more radical forms of performance pay is not apparent in the public services.

Institutional changes

A second way in which public service workers may be becoming more insecure is through the erosion of institutions of worker protection. In this section we want to examine the pattern of institutional change within public services and establish the extent to which employment law, trade unionism and collective bargaining have ceased to provide effective protection for public service employees. With regard to employment law, our primary focus is not on the general deregulation of the labour market but on statutory and other reforms which have been targeted specifically at public service workers. With regard to trade unionism and collective bargaining, our main concern is with the trend in union density and coverage by collective bargaining and, again, we review the extent to which public services have converged with the private sector and public sector workers have lost any 'security advantage' which they previously enjoyed.

Employment law

Unlike their counterparts in some other countries, British public servants have never been endowed with a set of specific rights to protection or with a legal guarantee of secure employment (Blenk 1987). The one exception has been university academics, and security of tenure for this group was withdrawn by the Education Reform Act 1988 (Keep and Sisson 1992). For other groups of public servants the most significant change has been either legislative or administrative exposure of services to competitive tendering, which has been compounded by a series of other reforms designed to force competition on the basis of cost with private sector suppliers. In the 1980s, the positive requirement for public services to compete with the private sector was accompanied by a series of deregulatory measures to ensure this new competitive discipline was as sharp as possible.

First, the Fair Wages Resolutions were rescinded with effect from 1983, which ended the requirement for public service contractors to offer rates of pay established by relevant collective agreements and to recognise their workers' freedom to join trade unions (Fredman and Morris 1990). This change was accompanied by the Thatcher government's denunciation of International Labour Organisation Convention No. 94 on Labour Clauses in Public Contracts. Second, the Local Government Act 1988 made it unlawful for local authorities and several other public bodies to use policies of 'contract compliance' or to consider 'non-commercial matters' when choosing and dealing with contractors (*ibid.*). These 'non-commercial matters' included the wages of contractors' employees and policies on trade union membership and equal opportunities. Third, when the government unwillingly transposed the European Acquired Rights Directive into the TUPE Regulations in 1981, it excluded public services from coverage so that employees transferred from public to private employment through competitive tendering would have no right to retain the terms of their existing contract of employment (Cavalier 1997). These legislative changes, moreover, were compounded by a significant case, the North Tyneside judgment, which ruled that the award of extrastatutory redundancy payments to local authority workers was contrary to the fiduciary duty of councillors and that compensation for job loss for public service workers could no longer exceed the statutory maximum (Walsh and Davis 1993).

In combination, these changes amounted to a substantial weakening of the legislative protection that was afforded to public service workers, and were directed at ending their relatively 'privileged' position. Several measures, however, served not merely to remove the difference between public and private sector workers, but to place the former in a less advantageous situation. It is notable, for instance, that private sector employers, such as Marks and Spencer and Asda, remain at liberty both to protect their own workforces and to encourage good practice amongst suppliers through contract compliance (Fredman and Morris 1990).

Although the main thrust of statutory reform has been to expose public servants to competition from the private sector, there have been important counter-tendencies, and some aspects of the Conservative programme have been reversed by case law. The most significant reversal has been the extension of TUPE to public services (Cavalier 1997) and in the majority of local government and NHS contracts it is now assumed that TUPE applies. Moreover, unions have successfully used equal pay legislation to combat the greater adverse effect of CCT on female manual workers in local government (*People Management*, 9 January 1997). Court judgments have not restored the level of employment security enjoyed by public service workers prior to the onset of competition, and have not ended the loss of public service jobs or the erosion of employment conditions. They have provided some additional protection to public sector workers, however, and public sector unions now have a set of legal instruments which can be used to exert pressure on the process of competitive tendering. According to one recent assessment:

> [T]he use of TUPE in negotiations and selected legal cases since the early 1990s has acted as a constraint on employers' freedom of action. In many instances this has deterred contractors from bidding for contracts or enabled an in-house bid to succeed. In others, employees have still faced a change of employer, but the new employer has been inhibited (sometimes only temporarily) from reducing staff numbers or cutting pay, hours or conditions.
>
> (Cavalier 1997: 4)

Trade union membership

For much of this century public service employment has provided fertile territory for trade unions, and union membership has been actively encouraged by public sector employers (Beaumont 1992: 78–80). Today, the public sector provides the main redoubt of an increasingly embattled labour movement, but there is evidence that here, too, change is underway and that the general decline in trade union density across the economy (the proportion of employees who are union members) has been echoed within the public services. For the earlier part of the period under review (1979–87), for instance, Waddington (1992) reports a slight decline in density across the public services, from 79.6 to 78.9 per cent, with a drop of nearly 15 per cent in 'national government' and 5 per cent in 'local government and education'. Only 'health services' bucked the trend, with an increase from 70.7 to 72.9 per cent. More recent figures, calculated on a different basis, are available from the Labour Force Survey (Cully and Woodland 1998). These show a continuing gradual decline in public sector trade union density through the 1990s, from 64 per cent in 1993 to 61 per cent in 1997.

The evidence, therefore, points to an increasing proportion of public sector workers who are either discouraged from joining a trade union or who are disinclined to take out membership. However, public sector workers are much more likely to be unionised than their counterparts in the private sector, where density has now fallen to 20 per cent. Table 5.7 shows the extent of the gap between public and private sector employment and indicates the much lower level of private sector density both across the economy and in individual service industries. Public sector workers may be becoming more insecure by virtue of steadily declining levels of trade union membership, but their level of protection on this indicator remains much higher than their private sector counterparts.

Collective bargaining

The primary function of British trade unions has been to regulate terms and conditions of employment through collective bargaining with employers, and collective bargaining has been the dominant form of job regulation in the public

Table 5.7 Trade union density in the public and private sectors, 1997

	All	*Private*	*Public*
All employees	30	20	61
Service industries			
Public administration	62	29	63
Education	54	27	58
Health	47	15	63
Other services	22	10	46

Source: Cully and Woodland (1998)

sector since the immediate aftermath of the First World War. Once again, however, there is considerable evidence of erosion and increasing numbers of public
service workers losing or abandoning the shield of collective regulation. There has
been a growth of more individualised forms of employment in the public sector,
with employees becoming more dependent on their own individual market power
or the unilateral decisions of public sector managers.

Evidence of the decline in coverage by collective bargaining in the public sector
is available from WIRS. In 1984, 91 per cent of public sector workplaces relied on
collective bargaining to determine the pay of manual workers, compared with 78
per cent in 1990. Equivalent figures for non-manual employees were 98 and 84 per
cent, respectively (Millward *et al.* 1992: 232). Much of the decline for non-manual
workers is accounted for in terms of the replacement of collective bargaining
with pay review bodies for nurses, midwives, professions allied to medicine and
schoolteachers. Subsequently, the coverage of the Senior Salaries Review Body
in the civil service has also been extended to include a further 2,300 senior
employees (Corby 1998). Views differ as to the efficacy of these arrangements
(Bailey 1994; Elliott and Duffus 1996; Ironside and Seifert 1995), but they pre-
serve the principle of collective pay determination, retain a role for trade unions
in submitting evidence and argument to the review body and in certain respects
may be 'captured' by the occupational groups with which they deal.

A less ambiguous erosion of collective bargaining can be seen in the spread of
personal contracts amongst senior managers in public services. Collective bargaining machinery was not established when general managers were introduced
into the NHS as part of the Griffiths reforms, and in central and local government
and education there has been a trend towards the detachment of senior
employees from collective agreements, often as part of a movement towards
the introduction of IPRP (Burchill and Casey 1996; Farnham and Giles 1996;
Farnham and Horton 1996b; Jackson *et al.* 1993; LACSAB 1990b). Erosion of
collective bargaining can also be seen at the base of the occupational hierarchy
where CCT has led to departure from national collective agreements on pay
and conditions of employment for manual workers (Escott and Whitfield
1995).

Not only has there been some withdrawal from collective bargaining in public
services, there has also been a change in bargaining structure and a movement
towards single employer and workplace bargaining. This change has been apparent in the civil service, where service-wide collective bargaining ended in April
1996 and was replaced by agency-level collective agreements (Corby 1998). Other
services have not proceeded so far, but decentralisation has been encouraged by
government and has occurred to some degree in all branches of the public service.
In the NHS, for example, there have been experiments with 'two-tier' bargaining,
with individual trusts negotiating supplements to national awards, and health care
assistants, an important new category of staff created in 1990, are employed
solely on local conditions of service (Thornley 1998). In local government, the
late 1980s and early 1990s witnessed the withdrawal from national collective
bargaining by more than thirty local authorities and, again, there is evidence of

CCT promoting the negotiation of local agreements within individual DSOs (Jackson *et al.* 1993; Walsh and Davis 1993).

The devolution of collective bargaining can contribute to worker insecurity to the extent that it produces outcomes which are less favourable than those secured through national agreements and when it results in the erosion of terms and conditions and rates of pay. National collective agreements can be viewed as safety nets, providing minimum standards across an industry, and local bargaining may allow undercutting by individual employers. It might also result in insecurity, by effectively providing managers with an opportunity to escape from joint regulation and operate at a level where union organisation is too weak to provide a counter to management decision-making.

Evidence of the impact of local bargaining on employment standards is limited, although there are findings from local government which suggest that bargaining within DSOs has resulted in some weakening of conditions and has occurred largely on management's terms (Colling 1993; Escott and Whitfield 1995; Walsh and Davis 1993). The extent to which local bargaining implies a transition from more to less effective union regulation has attracted more attention from researchers, but there are sharply contrasting viewpoints and findings. Case studies in local government have identified ineffective workplace trade union organisation and limited influence over management, where the determination of pay and conditions has been devolved to local level (Colling 1995; Heery 1997). In the civil service and NHS, however, there is evidence of decentralisation stimulating some renewal of workplace trade unionism, and local bargaining resulting in increased union membership and activism (Corby 1998; Thornley 1998). What these findings suggest is that the consequences of devolution will vary and will depend on both structural factors (e.g. size of workplace) and the tradition of collective organisation within individual service units. In at least a proportion of cases, however, it seems clear that decentralisation has facilitated management's escape from effective joint regulation and in this sense has contributed to an increase in worker insecurity.

Although the system of collective bargaining in public services has been buffeted and restructured over the past two decades, it remains substantially in place and the continued centrality of joint regulation distinguishes public services from the private sector. Table 5.8 shows estimates from LFS for the percentage of employees covered by collective bargaining across the economy and in large and small workplaces in the public and private sectors. A consistent pattern is revealed of far lower coverage in the latter, where collective bargaining affords protection for only small minorities of employees in many industries. It should also be noted that the decentralisation of bargaining has proceeded much further in the private sector, where multi-employer bargaining has collapsed in a range of industries since 1980, leading some to pronounce the 'end of institutionalised industrial relations' (Purcell 1995). While the erosion of collective industrial relations may be heightening worker insecurity in public services, change is more pronounced in the private sector and, once again, on this dimension public service workers appear more secure than their counterparts in other industries.

Table 5.8 Employees covered by collective bargaining in the public and private sectors, 1997 (percentages)

	All	Private sector workplaces		Public sector workplaces	
		Less than 25 employees	25 or more employees	Less than 25 employees	25 or more employees
All employees	36	7	32	60	79
Service industries:					
Public administration	80	*	*	67	84
Education	65	10	32	63	74
Health	51	6	11	60	78
Other services	27	4	19	48	71

Source: Cully and Woodland (1998)

Note: * Base too low to provide a reliable estimate.

Insecure workers

A final way of assessing the level of insecurity of public service employees is to consider their attitudes and examine the extent to which public sector workers regard their jobs as insecure and express concern or dissatisfaction with their level of job security. Given the broad pattern of change in public service employment described above, it might be hypothesised that public service workers will exhibit high levels of dissatisfaction with job security, and that an increasing proportion will regard their jobs as insecure. One might also expect a pattern of convergence with the private sector and perhaps even higher levels of dissatisfaction amongst public sector workers, to the extent that public service employment has attracted employees who valued its traditional stability and who are relatively risk averse. Accordingly, in this section we review available evidence on the levels of perceived insecurity and dissatisfaction amongst public service workers, the trend in these attitudes over time and the extent to which public service workers regard themselves as more or less secure than their private sector counterparts.

The amount of published data on the attitudes of public sector workers to job insecurity is not extensive. The 1996 *Eurobarometer* survey, however, contained a question which asked respondents in 'public administration' to state whether they agreed or disagreed that 'my job is secure' (OECD 1997: 133). Across the United Kingdom, 59.4 per cent failed to agree strongly with the statement, a figure which exceeded the European average for public sector workers of 44.7 per cent and which was surpassed by only three other countries, Portugal (75.2), Finland (63.7) and Sweden (85.2). The figures indicate that less than half the public sector workforce in Britain has a high degree of confidence in their future job tenure. The comparison with other countries is also instructive because it suggests that the restructuring of public services, which has been particularly acute in Britain, has generated a relatively high perception of diminished job security.

With regard to trends over time, there is no published source which provides time series data on attitudes to insecurity of public sector workers. At best, trends can be inferred from general surveys of employee attitudes, most of which point to a rise in employee perceptions of insecurity in recent years, once the cyclical effect of trends in unemployment are controlled for. Thus, Felstead *et al.* (1998) report findings from two representative samples of British employees in 1986 and 1997, which demonstrate stability in the aggregate reported level of job insecurity, despite a substantial drop in unemployment between these two years. Similarly, Bryson and McKay (1997: 28) report that data from British Social Attitudes demonstrate an underlying increase in employee concern over job insecurity since the early 1980s. And the OECD (1997: 136) reports findings from the British Household Panel Survey which show a rise in the percentage of employees who were not 'completely satisfied' with job security from 61.7 to 78.4 per cent between 1991 and 1995, a period of economic recovery. Of course, these sources do not demonstrate conclusively that concern over job insecurity has risen amongst public service workers in the past two decades, but none mention a distinctive pattern in the public sector and it seems reasonable to conclude that the attitudes of public service workers have followed the general trend, particularly given the reduction in employment levels and extensive restructuring which have taken place.

While it can be inferred that the percentage of public service workers who feel insecure has risen, it remains the case that employees in the public sector are less likely to report perceptions of this kind than their counterparts in the private sector. Thus, the *Eurobarometer* findings for 'industry' and 'services' indicate that 65 and 69 per cent of employees, respectively, do not agree strongly that their jobs are secure, compared with the 59 per cent in 'public administration' (OECD 1997: 133). Results from the *Employment in Britain* survey of 1992 reported by Gallie *et al.* (1998: 140, 145) tell a similar story. This research used two measures of job insecurity, a measurement of the ease with which individuals reported they could be dismissed from their jobs, and a measurement of dissatisfaction with job security. Multivariate analysis indicated that public sector employment was associated statistically with low scores on both indicators, suggesting that public service workers are less likely to perceive themselves at risk of job loss and more likely to be satisfied with their level of security. However, there was one exception to this pattern: public sector women were no more likely than their private sector equivalents to report satisfaction with job security, which supports the contention that the effects of CCT and other restructuring initiatives have fallen disproportionately on women workers (Escott and Whitfield 1995).

To summarise, therefore, less than half the public sector workforce in Britain is confident about its future job tenure and British public sector workers appear more insecure than their counterparts in most other European countries. It is probable, but not certain, that perceptions of insecurity have risen amongst public service workers in recent years in line with the general trend across the workforce, but public service workers, on average, continue to regard themselves as more secure than private sector employees. The former are less likely to perceive a risk to their employment, and male public sector workers, at least, exhibit less dissatisfaction with job security. These patterns, moreover, are broadly in line with the account of 'objective' insecurity presented above and provide little support for the belief that risk-averse public sector workers are peculiarly sensitive to threats to their security of employment.

Insecurity and the public service ethos

Critics of public sector reform in Britain have claimed repeatedly that it has generated perverse effects and has served to hinder, not promote, lasting improvements in the effectiveness and quality of public services. While reform has imposed costs on the public sector workforce, which has become more insecure, it is argued that this change has not been balanced by substantial or sustainable benefits for citizens who fund and consume public services. Thus, it has been variously claimed that cost savings and efficiency improvements resulting from CCT have been exaggerated, that reliance on a contingent workforce is serving to erode quality, skill formation and levels of performance and that the use of financial incentives is both channelling management effort towards cost reduction and demotivating public sector workers (e.g. Bach 1989; Escott and Whitfield 1995; Husbands 1998; Ironside and Seifert 1995; Keep and Sisson 1992; Marsden and Richardson 1994; Sinclair *et al.* 1995).

Central to this argument is a belief that changes in employment practice are producing a fundamental shift in the orientation to work of public service workers and a collapse of traditional sources of motivation and commitment, in what might be termed the 'public service ethos'. As public sector employers withdraw from long-term commitment to employees, the argument goes, so employees are abandoning their own diffuse commitment to public service and a more instrumental, calculating orientation is taking its place. In this final section we wish to review the evidence for a fundamental change in work attitudes amongst public service workers together with the extent to which the spread of insecure employment has eroded worker commitment. We also examine public sector workers' attitudes in relation to those of employees in the private sector and establish whether there has been a convergence; whether exposure to the new public management has generated a new public sector workforce with attitudes similar to those found in private industry.

Systematic longitudinal data on the work attitudes of public sector workers is not available, but there is evidence that many public service workers continue to adhere to a distinctive set of work values. A key study, in this regard, is that by Pratchett and Wingfield (1996) which used survey and focus group research in local government to test the degree to which employees subscribed to a 'public service ethos' made up of five elements: acceptance of accountability through the political process; adherence to bureaucratic norms of honesty, integrity, impartiality and objectivity; commitment to the public good; intrinsic and altruistic motivation; and loyalty to an occupation, profession or service. Their findings suggest that about three-quarters of local government officers believed a public service ethos existed, though a third of these felt that it generated inefficient and inflexible work behaviour. The authors conclude from the research that traditional public sector values have proved surprisingly robust 'given the changes which have swept across local government in the last two decades' (*ibid.*: 644), but also note signs both of erosion and evolution in the public service ethos. For example, employees most exposed to market-based reforms in local authority DSOs were least likely to believe in or support traditional public service values. Also, there was a current amongst the survey population who stressed the need for improvements in management and for the adoption of a more commercial, entrepreneurial approach to service delivery as a means of satisfying traditional public service objectives.

A more direct test of the impact of changes in employment practice on worker attitudes can be found in Gallie *et al.*'s (1998) analysis of the *Employment in Britain* survey. This research examined the impact of a number of influences on the organisational commitment of 'social sector' workers, employees in public services plus those of charities, trade unions and churches and creative people in the artistic and literary professions. Commitment was measured along three dimensions: a preparedness to work flexibly and accept different job assignments, identification with the employing organisation and its values, and a readiness to put in effort beyond the level contractually required. Perhaps surprisingly, these commitment measures were not found to be associated with a series of measures of worker insecurity. 'Flexibility' and 'value' commitment were lower amongst employees of 'social sector' organisations which had undergone workforce reduction, but staff cuts and changes in work organisation which affected respondents' own work and working on a temporary or fixed-term contract were found to have no statistical association with any of the three commitment measures. Indeed, one of the measures of insecurity used in the analysis, employee anxiety about the prospect of dismissal, was found to be positively associated with both 'flexibility' and 'effort' commitment, a finding which the authors account for in terms of 'selective attention'; i.e. 'those who are insecure are more aware of the value of their jobs and so feel more committed' (*ibid.*: 245).

While perceptions of insecurity were found to have a modest, depressing effect on attitudinal commitment, other factors proved to be more significant. All three measures of commitment were positively associated with employee assessments of management style, with supportive supervision and open communications showing a particularly strong influence. An even stronger influence was found to be exerted by employee assessments of the broad values of their employing organisation. What Gallie *et al.* describe as 'social values' were particularly influential and high levels of employee commitment were associated statistically with a belief that management shared decision-making power with employees, that the organisation cared about its employees' welfare and that the service delivered was socially beneficial. The authors conclude from the analysis that 'organisational commitment is less a matter of personnel policies and more a matter of broad values. Even after controlling for a wide range of policies, and for various facets of job satisfaction, it was these values which had by far the strongest relationship with commitment' (*ibid.*: 260; see also Benson 1998; Guest, this volume).

This analysis suggests is that the commitment of public service workers may prove surprisingly robust in the face of labour market change and the emergence of a more contingent employment relationship. It seems that the commitment of 'social sector' workers arises in large part because they identify with the broad social goals of their organisations, and this identification may survive changes in employment practice which impinge negatively on employees (Heery 1998). However, aspects of public service restructuring may, in the longer term, serve to erode employee commitment. The latter is likely to occur if a more directive, non-participative management style becomes the norm and if public service employers cease to display concern for the well-being of their employees. If public service organisations abandon the kinds of employment practice which have differentiated them from their private sector equivalents, and which are described above, such as the avoidance of redundancy, then a likely effect will be a reduction of employee commitment.

The *Employment in Britain* survey also contains information on the relative attitudes to work of 'social' and 'commercial' sector employees and indicates that the former are distinctive. Thus, social sector workers are much more likely to describe their employing organisation in terms of social utility. Two-thirds report that they are satisfied or very satisfied with their 'chance to do something worthwhile in life', compared with less than 50 per cent in the commercial sector (Gallie *et al.* 1998: 240). There are also indications in the survey that the commitment of social sector workers is more robust and less liable to erosion through rising insecurity than that of commercial sector workers. Fixed-term contract workers in the commercial sector *do* report lower levels of commitment than permanent employees, and across the commercial sector workforce dissatisfaction with job security is associated with low levels of flexibility and value commitment. In the social sector, in contrast, 'satisfaction or dissatisfaction with job security had no influence on organisational commitment' (*ibid.*: 246). Once again, these findings suggest that the distinctive characteristics of the public sector serve to insulate employee attitudes from the drift towards more insecure employment.

To summarise, the attitudes to work of public service workers appear to be distinctive and to be shaped by a public service ethos, in which the theme of social utility looms large. Although there are some indications of attitude change among public service workers, there is little evidence of a collapse in organisational commitment as a result of heightened insecurity. Neither is there evidence of convergence in work attitudes with those of employees in the private sector. Rather, there are indications that the distinctive attitudes of public service workers have caused them to respond to labour market change in a different way and that the commitment of public service workers is less susceptible to erosion through perceived insecurity and contingent employment than that of employees in other parts of the economy.

Conclusion

The purpose of this chapter has been to establish whether employees in UK public services have become more 'insecure' in three senses: as a result of changes in the structure of public service jobs which have made employment and earnings more uncertain, through the removal or attenuation of protective regulation, and through changes in the beliefs and attitudes of public service workers themselves who may regard their employment as precarious. The available evidence, we believe, demonstrates that there has been significant change along at least two of these dimensions and that it is accurate to describe the public service workforce in Britain as increasingly insecure. Thus, with regard to changes in jobs, there has been a reduction in public service employment and increased resort by employers to redundancy, the exposure of many jobs to competition with a resultant erosion in terms and conditions of employment, an increase in contingent working and the introduction of performance-related pay for categories of employee who have never experienced this form of remuneration before. With regard to protective regulation, the public services have witnessed a decline in trade union density over the past two decades and some withdrawal of the system of joint regulation through collective bargaining, while a series of changes in employment law have required public servants to compete with workers in the private sector, primarily on the basis of low labour costs. The evidence for growing insecurity is weakest with regard to attitude change. It is clear that British workers in general have come to regard their jobs as more insecure and, while it is likely, it is not certain, that this general trend has encompassed employees in the public sector. It is the case, however, that public servants in Britain regard themselves as less secure than their counterparts in most other European countries.

A second objective of the chapter has been to gauge the degree of convergence with the private sector along each of the three dimensions of insecurity. The principle finding here is that, notwithstanding the restructuring of employment relations in the public services, employees remain substantially more secure than their private sector counterparts. Thus, the risk of redundancy is less in the public services, public service contractors tend to provide more advantageous employment conditions, performance pay is less widely used and exposes a smaller proportion of salary to risk, and trade union membership and collective bargaining are much more extensive. These objective differences, moreover, are reflected in the attitudes of public service workers, who are less likely to regard themselves as insecure than employees in the private sector. The belief that public service workers continue to enjoy a 'security advantage', however, needs to be qualified in two important ways. Public services are the main users of fixed-term contract staff and, in certain respects, the legal protection afforded public employees is less than that enjoyed in the private sector.

A third objective of the chapter has been to consider some of the consequences of heightened worker insecurity in public services and to examine whether changes in the employment relationship have led to changes in worker attitudes.

Our conclusions here must be tentative, given the limited amount of information available, but available survey data suggest that employees continue to subscribe to the 'public service ethos' and that levels of commitment have been surprisingly immune to changes in employment conditions and management policy. It should be noted, however, that organisational commitment amongst public servants is associated with a belief that the employer cares for employee well-being and that, if current trends continue, this perception may weaken, with adverse consequences for the attitudes and motivation of public service workers.

The final objective of the chapter has been to relate the issue of worker insecurity to wider debate over the degree and significance of change in public sector employment. Discussion of this issue has frequently centred around the concept of the 'good' or 'model' public sector employer, with some claiming that there has been a fall from grace and a collapse in employment standards since the early 1980s (Fredman and Morris 1989) and others questioning the utility of the concept and the assumption that public sector managers have voluntarily and consistently developed high employment standards (Ironside and Seifert 1995: 123; Lloyd and Seifert 1995: 360). The preceding review sheds light on two issues relevant to this debate. First, there has been a decline in employment standards in the public service over the past two decades, and much of the restructuring of the public sector has taken place at the expense of employees. Particularly noteworthy, we feel, have been the reductions in employment levels and standards as a result of competitive tendering and the increased reliance on contingent forms of labour. If the notion of a 'good employer' is informed by a comparison with absolute standards of best practice, then clearly there has been a deterioration in recent years. It remains the case, though, that public service workers are more secure than their private sector counterparts on many 'objective' indicators, that they are more likely to regard themselves as secure and that they continue to display distinctive work attitudes which rest, in part, on the traditional perception of public services as 'good employers'. If the notion of the 'good employer' is informed by a relative standard and comparison with the private sector, then the distinctiveness of the public sector is still apparent, notwithstanding recent change. There has been a deterioration of public service employment, therefore, but convergence with private sector employment practice has not yet occurred. Expressed differently, the public services are less good employers than they once were, but they continue to be better employers, on average, than the bulk of private sector companies.

References

Allen, J. and Henry, N. (1996) 'Fragments of industry and employment: contract service work and the shift towards precarious employment', in R. Crompton, D. Gallie and K. Purcell (eds) *Changing Forms of Employment: Organisations, Skills and Gender*, London: Routledge.

Bach, S. (1989) *Too High a Price to Pay? A Study of Competitive Tendering in the NHS*, Warwick

Papers in Industrial Relations No. 25, Coventry: Industrial Relations Research Unit, University of Warwick.

Bach, S. and Winchester, D. (1994) 'Opting out of pay devolution? The prospects of local pay bargaining in UK public services', *British Journal of Industrial Relations*, 32, 2: 263–82.

Bailey, R. (1994) 'Annual review article 1993: British public sector industrial relations', *British Journal of Industrial Relations*, 32, 1: 113–36.

Beaumont, P.B. (1992) *Public Sector Industrial Relations*, London: Routledge.

Benson, J. (1998) 'Dual commitment: contract workers in Australian manufacturing enterprises', *Journal of Management Studies*, 35, 3: 355–75.

Blenk, W. (1987) 'Labour relations in the public service in the Federal Republic of Germany', in T. Treu (ed.) *Public Service Labour Relations: Recent Trends and Future Prospects*, Geneva: International Labour Office.

Blundell, B. and Murdock, A. (1997) *Managing in the Public Sector*, Oxford: Butterworth-Heinemann.

Boyne, G., Jenkins, G. and Poole, M. (1999) 'Human resource management in the public and private sectors: an empirical comparison', *Public Administration*, forthcoming.

Bryson, A. and McKay, S. (1997) 'What about the workers?', in R. Jowell, J. Curtice, A. Park, L. Brook, K. Thomson and C. Bryson (eds) *British Social Attitudes: the 14th Report*, Aldershot: Ashgate.

Burchill, F. and Casey, A. (1996) *Human Resource Management. The NHS: A Case Study*, London: Macmillan Business.

Casey, B., Metcalf, H. and Millward, N. (1997) *Employers' Use of Flexible Labour*, London: Policy Studies Institute.

Cavalier, S. (1997) *Transfer Rights: TUPE in Perspective*, London: Institute of Employment Rights.

Colling, T. (1993) 'Contracting public services: the management of compulsory competitive tendering in two county councils', *Human Resource Management Journal*, 3, 4: 1–15.

—— (1995) 'Renewal or *rigor mortis*? Union responses to contracting in local government', *Industrial Relations Journal*, 26, 2: 134–45.

Colling, T. and Ferner, A. (1995) 'Privatization and marketization', in P. Edwards (ed.) *Industrial Relations: Theory and Practice in Britain*, Oxford: Blackwell.

Corby, S. (1996) 'The National Health Service', in D. Farnham and S. Horton (eds) *Managing People in the Public Services*, London: Macmillan Business.

—— (1998) 'Industrial relations in the Civil Service agencies: transition or transformation', *Industrial Relations Journal*, 29, 3: 194–206.

Cousins, C. (1988) 'The restructuring of welfare work: the introduction of general management and the contracting out of ancillary services in the NHS', *Work, Employment and Society*, 2, 2: 210–28.

Cully, M. and Woodland, S. (1998) 'Trade union membership and recognition 1996–97: an analysis of data from the Certification Officer and the LFS', *Labour Market Trends*, July: 353–62.

Davies, A. and Kirkpatrick, I. (1995) 'Performance indicators, bureaucratic control and the decline of professional autonomy: the case of academic librarians', in I. Kirkpatrick and M. Martinez Lucio (eds) *The Politics of Quality in the Public Sector: The Management of Change*, London: Routledge.

Dawson, S., Winstanley, D., Mole, V. and Sherval, J. (1995) *Managing in the NHS: A Study of Senior Executives*, London: HMSO.

Dowling, B. and Richardson, R. (1997) 'Evaluating performance pay for managers in the

National Health Service', *The International Journal of Human Resource Management*, 8, 3: 348–66.

Elliott, R. and Duffus, K. (1996) 'What has been happening to pay in the public service sector of the British economy? Developments in the period 1970–1992', *British Journal of Industrial Relations*, 34, 1: 51–85.

Escott, K. and Whitfield, D. (1995) *The Gender Impact of CCT in Local Government*, Equal Opportunities Commission Research Discussion Series No. 12, Manchester: Equal Opportunities Commission.

Farnham, D. and Giles, L. (1996) 'Education', in D. Farnham and S. Horton (eds) *Managing People in the Public Services*, London: Macmillan Business.

Farnham, D. and Horton, S. (1996a) 'Continuity and change in the public services', in D. Farnham and S. Horton (eds) *Managing People in the Public Services*, London: Macmillan Business.

—— (1996b) 'Towards a new people management?', in D. Farnham and S. Horton (eds) *Managing People in the Public Services*, London: Macmillan Business.

Felstead, A., Burchell, B. and Green, F. (1998) 'Insecurity at work: is job insecurity really much worse now than before?', *New Economy*, 5: 180–4.

Ferlie, E., Ashburn L., Fitzgerald, L. and Pettigrew, A. (1997) *The New Public Management in Action*, Oxford: Oxford University Press.

Fredman, S. and Morris, G. (1989) *The State as Employer: Labour Law in the Public Services*, London: Mansell.

—— (1990) 'The state as employer: is it unique?', *Industrial Law Journal*, 19, 2: 142–53.

Gallie, D., White, M., Cheng, Y. and Tomlinson, M. (1998) *Restructuring the Employment Relationship*, Oxford: Oxford University Press.

GSS (1998) *Civil Service Statistics 1997*, London: Government Statistical Service.

Healy, G. (1997) 'The industrial relations of appraisal: the case of teachers', *Industrial Relations Journal*, 28, 3: 206–20.

Heery, E. (1996) 'Risk, representation and the new pay', *Personnel Review*, 25, 6: 54–65.

—— (1997) 'Performance related pay and trade union membership', *Employee Relations*, 19, 5: 430–42.

—— (1998) 'A return to contract? Performance related pay in a public service', *Work, Employment and Society*, 12, 1: 73–95.

Heery, E. and Warhurst, J. (1994) *Performance Related Pay and Trade Unions: Impact and Response*, Occasional Paper, Kingston-upon-Thames: Kingston University Business School.

Horton, S. (1996) 'The Civil Service', in D. Farnham and S. Horton (eds) *Managing People in the Public Services*, London: Macmillan Business.

Husbands, C.T. (1998) 'Job flexibility and variations in the performance motivations of longer-term part-time teaching auxiliaries at the London School of Economics and Political Science', *Work, Employment and Society*, 12, 1: 121–44.

IDS Public Sector Unit (1989) *Paying for Performance in the Public Sector: A Progress Report*, London: Incomes Data Services and Coopers & Lybrand.

Ironside, M. and Seifert, R. (1995) *Industrial Relations in Schools*, London: Routledge.

Jackson, M.P., Leopold, J.W. and Tuck, K. (1993) *Decentralization of Collective Bargaining: An Analysis of Recent Experience in the UK*, London: Macmillan.

Keep, E. and Sisson, K. (1992) 'Owning the problem: personnel issues in higher education policy-making in the 1990s', *Oxford Review of Economic Policy*, 8, 2: 67–78.

Kessler, I. (1991) 'Workplace industrial relations in local government', *Employee Relations*, 13, 2: 1–31.

Kessler, S. and Bayliss, F. (1995) *Contemporary British Industrial Relations* (second edition), London: Macmillan Business.

Kirkpatrick, I. and Martinez Lucio, M. (1995) 'The uses of "quality" in the British government's reform of the public sector', in I. Kirkpatrick and M. Martinez Lucio (eds) *The Politics of Quality in the Public Sector: The Management of Change*, London: Routledge.

—— (1996) 'Introduction: the contract state and the future of public management', *Public Administration*, 74, 1: 1–8.

LACSAB (1990a) *Performance Related Pay in Practice: Case Studies from Local Government*, London: Local Authorities Conditions of Service Advisory Board.

—— (1990b) *Performance Related Pay in Practice: A Survey of Local Government 1990*, London: Local Authorities Conditions of Service Advisory Board.

LGMB (1997a) *Flexible Working: Working Patterns in Local Authorities and the Wider Economy*, London: Local Government Management Board.

—— (1997b) *Survey Report No. 15*, Service Delivery and Competition Information Service, London: Local Government Management Board.

Lloyd, C. and Seifert, R. (1995) 'Restructuring the NHS: labour utilisation and intensification in four hospitals', *Work, Employment and Society*, 9, 2: 359–78.

Marsden, D. and Richardson, R. (1994) 'Performing for pay? The effects of "merit pay" on motivation in a public service', *British Journal of Industrial Relations*, 32, 2: 243–62.

Millward, N., Stevens, M., Smart, D. and Hawes, W.R. (1992) *Workplace Industrial Relations in Transition*, Aldershot: Dartford.

Morgan, P. and Potter, C. (1995) 'Professional cultures and paradigms of quality in health care', in I. Kirkpatrick and M. Martinez Lucio (eds) *The Politics of Quality in the Public Sector: The Management of Change*, London: Routledge.

OECD (1997) *Employment Outlook*, Paris: Organisation for Economic Cooperation and Development.

Pollert, A. (1988) 'The "Flexible Firm": fixation or fact?', *Work, Employment and Society*, 2, 3: 281–316.

Pollitt, C. (1993) *Managerialism in the Public Services* (second edition), Oxford: Blackwell.

Potter, C. and Morgan, P. (1997) 'Deprofessionalising the NHS: has the internal market reduced professionals to the role of employee?', paper presented at the Cardiff Business School, Public Sector Research Unit Conference, Public Dimensions of Public Service: Issues of Equity, Accountability and the Role of the Professions, 26–27 March.

Pratchett, L. and Wingfield, M. (1996) 'Petty bureaucracy and woolly-minded liberalism? The changing ethos of local government officers', *Public Administration*, 74, 4: 639–56.

Purcell, J. (1995) 'The end of institutional industrial relations', *Political Quarterly*, 64, 1: 6–23.

Purcell, J. and Ahlstrand, B. (1994) *Human Resource Management in the Multi-Divisional Company*, Oxford: Oxford University Press.

Sinclair, J., Ironside, M. and Seifert, R. (1996) 'Classroom struggle? Market-oriented reforms and their impact on the teacher labour process', *Work, Employment and Society*, 10, 4: 641–61.

Sinclair, J., Seifert, R. and Ironside, M. (1995) 'Market-driven reforms in education: performance, quality and education in schools', in I. Kirkpatrick and M. Martinez Lucio (eds) *The Politics of Quality in the Public Sector: The Management of Change*, London: Routledge.

Thornley, C. (1998) 'Contesting local pay: the decentralization of collective bargaining in the NHS', *British Journal of Industrial Relations*, 36, 3: 413–34.

Townley, B. (1990/91) 'The politics of appraisal: lessons of the introduction of appraisal into UK universities', *Human Resource Management Journal*, 1, 2: 27–44.

Waddington, J. (1992) 'Trade union membership in Britain, 1980–1987: unemployment and restructuring', *British Journal of Industrial Relations*, 30, 2: 287–324.

Walsh, K. (1995) *Public Services and Market Mechanisms: Competition, Contracting and the New Public Management*, London: Macmillan.

Walsh, K. and Davis, H. (1993) *Competition and Service: The Impact of the Local Government Act 1988*, London: HMSO.

White, G. (1996) 'Public sector bargaining: comparability, decentralization and control', *Public Administration*, 74, 1: 89–111.

——— (1999) 'The remuneration of public servants: fair pay or new pay?' in S. Corby and G. White (eds) *Employee Relations in the Public Services: Theories and Issues*, London: Routledge.

White, G. and Hutchinson, B. (1996) 'Local government', in D. Farnham and S. Horton (eds) *Managing People in the Public Services*, London: Macmillan Business.

Winchester, D. and Bach, S. (1995) 'The state: the public sector', in P. Edwards (ed.) *Industrial Relations: Theory and Practice in Britain*, Oxford: Blackwell.

Acknowledgements

Thanks to Peter Thomas of the Greater London Employers' Association and Jo Roper of HESA Services Ltd. for providing data and advice on sources. Thanks also to George Boyne for commenting on an earlier draft.

6   Gendered employment insecurity?

Kate Purcell

Introduction

The objective of this chapter is to assess the extent to which the insecure work-force is gendered, drawing mainly on UK data. As is discussed elsewhere in this volume, 'the insecure workforce' is difficult to define. In the UK, progressive employment deregulation in the 1980s led to a situation where employees with less than two years' continuous employment with the same employer have no legal rights to job security, regardless of their contractual status. Most of the analysis in this chapter will therefore be confined to consideration of recent trends in tem-porary employment, covering fixed-term, seasonal, agency, casual and other tem-porary work; forms of employment which are unequivocally insecure, whether or not they are freely chosen. However, in order to make sense of recent trends in the gendering of temporary employment, it is useful to consider the evolution of women's labour force participation, particularly in the context of industrial and workforce restructuring.

The first section of the chapter considers the pressures and resistances which have cumulatively led to women's current participation in paid work. This is followed by an examination of recent trends in UK employment patterns, with particular reference to differences within the female population of working age and the incidence and distribution of part-time employment. Recent trends and gender differences in temporary employment are then considered against this broader background. Finally, this evidence is considered in relation to arguments that atypical employment provides opportunities for women's increased labour force participation and the practical reconciliation of employment and family roles and relationships.

Women and employment

A major theme of the writing on women's employment has been the impact of the historic and symbolic distinction between private and public: the household and institutions in the public domain. Opinion polls and surveys continue to use statements such as 'A woman's place is in the home' as a social indicator of gender attitudes, and substantial minorities of respondents (albeit more males than females) continue to agree with them (Scott *et al.* 1996: 486). Although there is ample evidence that women's economic activity, whether recognised as such or not, has made a substantial contribution to social production as well as reproduction at most stages of history and in most cultures, all known societies have, to a greater or lesser extent, been characterised by a gendered division of labour. In most – and certainly in all developed countries for most of the twentieth century – gender roles have emphasised women's pre-eminence in the private and men's in the public spheres. The corollary of this has been that women have often been seen, and have seen themselves, as tangential members of the labour force. This has particularly been the case in industries and occupations where they are heavily outnumbered by men. Male resistance to and resentment of women colleagues and the psychological insecurity and harassment experienced by women in gender-atypical jobs have been well documented (Cockburn 1991; Collinson and Collinson 1996; Devine 1992; Hearn *et al.* 1989). More generally, there has been ample evidence of management (Collinson *et al.* 1990) and trade union (Cunnison and Stageman 1993) perceptions of women's allegedly lower commitment (and implicitly, right) to paid work. 'The family wage' was predicated upon the perception that men were the primary breadwinners, and much social welfare provision continues to assume 'traditional' gendered divisions of labour within 'traditional' two-parent families.

The Marxist theory that women in paid work largely constituted a reserve army of labour, drawn upon in times of labour shortage and discouraged from the workforce during periods of over-supply – thus by definition subject, in general, to greater employment insecurity than men (Beechey 1987; Bruegel 1979) provided considerable insight into trends in women's economic activity, relating to major challenges to the labour supply such as war (Riley 1984; Summerfield 1984). However, technological change and industrial restructuring as well as demographic pressures have led to increased demand for women's labour and, in some cases, employer preference for female employees (Glucksman 1990; Humphries and Rubery 1992). The decline of manufacturing employment, accompanied by expansion in private services industries, has been characterised by progressive decline in full-time traditionally male jobs and an increase in part-time jobs mainly filled by females. Women's labour has historically been cheaper than men's, in acknowledgement of the male breadwinner model, and despite equal pay and equal opportunities legislation, female average earnings and hourly pay remain substantially below that of males (Elias and Gregory 1994). Women are twice as likely to be in low-paid jobs than men, and low pay is concentrated in numerically female-dominated sectors such as retail and hospitality (Metcalf 1998: 7). Of the two million employees who earn below the agreed minimum wage of £3.60, 55 per cent are women in part-time employment (Low Pay Commission 1998: 5). The overwhelming majority of those earning below the National Insurance Lower Earnings Limit – the level at which employers and employees are required to pay contributions and at which employees become eligible for employment-related benefits such as sick pay, maternity benefits and employment-related pensions are also women (McKnight *et al.* 1998). It is clearly the case that there has been some substitution of female for male labour on the basis of cost and deliberate construction of new jobs as 'women's jobs' in order to minimise labour costs. An example of the feminisation of occupations being accompanied by loss of status and relative wages is in the move from 'white' to 'pink-collar' employment of secretarial and clerical work since the earlier part of the century (Crompton 1988). The polarising impact of technology and employment restructuring has had the effect of upskilling some secretarial and administrative jobs while eliminating, intensifying or deskilling many others (Greenbaum 1998; Warhurst and Thompson 1998).

Humphries and Rubery (1992) argue that the net effect of industrial restructuring and progressive deregulation of the UK labour market has been increased integration, differentiation and polarisation of women in the labour market. On the one hand, although women's economic activity rates have increased, their employment remains considerably more concentrated than men's, either in low-paid 'complementary wage' jobs (Siltanen 1994) or in 'sex-typed' jobs which explicitly require attributes believed to be held more often by women than men, deriving from 'natural' or gender-socialised aptitudes (Crompton and Sanderson 1990). For example, in the growing services sector, sexuality (Adkins 1996) and the capacity and willingness to engage in emotional labour (Hochschild 1983) have been argued to be implicit prerequisites for a wide range of gendered jobs (Purcell 1996), a high proportion of which are also low-paid, predominantly part-time jobs. On the other hand, substantial numbers of women entered managerial and professional employment in the 1980s, and over half the growth in women's jobs between 1983 and 1990 was in these categories (Humphries and Rubery 1992: 245). At a broad occupational level, there is some evidence that occupational segmentation by gender has become less pronounced (Hakim 1994) as women have been entering an increasingly wide range of occupations and rising within occupational hierarchies at an unprecedented, though still modest, scale. However, permeation by women of the 'glass ceiling' between middle and upper management levels remains rare (Wajcman 1996) and women's employment in professional and management jobs has been observed to tend to concentrate in occupational niches which are more likely to be associated with the exercise of expertise rather than power (Crompton with Le Feuvre 1996; Savage 1992).

Rubery and Fagan (1994), after a detailed examination of occupational segregation in six areas – teaching, computer professionals, bank clerical workers, civil service clerical and administrative staff, catering workers and drivers – concluded that the change in gender ratio at aggregate occupational level cannot be assumed to indicate substantial reduction of gender segregation:

> [T]he entry of women into previously male-dominated job areas usually involves a transformation in the organisation of that occupation. Evidence of changes in the occupational sex mix does not necessarily imply a move towards integration but may herald the development of a new occupational subdivision or indeed a long term trend towards feminisation.
>
> (*Ibid.*: 40)

Lindley (1994: 116–17) points out that the expansion in women's employment has involved organisational and occupational restructuring involving relabelling of previously clerical grade administrative posts, delayering of middle-level posts leading to less promotion opportunities and selective feminisation of some areas, and has occurred disproportionately in relatively low-pay, low-status sectors.

The arguments have thus moved on somewhat since the polarised juxtaposition of competing predominantly labour supply or demand-related explanations for occupational gender segmentation and women's lower economic activity in comparison to men's – 'women's two roles' (Myrdal and Klein 1956) versus 'the social construction of jobs' (Beechey and Perkins 1987). Male and female economic activity rates have been increasingly converging in most developed countries in the last four decades. Women now constitute over 40 per cent of the workforce in most developed countries and almost half in several, including the UK. In the UK, Labour Force statistics indicate that over 70 per cent of women and 84 per cent men of working age were in paid employment in 1997. Male and female economic activity rates and work histories have converged substantially (Bridgewood and Savage 1993; Thomas *et al.* 1994). Yet it remains clear that although the cultural mandate that women should take primary responsibility for social reproduction may be considerably weaker than it was in previous decades, and women's participation in the labour force has become a normal rather than a minority activity, the relationship between employment and unpaid work in the home remains considerably stronger for women than for men (Baxter 1992), as the following examination of recent UK employment trends reveals.

Employment in Britain

MacInnes (1998: 2) has defined the primary breadwinner system as:

> [T]he process whereby men have typically entered the labour market on finishing their education and remained in it permanently until they retire, usually seeking full-time hours jobs with no fixed time limit; while women of working age have routinely prioritised, or been expected to prioritise, both the daily reproduction of their partners and the generational reproduction of the labour force, together with the care needs of other dependent family members, over their own labour market careers.

This, claims MacInnes, has been the explanation in the past for women's greater propensity to work part-time or participate only intermittently in the labour market.

In terms of the structural underpinning of gender relations and household divisions of labour, the UK has been characterised as having a 'modified breadwinner' system (Rubery *et al.* 1996), with contradictory pressures on women's propensity to be economically active over the family life cycle. Equal opportunities policies and individual taxation coexist with means-tested benefits and negligible pre- and after-school child care provision (Perrons and Hurstfield 1998: 125–6).

Until the beginning of the 1980s, the majority of women in Britain tended to be economically active until the birth of their first child, to leave paid employment for a substantial part of their family-building period and to re-enter the labour market when they regarded their youngest child as sufficiently established at school. But this 'bimodal' pattern has been becoming progressively less distinct, to a point at which, by 1988, around two-thirds of mothers were economically active and half of women who had given birth had returned to employment within nine months (McRae 1991).

The most substantial increase in women's economic activity rates in the last decade has been amongst mothers of under-fives, but full-time, continuous employment remains least common among mothers of young children. Economic activity and whether women work full or part-time is clearly correlated with educational and occupational qualifications (Corti *et al.* 1995; Dale and Egerton 1997). In 1997, 86 per cent of women with 'A' level or higher qualifications were economically active, compared with 52 per cent of those with no formal qualifications (Sly *et al.* 1998: 113). Of mothers whose youngest dependent child was under five, 55 per cent were economically active and of these, just under a third were in full-time employment and approximately two-thirds were in part-time employment. This compares with figures for all women of 71 per cent economically active, of whom almost 60 per cent worked full-time. Table 6.1 shows how women's economic activity, though clearly related to responsibility for dependent children, has continued to increase in the last ten years, particularly for women with young dependent children, as men's activity rates have declined (*ibid.*: 110). As Table 6.1 shows, there are not only substantial differences between the propensity of women and men to be economically active and to work full-time or part-time, but also systematic differences within the female population.

The analysis from which this table is derived also revealed the extent to which the most recent cohorts of mothers have been working continuously through their family-building life-cycle stage. One-fifth of women whose youngest child was under school age had remained in employment and presumably taken advantage of maternity leave to a greater or lesser extent during the childbirth and neonatal periods, and more than 40 per cent had been with their current employer for more than five years (*ibid.*: 102). This contrasts with a very low incidence of employment among mothers of very young children which scarcely rose between the immediate post-Second World War period and the late 1970s (Brannen 1998: 77). Two points stand out, in terms of the changing pattern of jobs. Women's part-time employment has grown more among the mothers of under-fives than has full-time employment: and male part-time employment has almost doubled, albeit from a low base. Men are considerably more likely to work part-time if they are under 24 or, to a lesser degree, over 50. Mothers with children under ten tend to work few hours, and this is accompanied by fathers' propensity to work very long hours (*ibid.*: 78–9).

Table 6.1 Economic status by age of youngest dependent child: UK spring 1987, 1992, 1997 (not seasonally adjusted)

Spring 1987	All women	Child 0–4	Child 5–10	No dependent child	All men
Economically active	68.9	42.4	67.2	76.1	87.6
In employment	61.7	32.3	59.8	69.3	77.7
• Full-time	35.4	10.0	16.2	49.1	74.1
• Part-time	26.2	22.3	43.5	20.1	3.5
Self-employed	4.2	4.0	5.9	3.5	12.1
Govt-supp. training	1.1	—	—	1.8	1.8
Unemployed (ILO)*	7.2	10.0	7.4	6.8	9.9
Economically inactive	31.1	57.6	32.8	23.9	12.4

Spring 1992	All women	Child 0–4	Child 5–10	No dependent child	All men
Economically active	70.6	48.4	70.9	75.7	86.3
In employment	65.4	42.4	64.7	70.5	76.3
• Full-time	37.5	13.5	21.4	48.6	71.8
• Part-time	27.8	28.9	43.2	21.9	4.4
Self-employed	4.3	3.9	5.8	3.8	12.7
Govt-supp. training	0.8	—	—	1.2	1.4
Unpaid family workers	0.6	0.9	0.7	0.4	0.2
Unemployed (ILO*)	5.3	6.0	6.2	5.2	10.1
Economically inactive	29.4	51.6	29.1	24.3	13.7

Spring 1997	All women	Child 0–4	Child 5–10	No dependent child	All men
Economically active	71.4	55.0	70.9	75.1	84.4
In employment	67.2	51.1	65.9	70.7	77.4
• Full-time	37.9	17.9	22.8	48.1	71.2
• Part-time	29.2	33.2	43.0	22.7	6.2
Self-employed	4.6	4.6	6.1	4.0	12.6
Govt-supp. training	0.5	—	—	0.7	0.7
Unpaid family workers	0.4	0.5	0.5	0.3	0.2
Unemployed (ILO)*	4.2	3.9	5.0	4.3	6.9
Economically inactive	28.6	45.0	29.1	24.9	15.6

Source: Sly *et al.* 1998: Table C, p. 110

Part-time working

Women's activity rate in the UK – as more widely – is linked to the extent of part-time working (O'Reilly and Fagan 1998). Sly *et al.* (1998: 101) reflect that, 'There has been a shift [between 1987 and 1997] from full-time to part-time employment coinciding with an increase in the number of women wishing [*sic*] to work.' But neither women's nor men's work preferences can be presumed to be reflected by their actual work patterns, as the proportion of involuntary part-time working indicated in Sly *et al.*'s (*ibid.*: 115) analysis shows clearly. There has been a recent renewal of the debate about the lesser centrality of employment and career development for women and the possibility that women either choose between full-time continuous work histories or more flexible employment which enables them to give precedence to their family-raising roles (Hakim 1996; Hakim and Jacobs 1997) or gravitate (with or without their collusion) into particular career trajectories as a result of their occupational choices and domestic constraints (Crompton with Le Feuvre 1996). Highly qualified women (who have the greatest propensity to work continuously and full-time throughout their working lives) tend to have access to career rather than job opportunities and also tend to have access to breadwinner earnings. They are likely to have equally highly qualified (and higher-paid) partners (Paci and Joshi 1996), which enables them to buy in high-quality substitute domestic work and child care (Gregson and Lowe 1994).

Of those working part-time in spring 1997, 10 per cent of women aged 16–59 and 28 per cent of men aged 16–64 were doing so because they could not find a full-time job. Among women, the proportions were highest for those who did not have dependent children, but we cannot assume that women not looking for full-time work because of the constraints imposed by dependants would not prefer either to work full-time or opt for economic inactivity. Previous research suggests that significant proportions of women in part-time employment would prefer full-time jobs (Rubery and Fagan 1994) and many are constrained by caring responsibilities (McRae 1991), rather than exhibiting a preference to work part-time.

The fact that there has been growth in male part-time working in the same period is indicative of restructuring of the labour force at both ends of the age scale. Changes both in the scale and funding of higher education have led to an increasing proportion of school-leavers entering higher education rather than employment and seeking term-time employment compatible with their studies. The combination of financial hardship (Lucas 1997) and employers' increasingly articulated preference for graduate recruits with work experience (Harvey *et al.* 1998) has amplified this supply of generally high-quality part-time labour, and employers in some sectors, particularly hotels and catering, have drawn upon it with enthusiasm (Hogarth *et al.* 1999). Most part-time males who are not students are older workers who have retired early or who have negotiated part-time working arrangements prior to retirement. The participation of such peripheral members of the labour force has advantages both for employers and the employees concerned, but it may reduce the availability of work for traditional low-skilled applicants, and threaten the overall quality of jobs (Rubery 1998).

The definition of part-time work varies (Blossfeld and Hakim 1997; Fagan and O'Reilly 1998) and, in the case of LFS data, derives from the self-classification of respondents, reflecting fixed and variable weekly hours which range from less than five to over thirty-two. Part-time work is clearly not by definition insecure employment, but employment where the worker's short- and longer-term welfare is ultimately dependent upon their continued availability for work is inherently insecure. Those who work relatively few hours weekly or whose earnings are below a specified level (£64.00 per week in 1998) are liable to be excluded from the National Insurance system. There is evidence that employers and employees collude in negotiating working hours which fall below National Insurance and tax thresholds, and that most employees involved are women (McKnight *et al.* 1998; Ginn and Arber 1998). There are clearly financial benefits for employers and, in the short term, for employees. For some employees, whose paid work is clearly contingent to other aspects off their lives (such as students or second-wage earners), lack of eligibility for benefits may not present immediate problems. However, by reinforcing women's dependency, such arrangements have potential medium- and long-term costs which can be catastrophic when marital breakdown occurs or those in vulnerable, 'flexible' employment lose their jobs as organisations downsize or contracts are lost to competitors. Among the least advantaged groups of employees and the unemployed, social security legislation reinforces women's dependency (Lister 1992; Duncan *et al.* 1994) and women's employment patterns result, even amongst the most privileged groups, in women having access to less non-state pension income than men (Ginn and Arber 1998). Part-time work for women has been shown to be associated with downward occupational mobility (Joshi 1984).

Although part-time employment has most often been included in discussion of flexible and 'non-standard' employment, it has been pointed out (for example, by Gallie and White 1994) that, while part-time employees are more likely than full-time ones to be employed on a temporary basis (see Figure 6.1), over 60 per cent of part-timers are in permanent employment. Given that 45 per cent of women in employment and just under a quarter of employees in employment work part-time (many as a core and stable element in workplaces where part-timers are a

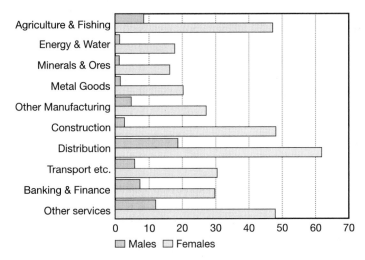

Figure 6.1 Proportion of employees working part-time, by sector and gender

Source: LFS 1996 (spring)

significant proportion), it is paradoxically becoming increasingly a standard form of working, particularly in industries such as retail (Perrons and Hurstfield 1998; Reynolds 1998). Part-time employment is certainly one of the mechanisms used by employers to achieve numerical flexibility and to match staffing to peak demand for goods or services, and it is also the main way in which those whose other responsibilities or schedules rule out full-time employment have been enabled to undertake paid work in the UK.

Part-time employment is nevertheless more common among those with the most tenuous attachment to the labour market. It is most common among both females and males in casual employment, seasonal employment and other temporary work, and rarely found among men in permanent, fixed-term contractual and agency temporary work. Agency placements are an interesting anomaly, clearly concerned predominantly with the provision of full-time temporary workers – although even here, 37 per cent of women worked part-time. Male temporary workers are most likely to be full-time employees unless they are employed on a casual basis, of which category 70 per cent of males worked part-time compared, at the other extreme, to only 16 per cent of those on fixed-term contracts. Women in temporary employment, conversely, are more likely than not to work part-time, even if on fixed-term contracts (51 per cent of whom were part-timers), and over two-thirds of women in casual and seasonal employment worked part-time.

Figure 6.1 compares part-time employment by industry sector and reveals substantial differences between women and men. The female workforce includes almost as many part-time as full-time employees in agriculture, construction and other services, while around two-thirds of women in distribution are part-time. Men's part-time employment, conversely, represents a negligible proportion in most sectors. Only in other services and distribution is it more than 10 per cent, whereas female part-timers range from 15 per cent of the small number of women employed in minerals and extraction, to over 60 per cent of the considerably larger female distribution workforce. A comparison of the gendering of part-time employment by occupation (see Figure 6.2) clarifies this picture further by revealing that part-time employment, particularly for women, is most common in lower-level service occupations.

In fact, over 80 per cent of all part-time female employees are concentrated in clerical and secretarial, personal and protective services, sales occupations and other occupations: occupations where demand has been declining because of restructuring and technology, or where male part-time employment has also been increasing, albeit from a low base (Wilson 1998). In retail distribution, a third of all employment growth between 1993 and 1995 consisted of male part-time employment (Perrons and Hurstfield 1998: 123). Although there are clearly substantial numbers of highly qualified women employed on a part-time basis, they are likely to be in the lower level and least secure occupational niches of their professions, rather than in 'fast track' positions – though they may have access to better jobs or career ladders than the majority of part-timers. Even in retail distribution, where women comprise almost two-thirds of employees, there is little

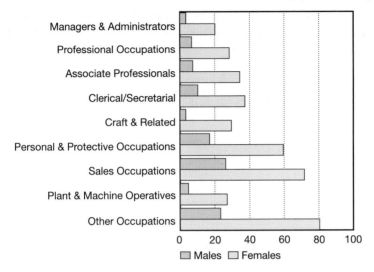

Figure 6.2 Percentage of occupational group who are part-time, by gender

Source: LFS 1996 (spring)

evidence that the lack of formal obstacles is conducive to part-time career development, with few instances of part-timers having been promoted or managerial jobs restructured as part-time posts (Perrons and Hurstfield 1998: 146, 157 ff.).

Part-time employees provide structured flexibility, but may be regarded by employers as the least flexible component of their workforces (Edwards and Robinson 1998; Hogarth *et al.* 1999). Nevertheless, part-time employment virtually always provides employers with cost advantages, even in circumstances where part-time employees are afforded *pro rata* terms and conditions of employment, in line with the European Directive on part-time employment. Meal-breaks and other such ambiguous 'benefits' are rarely paid for and it appears that part-time workers may be likely to both receive less training and development and require more in order to operate effectively (Edwards and Robinson 1998).

Temporary employment

Temporary employment is unequivocally insecure. Male permanent employment and full-time employment as a whole have fallen, whereas temporary employment, particularly fixed-term contact employment, has grown substantially, reflecting changes in public sector management and perhaps a more formal approach to temporary employment, where jobs that were previously casual or seasonal have been redefined as fixed-term. As this indicates, temporary employment is not a homogeneous category. Figure 6.3 shows women's and men's distribution among the categories of temporary employment used for Labour Force Survey (LFS) classification.

The figure shows that men are more likely to work on fixed-term contracts and

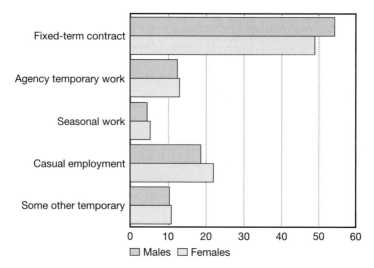

Figure 6.3 Type of temporary employment, by gender

Source: LFS 1996 (spring)

women somewhat more likely to be in the other, generally more casual categories. Both the distribution of temporary employees among these categories and indeed, the LFS self-classification into permanent and 'in some way not permanent' need to be regarded with caution, given changing boundaries between organisations (Colling 1995). Recruits to subcontracted organisations taken on to work on specific tasks in an insecure product market may not have temporary contracts, although their continued employment is contingent on customer demand. The increasing use of labour supply contracts between employers and intermediaries such as employment agencies complicates the employment relationship. Most agencies do not employ the staff they supply to clients, but some – including Manpower, one of the biggest – employ many of their 'temps' directly. On balance, such increasingly complicated relationships between organisations requiring work to be done and the people who actually do it, almost certainly leads to an underestimate of temporary employment, which by any workable definition cannot encompass all contingent and vulnerable employees.

As would be expected, the incidence of types of temporary employment varies considerably among industry sectors and, within these, between women and men. Temporary employment overall constituted a virtually stable proportion of the workforce until the early 1980s (Beatson 1995) but has grown substantially from a base of 5–6 per cent since then. Figure 6.4 shows changes between 1992 and 1996 in male and female distributions among the categories for all sectors and echoes the gender differences illustrated in Figure 6.3. The growth and reversal of fixed-term contract work clearly show the impact of public sector compulsory competitive tendering (CCT), health service management restructuring and other public spending constraints: a finding reinforced by examining the particular

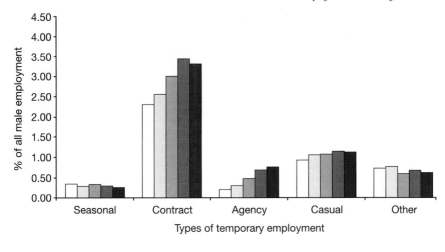

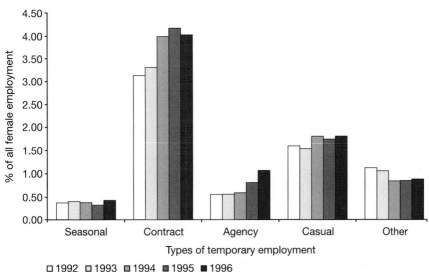

□ 1992 □ 1993 ▦ 1994 ▨ 1995 ■ 1996

Figure 6.4 Temporary employees as a percentage of male and female employees, all sectors

temporary employment profiles of the sector in question. Men are twice as likely as women to be on fixed-term contracts in health and social work, whereas growth followed by decline in male fixed-term contract employment in other community and personal services appears to have been accompanied by recent substantial increases in casual employment among men and, even more, women.

The incidence of temporary working and the types of temporary working found vary considerably by sector. The growth of temporary employment since the early 1990s has been greatest in sectors characterised by change – indicative of industrial restructuring, or technical, organisational or occupational changes which have led to or are projected to lead to either an increase or a decline in demand for labour (Purcell 1998). This could indicate a temporary fluctuation in confidence or employers' increasingly cautious recruitment, rather than long-term decline in demand for more secure labour, and there is evidence that both factors are relevant in some employment contexts. Thus, primary and extractive industries (such as agriculture), the privatised utilities (electricity, gas and water supply), other predominantly public sector areas (such as education), hotels and catering, other community and personal services, research and development, and computing and business services had higher than average proportions of temporary employees and all (apart from hotels and catering) had exhibited growth in the proportion of their workforces employed on a temporary basis between 1992 and 1996. The most consistent growth in all kinds of temporary employment categories in the 1992–6 period was male employment in computing and business services.

Figure 6.5 shows the proportion of each broad sector of the workforce employed in temporary work, comparing proportions of males and females. The enormous growth of temporary employment in the energy and water sector reflects public sector privatisation and the way that it has been managed, but it should also be borne in mind that here (and in agriculture and fisheries) the proportion of the workforce employed is small and has been declining for many decades. It is nonetheless notable that in all sectors, women are more likely than men to be employed on a temporary basis. Women are noticeably more likely to be employed temporarily in manufacturing – particularly in agency and casual work, which have fluctuated dramatically over the five-year period, possibly indicating substitution between categories. The similarity of male and female

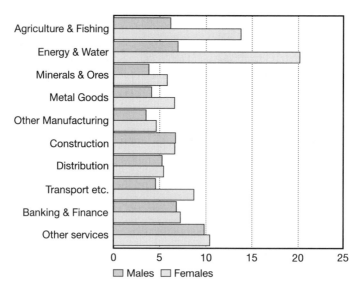

Figure 6.5 Proportion of workforce in temporary employment, by sector and gender
Source: LFS 1996 (spring)

temporary proportions in construction is initially surprising, until it is remembered that women are less than 10 per cent of the construction workforce (Briscoe 1998).

Distribution is a broad and disparate category whose component sub-sectors share fluctuating patterns of demand over the working day, week and year. Employment flexibility has increasingly been achieved by part-time rather than temporary employment in the predominantly female retail distribution sector, by variable working in the predominantly male transport industry and by both part-time and temporary employment in hotels and catering. As noted above, temporary employment has remained remarkably stable over the period studied, but there have been fluctuations between different temporary categories. This is one of the areas where it looks as if male casual employment may be being substituted for similar female employment, despite the fact that it is an industry with a distinctively gendered workforce (Purcell 1996). The hotels and catering sector is also distinctive, in that well over half of all temporary employees are casual workers, and a higher proportion are seasonal than in any other sector.

By contrast, the pursuit of flexible employment in financial services is a relatively recent development, reflecting radical technological, organisational and product market changes in the sector. The most recent year shows very dramatic changes, particularly in the use of agency temporary employees, which reflects a significant decline in permanent employment in the industry mediated and succeeded by the increased use of outsourcing telesales and routine clerical posts via labour supply contracts with employment intermediary agencies. There are obviously new patterns of labour use evolving here, with possible substitution of male and female agency and male fixed-term contract staff for employees on permanent contracts. Within other services, computing and business services indicate a distinctly gendered temporary labour force, with males more likely to be employed on fixed-term contracts and women in agency or casual employment, probably in lower-level posts. There is a clear upward trend in fixed-contract, agency and casual male employment, whereas for women the trend appears to be substitution between categories rather than growth in demand for temporary employees.

In health and social work, the size of the female workforce is considerably greater than that of males and the ratio of temporary to permanent employment is higher than in most other sectors. Males in the sector have a greater probability of being employed in fixed-term contract employment than women, and women are more likely to be casuals. Other community and personal services is another female-dominated sector with relatively high ratios of temporary to permanent employment, where males are more likely to be temporary than females in all but agency work.

To get a clearer picture of relative employment insecurity, it is necessary to look at occupational differences. The largest concentrations of male temporary employment are in professional occupations, clerical and manual categories. Women are most likely to be in professional, clerical and personal and protective services: in 'gendered niches' (Crompton and Sanderson 1992) even in the professional category, where the overwhelming majority are in teaching and health professions. If we look within each of the occupational categories, this picture of gendered temporary employment is reinforced. Figure 6.6 shows the proportions of male and female employees in each broad occupational category in non-permanent employment.

The figure shows very clearly that women professionals – that is, highly quali-fied women who have invested in acquiring human capital – are nearly twice as likely as their male peers to be in temporary employment. Although there is an increasingly wide range of employees in temporary employment, from manager-ial and professional staff through to the least skilled casual employees, the LFS statistics revealed that the majority, particularly in the case of women, remain at the lower-skill–low-paid end of the spectrum. Employer-led flexible employment thus applies mostly to lower-paid women and increases their labour market vul-nerability and economic dependency. Where highly qualified women work part-time, the net effect is broadly similar, although they are less immediately precarious. Males in secretarial and clerical employment (a relatively small group) and in other occupations (that is, predominantly unskilled work) are the only men to be more likely than their female workmates to be employed on a temporary basis.

The significance of age in relation to temporary employment

An examination of the age distribution of temporary employees throws further light on these patterns. Table 6.2 gives a simple comparison of age by gender, and

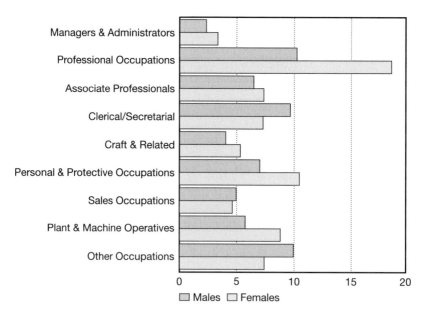

Figure 6.6 Percentage of occupational group in temporary employment, by gender

Source: LFS 1996 (spring)

Table 6.2 **Reason for taking a temporary job, by age and gender**

Age group	Contract included training		Could not find permanent job		Did not want permanent job		Other	
	Male	*Female*	*Male*	*Female*	*Male*	*Female*	*Male*	*Female*
22 and under	11.3	7.1	31.8	25.6	38.4	44.7	18.5	22.6
23–25	10.2	12.3	47.8	46.0	21.3	20.2	20.8	21.5
26–30	8.0	6.9	46.5	43.5	12.6	22.6	32.9	27.0
31–5	7.3	4.0	52.8	32.6	9.2	27.0	30.7	36.4
36–40	4.4	3.3	60.9	34.9	8.7	32.7	26.0	29.0
41–50	3.8	1.0	52.3	41.0	13.9	32.1	30.0	25.8
51–60	0.7	0.3	55.1	28.4	23.2	48.0	21.0	23.2
Over 60	0.0	0.0	14.1	9.8	57.0	61.9	28.9	28.3

Source: LFS 1997 (spring)

Table 6.3 gives the main reasons for taking temporary employment, by age and gender.

The groups least likely to work on a temporary basis are interestingly different: women between 23 and 25 and men between 36 and 40. Their main reasons for taking temporary work show a predictable difference in the ratios of those who could not find and did not want (or who did not consider themselves free to want) permanent employment, but these responses vary significantly by age group, with younger and older employees of both sexes most likely to be voluntarily temporary and significant proportions of both sexes aged 23–40 stating that they could not find a permanent job. Older men were significantly more likely than women to be involuntarily temporary, but both men and women in the 41–50 age group were most likely of their sex to give this as their main reason.

Males with no formal qualifications, or low ones (NVQ level 1 or less), are more likely than most other groups to have said that they could not find permanent employment, but they are closely followed by the most highly qualified groups (NVQ level 5). Perhaps these are Handy's (1995) 'portfolio workers', but reference to the occupational structure suggests that they are more likely to be younger professionals in service sector and/or public employment, such as education or the health service. The pattern is broadly similar for women, with those at the intermediate levels least likely to be involuntarily temporary and most likely to have said that they did not seek permanent employment. In both the low and high qualified categories, women are more likely to be in non-permanent employment than men.

Discussion

The LFS evidence thus indicates that both standard and atypical contractual relations, and thus employment insecurity, are gendered. Casey *et al.* (1997), in addition to examining LFS data for the early 1990s, compared employers' use of flexible labour in the Workplace Industrial Relations Surveys (WIRS) of 1984 and 1990 and carried out case study investigations in twenty-five establishments. From a consideration of their findings from these three sources, they concluded that employers' use of flexible forms of working had been increasing, particularly in medium and large companies. They also identified increased use in newer, labour-intensive areas of employment: those which tend to employ high proportions of women. Their case study findings revealed that the forms of flexible resourcing used by employers depended significantly upon the gendering of the workforce. That is, jobs were constructed to take implicit account of gender divisions of labour and responsibility in the household. Thus, it would seem that male and female 'breadwinning' responsibilities are liable to remain asymmetrical. As several chapters in this volume show, some categories of employees are disadvantaged more than others by such developments, while a very few are empowered in the downsized, delayered organisation.

Table 6.3 Type of employment contract by working arrangements, by gender.

Age group	Permanent		Fixed contract		Agency temporary		Other	
	Male	*Female*	*Male*	*Female*	*Male*	*Female*	*Male*	*Female*
Flexitime	8.6	11.6	14.4	12.6	7.0	9.2	5.2	8.7
Annualised hours	4.2	3.9	3.6	4.4	2.2	0.8	0.8	1.0
Term-time working	1.1	6.4	4.5	23.4	1.3	1.8	4.7	13.4
Job-sharing	0.1	1.3	0.2	2.0	0.0	0.8	0.0	0.9
Nine-day fortnight	0.5	0.1	0.4	0.1	0.0	0.3	0.0	0.0
Four and a half day week	2.6	1.6	2.1	0.7	3.4	0.4	1.8	0.4
Zero hours	0.6	0.6	1.3	1.0	4.0	4.8	3.8	5.2
None of these	82.3	74.8	73.4	55.9	82.6	81.9	82.3	70.5

Source: LFS 1997 (spring)

The implications for equal opportunities

In a comparative analysis of employment, flexibility and gender in EU member countries, Drew and Emerek (1998) argue that the main impetus for labour market change has been the shift in employment from agricultural and manufacturing to service industries, where there are both greater inherent and potential variations in labour demand over the working day and week. In essence, they conclude that the net effect of women's increased economic activity has been the emergence of a dual breadwinner family model, to a greater or lesser extent in different European countries in relation to the industrial structure, traditions, norms, cultures and labour market regulation of each one. Their analysis suggests that atypical working has been a major characteristic of the increase in women's labour market participation in most of the countries studied and, indeed, the growth in atypical working patterns is strongly correlated with women's activity rates. In essence, Drew and Emerek (1998: 89) suggest that the growth of service sector industries which require extended hours operation with fluctuating demands for labour have been particularly conducive to the construction of part-time jobs and, thus, to the growth of women's employment. Their conclusion, in line with the earlier study by Meulders *et al.* (1994) appears to suggest that women's increased economic activity and breadwinning role have not been accompanied by a decrease in gender segregation or, by implication, increasingly equal opportunities. Diverse workforces have diverse needs in order to be able to make their social contribution.

This leads to the argument that increasing employment flexibility and, in particular, non-standard employment, is both responsive to the supply of, and creates opportunities for, previously under-represented groups – particularly women – to be economically active. An increasing range of documents have emerged from the European Commission which indicate that the big issue for the millennium will be the reconciliation of work and family life. For example, the White Paper *Growth, Competitiveness, Employment* proposed that a fifth of new jobs projected by the year 2000 could come from the expansion of services 'dealing with new needs . . . [arising from] changes in lifestyles, the transformation of family structures, the increase in the number of working women [*sic*] and the new aspirations of the elderly and very old people' (European Commission 1994, cited in Moss 1997: 22).

These debates connect with arguments for a rethinking of how work and employment are organised, allied to concern about falling fertility rates, the welfare of children and the care of those who are unable to care for themselves. Thus, 'family friendly' employment policies are seen to call for 'flexible employment' which is responsive to the needs of employees: and although the 'family friendly' policies lobby is invariably concerned to stress that the issues are of concern to all employees – men, women, mothers and fathers, daughters and sons – all evidence on the introduction and implementation of such policies suggests that both employers and employees see them as primarily related to women. The issues are approached from the point of view of the labour supply; particularly those employees who themselves desire flexibility in order to fit employment to other components of their lives – particularly women who are mothers and carers. Underlying the arguments for 'family friendly' policies is a recognition that 'standard' full-time employment is not easily compatible with responsible parenting, that the majority of mothers as well as fathers of dependent children are employed in paid work and that the role conflicts generated by such patterns may be socially and personally dysfunctional.

Does this reflect employers responding to change in the labour supply: more women 'wishing' to combine caring responsibilities and family life and, latterly, younger and older workers of both sexes 'wishing' to combine part-time employment with participation in higher education, or early retirement with some continued earning? The evidence cited earlier suggested that economic restructuring and employer demand relating to product rather than labour markets appear to be the main factors in changing female activity rates and the growth of part-time employment. The effects on women of increasing employment deregulation, industrial restructuring and privatisation have been to increase women's participation in the labour market but at the same time to make the position of many of them more vulnerable. Women's employment has increased as a result of the expansion of services, but the quality of jobs offered to them has deteriorated considerably, often amounting to exploitation with no prospects of improvement, as in the case of low-skilled and low-paid jobs. Recent research on employers' recruitment and resourcing practices reveals that in organisations where temporary employees form over half of the workforce (a small but significant minority), temporary employees never move to permanent contracts (Heather *et al.* 1996).

The number of part-time jobs has increased, particularly those with low hours or zero hours contracts where employees have no guaranteed minimum wage. Such employees are often paid below the National Insurance threshold, which means that they are ineligible for maternity pay, sick pay and the state pension. They are unlikely to be entitled to time off for national holidays or for meal breaks. Part-time work and other forms of flexible employment may enable those with caring responsibilities to juggle employment and family life, but it may be very far from reconciling work and family life. Donaldson (1996) has argued that the increasing use of part-time and shift-working arrangements to extend operating hours in manufacturing and service industries – far from providing flexibility for employees – has led to an intensification of household work effort as parents increasingly both have paid jobs which they have to manage, in addition to household and child-rearing responsibilities. Family life, community activities and 'own time', he argues, are thus being eroded.

Furthermore in the name of flexibility, new employment practices have spread, particularly short-term contracts and the use of agency temporary staff so that employees can be hired and dispensed with according to fluctuations in demand for products or services. A good example of this is the retail industry, where supermarket managers think in terms of covering hours, rather than appointing members of staff – relying heavily on a variety of types of contingent employees – older semi-retired employees, schoolchildren and students, as well as working mothers who seek employment hours compatible with family obligations.

Research on flexible employment in the retail and finance sectors (Perrons and Hurstfield 1998; Neathey and Hurstfield 1995), revealed that part-time and other women on 'non-standard' employment contracts were often under pressure to conform to requests for intensified effort and increasing flexibility to suit the needs of employers. These women also had poorer conditions of employment than those on 'standard' contracts and were in many cases excluded from sick pay and pension schemes. Dex and McCulloch (1995), in an earlier analysis of LFS and British Household Panel Survey (BHPS) data, found that 'non-standard' employees, most of whom were women, had lower hourly earnings, less job-related training and shorter average job tenure (and thus, greater likelihood of being ineligible for rights granted by the Employment Protection Act). Preliminary research (Purcell and Purcell 1998) indicates that temporary employees recruited via labour supply contracts from agencies rarely have comparable rights to those directly employed.

Marginalisation or diversity?

But the evidence also indicates that increasing numbers of women have been entering and remaining in the labour force in more highly paid and secure occupations. 'Family friendly' employment policies have had the active support of employers and trade unions (IPD 1997; TUC 1998) and, as was clear from the LFS data, women's and men's work histories have been converging. Examples of good practice exist among British employers who recognise that women's increased employment participation and equal opportunities lead to more productive workforces, greater economic prosperity and a healthier society. The leading initiative is Opportunity 2000, a self-financing business-led campaign launched in 1991 with the objective of increasing the quality and quantity of women's participation in the workforce by encouraging employers to set up programmes and identify goals within their own organisations, thus signalling a public commitment to advancing equal opportunities. There are currently around 300 member organisations and these represent virtually all major British employers; for example, almost all the major banks, government departments, universities, utilities, services and manufacturers. These programmes and goals are defined in terms of positive action rather than positive discrimination: for example, widening recruitment pools, making better use of resources by encouraging employees to participate in training and development to realise their potential, facilitating women's return to work after childbirth by offering flexible work arrangements, career breaks and the option of movement between part-time and full-time contracts. Employers pay a subscription to join Opportunity 2000 for the privilege of sharing best practice and learning from their peers, as well as benchmarking their progress. Their only obligation is to demonstrate willingness to set goals for the improvement of women's representation in the organisation and an action plan for achieving these and to agree to undertake periodic reviews of progress towards these goals.

This monitoring reveals that organisations which have made the Opportunity 2000 commitment demonstrate equal opportunities records above the UK norm. Opportunity 2000 does, however, have three inherent limitations which restrict its capacity to initiate wide-ranging or radical change. First, it is voluntary – and although leading employers set trends and ultimately force other companies which compete with them for labour to raise standards, this 'trickle effect' can be slow and is subject to local labour market conditions. Secondly, and more fundamentally, a commitment to equal opportunities based on the 'business case', which is not compulsory for all competitors, means that equality and justice motives are always subservient to the profit motive. Third (although the participants would probably wish to challenge this), the initiative appears to be primarily about providing opportunities for training and advancement and, as such, is unlikely to benefit the majority of women in employment, particularly those in 'non-standard' employment. In fact, a formal commitment to equal opportunities may result in little practical effect (Liff 1989); and Neathey and Hurstfield (1995) found that, while their case study employers claimed that part-time and temporary employees were eligible for training and promotion, they were invariably at a loss to give examples when challenged to illustrate the principle.

Evidence from a case study of an Opportunity 2000 company – Midland Bank (a major UK high street bank) throws some light on the strengths and weaknesses of the 'positive action'/voluntarist approach (Lewis *et al.* 1996). The bank has been at the forefront of equal opportunities 'good practice' since legislation was introduced in the 1970s, appointing its first Equal Opportunities Manager in 1979 and its first Equal Opportunities Director in 1988, and consistently providing conditions of employment well beyond the statutory minimum – for example, 46 weeks' maternity leave, compared to the 14 required nationally. Its record on 'family friendly' policies has also been exemplary and in 1996 they had over 100 nurseries around the country providing places for 850 children of employees who are also 'primary carers'. However, their policies have always been implemented on the 'business case' for equal opportunities, stimulated most particularly in the 1980s by concern about the impending 'demographic time bomb', when (due to a substantial fall in the birth rate in the late 1960s and early 1970s) fewer young people were projected to enter the labour market and employers were being advised to consider alternative staffing strategies. One main strategy which they adopted was the implementation of 'family friendly' policies to retain trained staff (which essentially meant women who became mothers). In this, they were spectacularly successful, moving from a situation in the early 1980s where only 29 per cent of women taking maternity leave returned to work, to one where, in 1995, 80 per cent did so (*ibid.*: 108). However, the priorities have changed in the 1990s, from staff retention to 'downsizing' and flexibility, so that equal opportunities are likely to be seen as less of a priority. In another Opportunity 2000 organisation, Digital UK, research revealed that equal opportunities initiatives had been cut back in the mid-1990s – a result of the recession (Noel 1996; see also Colling and Dickens 1998).

Another potential problem about 'family friendly' policies is that they will be taken advantage of predominantly by women, reinforcing the role of women as carers and 'slow track' employees. In the case of the Midland Bank, it seems that women are more likely than their male colleagues to have taken parental leave and career breaks, and comparative research among senior managers in a sample of Opportunity 2000 companies showed very different profiles for comparable samples of males and females (Wajcman 1996). The men were mainly married to women who were not in employment or who worked part-time, and had two or more children; the women were either unmarried, or were married to men in equally demanding jobs, and had no children or only one child. This illustrates clearly how high the costs of remaining on the 'fast track' are, for women. In addition, a substantial number of the organisations which subscribe to Opportunity 2000 are, equally enthusiastically, adopting outsourcing and labour-supply contract insourcing from the big employment intermediaries, which means that they are likely to be employing increasing numbers of women who, because they are not, strictly speaking, their employees (and are unlikely to work for them continuously for long periods) are not eligible to benefit from the family friendly policies (Purcell and Purcell 1998). Such organisations increasingly are becoming 'hollow giants' (Allen and Henry 1996), externalising operations and employment responsibilities.

Conclusion

In the UK, women currently constitute almost half of those in paid employment, but their work patterns and distribution throughout the workforce remain distinctly different to those of men and exhibit systematic differences within the female population. Indeed, women constitute well over half the 'flexible' workforce (however it is defined) and the overwhelming majority of employees in 'non-standard' employment. If the narrower definition of non-permanent employment is used, they represent more than half of the insecure workforce.

Women's employment remains considerably more concentrated than men's, and is largely found in two broad areas: traditionally low-paid, low-skilled manufacturing and service industries and public sector services. In the former, such as food, drink and tobacco, distribution and hotels, since the abolition of the statutory pay regulation in 1993, the number of very low-paid workers – particularly part-time employees – has grown: and most of the low-paid are women. The other main areas of female concentration are in public services, where job security and conditions of employment, previously good, have deteriorated substantially as a result of government expenditure cuts. The introduction of compulsory competitive tendering in many areas of local government services, for example, has particularly hit those in low-paid, relatively low-skilled jobs (Escott and Whitfield 1995). The evidence demonstrates unequivocally that within these industries and in the labour force generally, a high proportion of women in employment are further concentrated into low-paid, low-skill occupations.

It is indisputable that women's greater participation in employment indicates the growing significance of their paid work to the household economy, but another way of conceptualising this is in terms of the increasing decline of the family wage, long ago identified by Barratt and Mackintosh (1980) as incompatible with equal opportunities. Does this, then, indicate greater gender equality – or is atypical employment the last gasp (or latest version) of patriarchy? Do atypical employment patterns signify the emergence of a new, different system of inequality? The evidence supports Rubery *et al.*'s (1996) 'modified breadwinner' thesis; polarisation may be eroding differences between men and women in similar labour market situations, while extending the range of difference *within* the male and female workforces. With the erosion of the family wage, however, the balance of power in the effort/reward bargain has shifted perceptibly towards employers and shareholders, and away from employees. In households with disadvantaged access to the labour market, the requirement for individual effort in order to subsist has been intensified, as predicted by Humphries (1977), who identified this change as the main danger inherent in feminist challenges to the concept of the family wage. At the dual career end of the spectrum, it appears that the material improvement in the quality of life may have severe social and emotional costs, and generate employment which contributes further to labour market polarisation.

References

Adkins, L. (1996) *Gendered Work: Sexuality, Family and the Labour Market*, Milton Keynes: Open University Press.

Allen, J. and Henry, N. (1996) 'Fragments of industry and employment: contract work and the shift towards precarious employment', in R. Crompton, D. Gallie and K. Purcell (eds) *Changing Forms of Employment, Organisations, Skills, Gender*, London: Routledge.

Barrett, M. and Mackintosh, M. (1980) 'The "family wage": some problems for socialists and feminists', *Capital and Class*, 11: 51–72.

Baxter, J. (1992) 'Domestic labour and income inequality', *Work, Employment and Society*, 6, 2: 229–49.

Beatson, M. (1995) *Labour Market Flexibility*, Employment Department Research Paper No. 48, Sheffield: Employment Department.

Beechey, V. (1987) *Unequal Work*, London: Verso.

Beechey, V. and Perkins T. (1987) *A Matter of Hours*, Cambridge: Polity Press.

Blossfeld, H.-P. and Hakim, C. (1997) *Between Equalization and Marginalization: Women Working Part-time in Europe and the United States of America*, Oxford: Oxford University Press.

Brannen, J. (1998) 'Employment and family lives: equalities and inequalities', in E. Drew, R. Emerek and E. Mahon (eds) *Women, Work and the Family in Europe*, London: Routledge.

Bridgewood, A. and Savage, P. (1993) *General Household Survey 1991*, London: HMSO.

Briscoe, G. (1998) 'Employment trends in construction', in R. Wilson and R. Lindley (eds) *Review of the Economy and Employment 1997/98*, Coventry: Institute for Employment Research, University of Warwick.

Bruegel, I. (1979) 'Women as reserve army of labour: a note on recent British experience', *Feminist Review*, 3: 12–23.

Casey, B., Metcalf, H. and Millward, N. (1997) *Employers' Use of Flexible Labour*, London: Policy Studies Institute.

Cockburn, C. (1991) *In the Way of Women: Men's Resistance to Sex Equality in Organisations*, London: Macmillan.

Colling, T. (1995) *From Hierarchy to Contract? Subcontracting and Employment in the Service Economy*, Coventry: Warwick Papers in Industrial Relations No. 52.

Colling, T. and Dickens, L. (1998) 'Selling the case for gender equality: deregulation and equality bargaining', *British Journal of Industrial Relations*, 36, 3: 389–411.

Collinson, D. and Collinson, M. (1996) ' "It's only Dick": the sexual harassment of women managers in insurance sales', *Work, Employment and Society*, 10, 1: 29–56.

Collinson, D., Knights, D. and Collinson, M. (1990) *Managing To Discriminate*, London: Routledge.

Corti, L., Laurie, H. and Dex, S. (1995) *Highly Qualified Women*, Research Series No. 50, Sheffield: Employment Department.

Crompton, R. (1988) 'The feminisation of the clerical labour force since the Second World War', in E.G. Anderson (ed.) *The Feminisation of Office Work*, Manchester: Manchester University Press.

Crompton, R. with Le Feuvre N. (1996) 'Paid employment and the changing system of gender relations', *Sociology*, 30, 3: 427–43.

Crompton, R. and Sanderson, K. (1990) *Gendered Jobs and Social Change*, London: Unwin Hyman.

Cunnison, S. and Stageman, J. (1993) *Feminising the Unions*, Aldershot: Avebury.

Dale, A. and Egerton, M. (1997) *Highly Educated Women: Evidence from the National Child Development Study*, Sheffield: Department for Education and Employment.

Devine, F. (1992) 'Gender segregation in the engineering and science professions: a case of continuity and change', *Work, Employment and Society*, 6, 4: 557–75.

Dex, S. and McCulloch, A. (1995) *Flexible Employment in Britain: A Statistical Analysis*, Manchester: Equal Opportunities Commission.

Donaldson, M. (1996) *Taking Our Time*, Perth: University of Western Australia Press.

Drew, E. and Emerek, R. (1998) 'Employment, flexibility and gender' in E. Drew, R. Emerek and E. Mahon (eds) *Women, Work and the Family in Europe*, London: Routledge.

Duncan, A., Giles, C. and Webb, S. (1994) *Social Security Reform and Women's Independent Incomes*, Research Series No. 6, Manchester: EOC.

Edwards, C. and Robinson, O. (1998) 'Better jobs for part-time workers: a study of two essential services', *Proceedings of the International Industrial Relations Association 11th World Congress: Developing competitiveness and social justice: the interplay between institutions and social partners*, 2: 213–18.

Elias, P. and Gregory, M. (1994) *The Changing Structure of Occupations and Earnings in Great Britain 1975–90*, Sheffield: Employment Department Research Series 27.

Escott, K. and Whitfield, D. (1995) *The Gender Impact of CCT in Local Government*, Research Discussion Series No.12, Manchester: EOC.

Fagan, C. and O'Reilly, J. (1998) 'Conceptualising part-time work: the value of an integrated comparative perspective', in J. O'Reilly and C. Fagan (eds) *Part-time Prospects*, London: Routledge.

Gallie, D. and White, M. (1994) 'Employer policies, employee contracts and labour market structure' in J. Rubery and F. Wilkinson (eds) *Employer Strategy and the Labour Market*, Oxford: Oxford University Press.

Ginn, J. and Arber, S. (1998) 'How does part-time work lead to low pension income?', in J. O'Reilly and C. Fagan (eds) *Part-time Prospects*, London: Routledge.

Glucksman, M. (1990) *Women Assemble: Women Workers and the New Industries in Inter-War Britain*, London: Routledge.

Greenbaum, J. (1998) 'The times they are a'changing: dividing and recombining labour through computer systems', in P. Thompson and C. Warhurst (eds) *Workplaces of the Future*, London: Macmillan.

Gregson, N. and Lowe, M. (1994) 'Waged domestic labour and the recognition of the domestic division of labour in dual career households', *Sociology*, 28, 1: 55–78.

Hakim, C. (1994) 'A century of change in occupational segregation, 1891–1991', *Journal of Historical Sociology*, 7: 435–54.

—— (1996) *Key Issues in Women's Work*, London: Athlone.

Hakim, C. and Jacobs, S. (1997) *Sex-Role Preferences and Work Histories: Is There a Link?*, Department of Sociology Working Paper 12: London School of Economics and Political Science.

Handy, C. (1995) *The Empty Raincoat: Making Sense of the Future*, London: Arrow.

Harvey, L., Geall, V. and Moon, S. (1998) *Work Experience: Expanding Opportunities for Undergraduates*, Birmingham: Centre for Quality in Higher Education, UCE.

Hearn, J., Shepherd, D., Tancred-Sherriff, P. and Burrell, G. (eds) (1989) *Sexuality and Organisation*, London: Sage.

Heather, P., Rick, J., Atkinson, J. and Morris, S. (1996) 'Employers' use of temporary workers', *Labour Market Trends*, September: 403–12.

Hochschild, A. (1983) *The Managed Heart*, Berkeley and Los Angeles: University of California Press.

Hogarth, T., Purcell, K. and Simm, C. (1999) *Whose Flexibility? The Costs and Benefits of Different Contractual and Working Arrangements for Employers and Employees*, York: Joseph Rowntree Trust.

Humphries, J. (1977) 'Class struggle and the persistence of the working class family', *Cambridge Journal of Economics*, 1, 3: 241–58.

Humphries, J. and Rubery J. (1992) 'Women's employment in the 1980s: integration, differentiation and polarisation', in J. Michie (ed.) *The Economic Legacy: 1979–1991*, London: Academic Press.

IPD (1997) *Managing Diversity: An IPD Position Paper*, London: Institute for Personnel Development.

Joshi, H. (1984) *Women's Participation in Paid Work: Further Analysis of the Women and Employment Survey*, Research Paper No. 45, Department of Employment, London: HMSO.

Lewis, S. with Watts, A. and Camp, C. (1996) 'Developing and implementing policies: Midland Bank's experience', in S. Lewis and J. Lewis (eds) *The Work–Family Challenge: Rethinking Employment*, London: Sage.

Liff, S. (1989) 'Assessing equal opportunities', *Personnel Review*, 18, 1: 27–34.

Lindley, R. (1994) *Labour Market Structures and Prospects for Women*, Manchester: Equal Opportunities Commission.

Lister, R. (1992) 'Tracing the contours of women's citizenship: a social policy perspective', paper presented to the LSE Gender Group Seminar, London University.

Low Pay Commission (1998) *The National Minimum Wage: First Report of the Low Pay Commission: Summary and Recommendations*, London: Department of Trade and Industry.

Lucas, R. (1997) 'Youth, gender and part-time work: students in the labour process', *Work, Employment and Society*, 11, 4: 595–614.

MacInnes, J. (1998) *The Growth of Women's Employment and the Breakdown of the Male Breadwinner System in Europe, Evidence from Spain and Britain*, Edinburgh Working Papers in Sociology No. 12, Edinburgh: University of Edinburgh

McKnight, A., Elias, P. and Wilson R. (1998) *Low Pay and the National Insurance System: A Statistical Picture*, Manchester: Equal Opportunities Commission.

McRae, S. (1991). 'Occupational change over childbirth: evidence from a national survey', *Sociology*, 25, 4: 589–604.

Metcalf, D. (1998) 'The Low Pay Commission and the national minimum wage', paper presented at the British Universities Industrial Relations Association Annual Conference, Keele University.

Meulders, D., Plasman, O. and Plasman, R. (1994) *Atypical Employment in the European Community*, Aldershot: Dartmouth.

Moss, P. (1997) 'Reconciling employment and family responsibilities: a European perspective', in S. Lewis and J. Lewis (eds) *The Work–Family Challenge*, London: Sage.

Myrdal, A. and Klein, V. (1956) *Women's Two Roles: Home and Work*, London: Routledge.

Neathey, F. and Hurstfield, J. (1995) *Flexibility in Practice: Women's Employment and Pay in Retail and Finance*, Manchester: Equal Opportunities Commission.

Noel, C. (1996) 'The pursuit of equal opportunities policies and practices: the case of management training and development in two organisations', DPhil thesis, Oxford University, Hilary Term.

O'Reilly, J. and Fagan, C. (eds) (1998) *Part-time Prospects: An International Comparison of Part-time Work in Europe, North America and the Pacific Rim*, London: Routledge.

Paci, P. and Joshi, H. (1996) *Wage Differentials Between Men and Women*, London: Department for Education and Employment.

Perrons, D. and Hurstfield, J. (1998) 'United Kingdom', in D. Perrons (ed.) *Flexible Working and the Reconciliation of Work and Family Life – A New Form of Precariousness*, Final Report to Community Action Programme on Equal Opportunities for Women and Men (1996 to 2000), Brussels: European Commission.

Purcell, K. (1996) 'Women's employment in UK tourism: gender roles and labour markets', in T. Sinclair (ed.) *Gender, Work and Tourism*, London: Routledge.

—— (1998) 'Flexibility in the labour market', in R. Wilson and R. Lindley (eds) *Review of the Economy and Employment 1997/8*, Coventry: Institute for Employment Research, University of Warwick.

Purcell, K. and Purcell, J. (1998) 'In-sourcing, outsourcing and the growth of contingent labour as evidence of flexible employment strategies', *European Journal of Work and Organisational Psychology*, 7, 1: 39–59.

Reynolds, J. (1998) 'Sectoral perspectives: retailing', in R. Wilson and R. Lindley (eds) *Review of the Economy and Employment 1997/8*, Coventry: Institute for Employment Research, University of Warwick.

Riley, D. (1984) *War in the Nursery*, London: Virago.

Rubery, J. (1998) 'Part-time work: a threat to labour standards?', in J. O'Reilly and C. Fagan (eds) *Part-time Prospects*, London: Routledge.

Rubery, J. and Fagan, C. (1994) 'Occupational segregation: *plus ça change . . .?*', in R. Lindley (ed.) *Labour Market Structures and Prospects for Women*, Manchester: Equal Opportunities Commission.

Rubery, J., Smith, M. and Turner, E. (1996) *Bulletin on Women and Employment in the European Union*, No. 9, Brussels: CEC.

Savage, M. (1992) 'Women's expertise, men's authority: gendered organisations and the contemporary middle class', in M. Savage and A. Witz (eds) *Gender and Bureaucracy*, Oxford: Blackwell.

Scott J., Alwin, D. and Brawn, M. (1996) 'Generational changes in gender role attitudes: Britain in cross-national perspective', *Sociology*, 30, 3: 471–92.

Siltanen, J. (1994) *Locating Gender*, London: UCL Press.

Sly, F., Thair, T. and Risdon, A. (1998) 'Women in the labour market: results from the spring 1997 Labour Force Survey', *Labour Market Trends*, March: 97–119.

Summerfield, P. (1984) *Women Workers in the Second World War*, London: Croom Helm.

Thomas, M., Goddard, E., Hickman, M. and Hunter, P. (1994) *General Household Survey 1992*, London: OPCS.

TUC (1998) *The Time of Our Lives: A TUC Report on Working Hours and Flexibility*, London: Trades Union Congress Equal Rights Department.

Wajcman, J. (1996) 'Women and men managers: careers and equal opportunities', in R. Crompton, D. Gallie and K. Purcell (eds) *Changing Forms of Employment*, London: Routledge.

Warhurst, C. and Thompson, P. (1998) 'Hands, hearts and minds: changing work and workers at the end of the century', in P. Thompson and C. Warhurst (eds) *Workplaces of the Future*, London: Macmillan.

Wilson, R. (1998) 'Employment overview', in R. Wilson and R. Lindley (eds) *Review of the Economy and Employment, 1997/98*, Coventry: Institute for Employment Research, University of Warwick.

7 Management and the insecure workforce

The search for a new psychological contract

David Guest

Introduction: are managers to blame for insecurity?

Change at work seems to have become a more or less permanent feature of organisational life; and with it comes uncertainty and insecurity. Gurus like Tom Peters have promised – or perhaps threatened – us with a world turned upside down, a world of non-stop, turbulent change (Peters 1988). From Peters' perspective, managers have no choice; organisational survival depends on their ability to handle change. They are captives of the external environment and their only choice is how to ensure that they manage the process of change effectively.

From the same camp of American gurus, Bridges (1995) promises us the end of the job. If there are no jobs, job insecurity loses its meaning. Again, this change is a function of changes in work and society, more particularly the growth of the knowledge industries and of project-based work activity. Scenarios of this type are designed to galvanise managers to action. But at the same time, they absolve managers. Change is inevitable; job security is an outdated notion; the new rhetoric is about employability. In any case, attempts to provide job security are likely to fall on deaf ears, at least as far as key workers are concerned. Their commitment is to their skills, which are transportable; their security is their employability. But Peters has his roots in the transient world of McKinsey consultancy, and Bridges is a product of Silicon Valley. They represent one vision of the future – but one that is not yet widely shared or widely practised. Before we absolve managers from causing job insecurity, we must therefore consider the issues at a more prosaic level.

Throughout this volume, there is a tension between objective and subjective notions of job insecurity; and between the view that the world of work has changed fundamentally with respect to job security and that any shifts are minor in nature. Building on the objective analysis, it is possible to identify an 'at risk' section of the population. The causes of their insecurity lie largely beyond the control of individual organisations and their managers. They can be traced to social deprivation, lack of education, to changes in the structure of industry and to geography. There are also factors such as the economic cycle (Bryson and McKay 1997) and influences at the societal level that managers can do relatively little to control. For much of the 1980s and 1990s the rhetoric of free market economics, with its emphasis on elimination of constraints on the ability of organ-isations to hire and fire, helped to create a climate of job insecurity. Of course senior management in general can be criticised for acquiescing to, sometimes displaying enthusiasm for and on occasion actively advocating, these policies.

Yet within the national framework and within particular sectors of industry, it is still possible for organisations to display considerable variation in their policies on employment and job security. Management retains choice and must therefore accept its responsibility for managing both objective and subjective job security for the great majority of those in the labour market. The growth of interest in human resource management has helped to sharpen the choices for management. On the one hand, there is the market-driven philosophy, the kind of macho-management which favours a robust approach to employment whereby employees at all levels can be brought in and dispensed with in a swift and arbitrary, albeit sometimes quite expensive fashion. Experience in the USA offers a more extreme example of this. Within this framework, various forms of flexible employment and fixed-term contract will be looked upon favourably. The under-lying assumption is that the discipline of the market-place provides the incentive to perform. The rewards are considerable for those who succeed; but those who fail will find themselves back on the labour market very quickly.

In contrast, human resource management (HRM) places more emphasis on employees' commitment to the organisation. Antecedents of commitment are likely to include policies promoting job security and fairness of treatment. The argument from this camp is that a set of progressive human resource practices will lead to higher performance. Guarantees of long-term security of employment can lie at the heart of these practices. This is what is sometimes called the 'soft' as opposed to the 'hard' approach to HRM (Storey 1987), the latter being more aligned to market-driven policies and practices.

This contrast raises questions about which approach management is choosing to pursue. In considering these, we must be aware of a third route. This recognises the market imperatives but at the same time acknowledges that to attract and, for a while at least, retain key employees, organisations must provide an environment which allows opportunities to enhance employability. While the rhetoric may centre around concepts of self-development and therefore individual initiatives to enhance employability, companies may be expected to provide the resources, the experiences and the context in which to facilitate this development.

Whatever strategy managers adopt, they need to recognise that job or employ-ment insecurity is probably most usefully considered as a subjective phenomenon. It is something that people perceive and experience. Job loss and unemployment may be associated with employment insecurity, but they are not essential features of the context; indeed, insecurity is something that people feel and believe to exist even where the objective characteristics of insecurity are absent. Taking this a step further, it is useful to distinguish the cognitive dimension of insecurity from the affective dimension. The cognitive dimension is concerned with perceptions of the environment, including, for example, perceptions of the probability of job loss. The affective dimension is more concerned with the related feelings of concern and anxiety (Hartley *et al.* 1991). The cognitive expectation of job loss may not be associated with feelings of anxiety, either because the job is not valued or because of the perception that attractive alternatives are available. On the other hand, it is quite easy to distort perceptions and thereby heighten the sense of insecurity, perhaps by paying disproportionate attention to what is happening elsewhere rather than in a person's own organisation.

Whether the focus is on the cognitive or the affective dimension, job insecurity is based on perceptions and expectations and these can, to some extent, be managed; herein lies the responsibility of managers. They can manage expectations about job security/insecurity through their employment policies and practices and also through information processing. The mechanisms for the 'management' of job security will lie in the HRM policy and practice, in the organisational culture and in the kind of psychological contract that exists between the organisation and its employees.[1]

How does management policy and practice affect job insecurity?

As already suggested, job insecurity is best viewed as a subjective concept. It is concerned with expectations about the future and it is likely to be heavily influenced by employment trends inside and outside the organisation. In their analysis of the British Social Attitudes data series, Bryson and McKay (1997) construct what they call a 'security index' based on individual's expectations about what will happen in their organisation and what would happen if they were to seek employment elsewhere. They confirm that this index is strongly associated with the state of the external labour market and more specifically with the level of unemployment, but additionally claim that after controlling for this, the typical score on the index has deteriorated in recent years compared with the early 1980s. However, this still focuses on descriptive information rather than the feelings and anxieties associated with it. For this we need rather different data.

One attempt to capture the sense of job security has been reported in the annual IPD survey of the state of the employment relationship. This is a survey of a random sample of the working population in organisations employing ten or more people. When comparing it with some other surveys, it is worth bearing in mind that it therefore only covers those in employment. The 1997 survey (Guest and Conway 1997), contained two items concerned with perceptions of employment security that focus on the cognitive dimension, and four that focus on the affective dimension. The first two items parallel to some extent the kind of data collected by Bryson and McKay. The 1997 results are shown in Table 7.1.

One of the first things to note is that the reported level of job security is quite high. Only 14 per cent felt fairly or very insecure in their present job and 24 per cent admitted to being fairly or very worried about their job security. Reflecting the buoyant labour market in 1997, 42 per cent felt more secure than a year previously, compared with 22 per cent who felt less secure. In helping to understand the background to these feelings, it is worth noting that 25 per cent of the

Table 7.1 Job security in the 1997 IPD survey

Statement	Response	%
How likely do you think it is that you will be made redundant in the next couple of years?	very likely	4
	somewhat likely	8
	slightly likely	28
	not at all likely	57
	don't know	2
If you were to leave your current job, how confident are you that you could quickly get another job at about the same pay without having to move home?	very confident	20
	somewhat confident	37
	not too confident	24
	not at all confident	18
	don't know	1
How secure do you feel in your present job?	very secure	37
	fairly secure	49
	fairly insecure	10
	very insecure	4
How worried are you about your job security?	very worried	4
	fairly worried	20
	not very worried	33
	not at all worried	43
If you are worried or fairly worried about your job security, what is the main reason?	factors affecting your own job	19
	factors to do with the organisation	30
	the economy/wider employment issues	25
	personal factors	20
	other/don't know	6
Compared to a year ago, do you feel more or less secure in your job?	much more secure	19
	a bit more secure	23
	unchanged	35
	a bit less secure	16
	much less secure	6
	not working two years ago	2

sample had had personal experience of redundancy, mostly through compulsory redundancy, and 69 per cent said they had left their last job by personal choice, compared with 24 per cent who said they were forced to leave through circumstances which may or may not have included redundancy. Fifty-eight per cent had only worked for one organisation in the past five years and 56 per cent expected to stay with the same employer for the next five years. All in all, these results do not paint a picture of an insecure workforce and are very different from some of the alarmist surveys that have been reported in recent years.

When factor analysed, three of the four items concerning feelings of security, omitting the penultimate item in the table, emerge as a single factor.[2] Using the resulting scale as a single measure of job security, a regression analysis was conducted to determine the factors that explain differences in level of security and in particular to determine whether management policy and practice have an important influence. A number of variables together explained 38 per cent of the variation on the scale of job security. Five factors have a particularly important influence on job security.

Perhaps predictably in the light of our preceding analysis, the first key item concerns expectations about future security. This is based on the first two items in Table 7.1, and as noted earlier, it is somewhat similar to the security index of Bryson and McKay. Those with low expectations of being made redundant in the next two years, and high levels of confidence about their ability to find another job if necessary, are likely to feel more secure. The second item is the presence of a positive psychological contract. The state of the psychological contract is defined in terms of judgements about fairness, trust in management and beliefs about the extent to which management has delivered its promises with respect to items such as job security, career opportunities and job demands. Key factors explaining the state of the psychological contract are adoption of progressive human resource practices and a climate of employee involvement. Therefore, employees working in organisations adopting these practices and who as a result report a positive psychological contract, are more likely to display high levels of job security. A high involvement climate has an additional independent impact in its own right, constituting the third factor. The fourth factor is an explicit policy of avoiding compulsory redundancy. Finally, younger workers feel more secure than those who are older.

There are two further findings that are worth emphasising. Those on atypical contracts, including temporary and fixed-term contracts, are no more likely to report feelings of insecurity. Also, length of service just failed to reach significance in the regression analysis. However, longer service is associated with a greater sense of insecurity. It also correlates highly with age. In other words, older, long service workers tend to feel more insecure than those who are younger and who have moved around and tested the labour market. The explanation for these findings may be twofold. First, at least in a healthy labour market, those who have tested it and found it reasonably easy to find an acceptable job may have less fear about the consequences of subsequent job loss. At the same time, older, long-service workers may be anxious about a labour market which seems to favour younger workers, and may also feel that older workers are singled out in organisations when job cuts are in the air.

A key implication of these findings is that much of the management of job security lies in the hands of management. Building on these findings, which largely mirror the results from the IPD survey of the previous year, management should build confidence about future expectations of employment security, should build and maintain a positive psychological contract, should promote progressive human resource policies and practices, including guarantees of no compulsory redundancies and should create a climate of high employee involvement. In doing this, they should seek to safeguard in particular the older workers who may feel least secure. Based on the evidence from the IPD survey, organisations which can achieve this will see other spin-offs. They are likely to have a workforce that is more committed and satisfied, to have better employment relations and to have workers who are more highly motivated and more likely to engage in organisational citizenship. In other words there is an opportunity for everyone to win. Not all organisations are willing to make such commitments to their employees, but there are a number of management initiatives which illustrate what can be done. Many link directly to the antecedents of job security outlined above. The next section therefore explores some of these policy initiatives in more detail.

Management policies to minimise insecurity

Most research on insecurity has understandably adopted an employee perspective with an implicit or explicit criticism of management policy and practice. The rest of this chapter explores strategies that organisations might adopt to minimise insecurity. In so doing, it is indicating a rather different kind of research agenda, concerned more with evaluation of policy innovation. The three main approaches that are discussed are guarantees of employment security, an emphasis on employability, and the use of internal placement programmes. As we shall see, these are not necessarily independent and they can be integrated around the concept of the psychological contract. In a further section we consider how far managers indirectly and perhaps inadvertently contribute to employment insecurity through their own more general insecurity about what policies and practices to pursue. These might be more effective if characterised by a greater emphasis on continuity rather than change.

Guarantees of employment security

If organisations could guarantee that no one would be made compulsorily redundant, much of the fear of job loss might disappear. There is some evidence to support this from the IPD survey. A surprisingly high 44 per cent said their organisation had 'a stated policy of deliberately avoiding compulsory redundancies and lay-offs'. Set against this, 33 per cent said their organisation had no such policy, while 22 per cent did not know. Arguably, it is the perception of such a policy that matters in terms of its impact on job security. This is largely borne out by a comparison of those who report that their organisation does or does not have such a policy. For example, those working in organisations with an explicit policy of avoiding compulsory redundancy are significantly less likely to believe they will be made redundant in the next couple of years ($\text{Chi}^2 = 11.3$; $p < 0.02$) and significantly more likely to feel secure in their present job ($\text{Chi}^2 = 10.7$; $p < 0.02$).

A policy of avoiding compulsory redundancies is one thing. Guaranteeing employment security is quite another; and few firms are prepared to go this far. Early exemplars of this policy included a number of high technology firms such as IBM and Hewlett Packard. Over the years, IBM has found such a policy hard to sustain although Hewlett Packard continues to stand out as a notable exception to the general employment volatility experienced by much of the high technology sector during the past decade. In the UK, BT has shed tens of thousands of jobs in the years since privatisation without resort to compulsory redundancy. Generous severance packages combined with a variety of other signals have served to achieve management goals. This does not, of course, mean that levels of employment security within BT are high. Therefore, while a management guarantee of no compulsory redundancy is a useful first step, arguably more is needed to ensure a sense of employment security.

One promising route is the use of new deals between company and union. The process of arriving at the deal and the implications for some kind of wider package of issues linked to the concept of partnership can turn such arrangements into a much more public commitment by the company and as such makes it more difficult for the organisation to renege on the deal. One of the most widely publicised examples is Rover's New Deal. This has a number of components, including a guarantee of employment security. Although the New Deal now seems to be widely accepted by Rover employees, it should be remembered that it was initially agreed by the workforce and their representatives by the narrowest of margins. One important element in the New Deal is that employment security is linked to a wider package of arrangements including flexibility and training, some of which are discussed below. For Rover, the guarantee of employment security was a key component in the plan to increase flexible working and gain the commitment to quality and continuous improvement which was considered essential for survival.

Since the Rover New Deal, there have been others which have also been widely reported, such as those at Blue Circle Cement and Welsh Water. Increasingly they are set in the context of partnership at work, and are one key component in a new and closer working relationship between company and trade unions (Coupar and Stevens 1998). The union role is crucial since it is in part the guarantor of the deal and therefore critical in underpinning the sense of employment security. As the account of developments at Welsh Water indicates, the role presents new challenges for the union in moving from a traditional adversarial role to one of cooperation (Thomas and Wallis 1998).

In a study of the concept of the 'partnership company' among members of the Involvement and Participation Association, which has usually played a key role in setting up and supporting these new partnerships, Guest and Peccei (1998) found that there were wide variations in adoption of employment security guarantees. Among this particular sample of organisations, which can be expected to be the most progressive with respect to their policies and practices in this area, 27 per cent had a formal commitment to employment security over a fixed term and 19 per cent had a formal guarantee of no compulsory redundancy. The finding that employment security guarantees, when part of a larger package, are associated with a range of positive outcomes for employees and for the organisation, suggests that there is a pay-off in promoting job security. We need more research, particularly into the sustainability of such arrangements when the economic climate becomes more hostile. Rover promises to be an interesting case study. We also need to understand that employment security guarantees alone are probably not enough. They need to be backed up by the sponsorship and monitoring role of trade unions and they need to be part of a wider package. One element in that package may be steps to increase employability.

Enhancing employability

The concept of employability has come to the fore as concern grows about the feasibility of traditional organisational careers and the idea of a job for life and the sense of job security that they brought with them. The essential idea of employability is that workers continually enhance their knowledge, skills and experience to ensure that they maintain and if possible enhance their attractiveness in the labour market. In the present context, it is suggested that firms should take active steps to promote employability among their staff. This will help to minimise any sense of insecurity. Furthermore, it may act as a potent basis for recruitment. Firms that have a reputation for enhancing the employability of those who work for them are more likely to attract talented people. Over recent years, consultancy organisations have been successful in attracting highly able applicants partly because of this factor.

The case for employability is made in a slightly different way by writers such as Bridges (1994), who argues that as the concept of the job becomes less relevant, people need to develop a portfolio of competencies that ensure their marketability. By implication, companies can help in this process, but the initiative lies with individuals. In the context of an environment like Silicon Valley, from which Bridges drew many of his examples, this can mean managing the CV by, among other things, changing employer on a regular basis. In Silicon Valley, staying too long with a single employer can appear to raise questions about employability.

The UK, as already noted, is not Silicon Valley. Yet there are signs of change. Returning briefly to the IPD survey, the differences between younger and older workers might be explained partly in terms of perspectives on employability. Young workers focused on their employability in the labour market, and as a result were quite prepared to move between organisations and at the same time report high levels of security. In contrast, some older workers appeared to define security more traditionally in terms of job security and although they had not experienced job loss, insecurity derived from the possible threat of the loss of a long-held job in a specific organisation. By implication, those who think and act in terms of employability may feel less insecure. Of course, in a national employment culture that gives primacy to younger workers, this may be much easier for them than for those who, chronologically or psychologically, feel older.

This brief analysis of employability implies that it holds risks for employers. A culture of employability rests upon increased general skills and therefore marketability, creating the risk of loss of talented staff and, moreover, a possible loss of investment in the development of their employability. However, it should enhance the scope for functional flexibility, permit better utilisation of staff and therefore increase productivity. As already noted, it also provides a potential basis for attracting more talented staff.

What does employability mean in practice? What should firms do? The core focus will be on training and development. One of the best-known examples, already cited, is the Rover Learning Company, which was linked to the New Deal. The Rover Learning Company is the focus for education and training within Rover. One of its initial aims was to develop a sense of self-efficacy about the capacity to learn among employees who may have left school at the earliest opportunity after unhappy learning experiences but who need to become more flexible and adaptive to keep pace with changing systems of production and quality improvement. To achieve this, Rover encouraged staff to study anything they liked. Even improving skills in, say, fly fishing or country dancing demonstrates a capacity to learn. Once confidence in this capacity had been built up, it can be transferred to work-related learning. Potentially, however – and this is one of the purposes of the Rover Learning Company – it can go a great deal further, resulting in qualifications, language skills and a range of employable assets for individuals. The key for the organisation is to utilise these skills.

One of the elements implied in the Rover Learning Company is that everyone should spend some time in planned learning. This may be classroom learning or it may be planned experience. Some companies have gone further and insisted that everyone should undergo a minimum number of annual hours of education and training per annum. For many years, IBM specified a minimum as well as a proportion that must be concerned with broadly defined 'people skills'. Other firms such as Cathay Pacific have done the same. While this appears somewhat bureaucratic, it is designed to signal how seriously the company takes continuous updating. As yet, this practice is not widespread, though informal norms may exist. In a survey of greenfield sites (Guest and Hoque 1996), only 12 per cent of organisations said that they specified some sort of minimum.

The way many organisations have preferred to pursue issues of continuous updating of employees is through adoption of the concept of the 'learning organisation'. This holds more appeal from an organisational perspective, since it is more organisation- rather than individual-oriented. While this concept has attracted much attention – indeed one of its problems is that it is such an attractive concept that almost every organisation is happy to sign up to the aspiration to be a learning organisation – in fact it hides a range of very diffuse practices and is often poorly thought through. Some of the UK organisations that are often cited as learning organisations, partly because they have speakers who have taken to the management lecturing circuit, do not use the concept as a significant lever for change and development. These organisations, which include Rover, Hewlett Packard, Motorola and ICL, use the concept to complement their existing organisational culture (Mackenzie Davey 1999). In other words, they were already learning organisations in some key respects and the label can be a convenient way to describe their activities.

A few organisations have tried to signal their serious intent by setting up company universities. In the UK we have Unipart University and more recently the British Aerospace University. Motorola have had a 'virtual university' in Europe for some time, although it also has bricks and mortar in more exotic locations such as Hawaii. And of course, McDonald's have their Hamburger University. Rather like the 'learning organisation', the company university is often an alternative, up-market name for the training department. The problem in this context is that the important concept of employability can become buried beneath faddish organisational initiatives which do little good either for organisations or employees.

While the rationale behind employability is clear, we should not over-estimate the desire for more in-company training and development. The IPD surveys are revealing, if rather depressing in this respect. In 1996, 82 per cent said their employer provided them with opportunities for training and development. In 1997 we tried to tighten the question by asking 'Does your employer provide you with *sufficient* opportunities for training and development?' This time, 84 per cent said 'yes'.

In research for the Careers Research Forum, a consortium of leading organisations concerned about the future of the career and career management, we explored issues of employability in more detail. This revealed a number of examples of innovative practice, including those cited above, but it also revealed a number of problems that indicate both management incompetence and doubts about how far they either wish to, or are capable of pursuing policies to enhance employability. The first concern was that some organisations had set up 'learning centres' or resources to encourage learning which, while impressive on the surface, appeared to have a low level of use. Secondly, informal development was encouraged through mentoring systems, but organisational changes had typically extended spans of control and made managers busier than ever, leaving them little time to take mentoring seriously. Thirdly, the rhetoric of the learning organisation, and the search for 'packages' had sometimes proved to be a distraction from effective action to enhance employability. Indeed, for some organisations whose main concern is to enhance their reputation, the rhetoric of employability may be more important than the reality of actually making employees, especially key employees, more employable.

For effective enhancement of employability it seems likely that two things must be in place. The first is a coherent human resource strategy to pursue full utilization of the workforce. Employability relates to the 'quality' dimension of the model of human resource management set out by Guest (1987). An integrated strategy requires that this is complemented by policies to enhance organisational commitment, since these are likely to encourage people to stay with the organisation, and policies to enhance functional flexibility, since these are likely to ensure that people and their newly acquired skills are more fully utilised. A focus on employability alone may simply realise management fears that they are investing in portable general skills. The second element that should be in place is a formal system of monitoring. Ideally, trade unions have a role in ensuring that an appropriate system is in place and this role should be an element in the kind of partnership deal outlined above. To date, this is too seldom the case, and without it there may be grounds for continuing concern about how seriously organisations pursue employability and therefore whether the concept achieves its potential to improve the sense of security.

Internal placement

In the 1980s, organisations discovered outplacement – a means of using independent consultants to ease the transition of people out of the organisation while at the same time salving the conscience of the organisation. However, the sense of job insecurity is often associated with a prior stage, when uncertainty about the possibility of job loss causes anxiety. Outplacement does nothing to ease concerns at this stage in the process. Something that can help in this respect is the use of what is sometimes termed 'inplacement', or reallocation to new positions within the organisation.

Normal changes within organisations mean that from time to time certain positions become surplus to requirements, while elsewhere in the organisation new opportunities are opening up. Often this has meant expensive redundancy and all the anxieties of job loss and insecurity in one part of the organisation, and expensive recruitment elsewhere. The aim of inplacement is as far as possible to transfer people internally. However, it can go further than this by including an education and training facility and a temporary employment facility. The rationale for the former is self-explanatory. The latter becomes increasingly feasible as work is organised around temporary, multi-skilled project teams. Individuals may join these teams initially on a short-term basis, but this can lead on to a more permanent posting. In effect, what is being set up is an internal employment agency and an internal contingent workforce.

An organisation of this sort, called Resource Link, has operated in AT&T in the USA since 1992 (Smither 1995). It has proved so successful that although it was initially intended for those whose positions had disappeared, up to half of those joining the scheme applied to do so, attracted by the possibility of varied project work or by the opportunity to refocus and develop their career. About a quarter of those in the scheme moved on to other permanent jobs within AT&T during the first three years of the programme. Starting with just over thirty workers in 1992, the numbers had grown to 1,000 by mid-1996.

A rather different version was utilized by the Dutch bank, ABM-Amro, when it had surplus staff. An internal employment agency was set up and was the first port of call for departments requiring staff. However, the staff were also hired out to other organisations in the financial sector of Amsterdam. AT&T have also followed this route, linking up with MRI (Management Recruiters International) to allow some AT&T staff to work on external assignments and some MRI staff to work on a temporary basis within AT&T.

In the UK there are a number of examples of organisations that have adopted this route. One is ICL. It set up Linkwise, initially in the particularly volatile and innovative ICL Enterprises Division. The purpose was to encourage change, flexibility and innovation by taking away the fear of any personal impact on employment. Those whose project has come to an end or who work on a contract that may have been lost, and who in the past may have left the company can move into Linkwise, thereby retaining valuable knowledge and experience and sometimes saving redundancy costs. The unit provides assessment, career counselling, development and placement facilities. Its role is aided by strict control on external recruitment which is only permitted when it can be shown that there is no suitable internal candidate. During a two and a half year period, over 540 people have moved into Linkwise. Of these, 49 per cent obtained new permanent jobs within ICL, 21 per cent were offered assignments, 9 per cent resigned, 2 per cent chose early retirement and 19 per cent were eventually made redundant. In the past, the great majority of these people would have left ICL, mainly though redundancy. Linkwise has been successful in moving large numbers of people to other jobs within ICL, in reducing dramatically the numbers leaving the organisation, in saving greatly on redundancy, recruitment and temporary staffing costs and in reducing the levels of job insecurity and concern about change. It is important to note that some people cannot be placed, and leave the organisation. But they do so on a different and less threatening basis than in the past, and in circumstances where they have more control over the timing and flow of the process. One lesson from the experience of such schemes is that it requires credible and committed management and strong senior level support.

In summary, it appears that there is real scope for reducing the sense of insecurity by setting up internal systems to provide a buffer against loss of employment. Such systems complement the notion of employability and help to reduce the dependence on a specific job. In some respects they complement or even supersede organisations such as Manpower who have been able to provide security guarantees to employees who do not have a specific job but who are nevertheless highly employable.

Employment security through management of the psychological contract

It was noted earlier that a positive psychological contract is a key factor associated with a feeling of job security. The state of the psychological contract is reflected in employee evaluations of how far management can be trusted, how far it treats people fairly and to what extent it is delivering on its promises. In this context, promises affecting security have particular salience. In practice it is sensible to view the psychological contract as a two-way process, recognising that there are always at least two parties to a contract. This therefore implies mutual obligations. While the expectations and obligations that make up the psychological contract can be explicit and clearly set out – what is sometimes termed a transactional contract – in other contexts they will be implicit and unstated – what are termed relational contracts. Relational contracts imply a longer-term, more informal but deeper relationship of the sort that was often embedded in the idea of a lifelong career within a particular organisation. By implication, there is also a deeper and possibly more emotional investment in them. Much of the recent interest in the psychological contract has focused on contract violation (Morrison and Robinson 1997). When one side, and in this case it is usually management, fails to keep its promises, trust and the related sense of security go out of the window, with a range of negative consequences.

The issue of employment security can usefully be considered within the framework of the psychological contract. If management break promises about job security, whether implicit or explicit, the psychological contract is damaged and insecurity is one consequence. Herriot and Pemberton (1996) have argued that rather than making false promises or encouraging implicit beliefs about the offer, management and employees should engage in a process of formal contracting, possibly as part of the appraisal process, to set out clearly the shared understandings. These may explicitly exclude any promise of job security; but as an alternative they may focus on employability; or they may recognise that low security implies a reciprocal response of low employee contribution. In this context, the evidence about those on fixed-term contracts suggests that they are generally content with their contracts and certainly no less secure than executives who are uncertain about what is expected of them and what roles they must fulfil in order to succeed in the promotional tournament that persists in most organisations.

Where collective arrangements between company and union exist, some sort of partnership and employment security deal may be the most appropriate framework to promote a sense of security and at the same time enhance individual well-being and organisational performance. However, within this context, and more particularly where such arrangements are not in place, the concept of the psychological contract, with its implications for a two-way process of contracting, provides a framework within which to clarify expectations about employment security at the individual level. When it is allied to a range of progressive human resource practices as well as the kind of high-involvement organisational climate that reinforces trust and fairness, it creates a useful policy framework for management action and to help employees to understand and begin to manage their own careers and their own employability.

Managing security through stability

The preceding analysis has attributed part of the sense of insecurity to the pervasiveness of change. While we must recognise the inevitability of change, organisations have too seldom sought to provide buffers to ameliorate its more threatening impact. The steps outlined above present some of the ways in which change can become less threatening. However, organisations often need to go a step further. They need to shed the kind of management promulgated by Peters (1988) and others that advocates more or less permanent revolution. Instead of championing managers who see as their first priority on arriving in a new post the need to undo everything linked to their predecessor, organisations might benefit from valuing continuity and stability. The best organisations have always been able to do this by maintaining their core culture and configuration for as long as possible (Greenwood and Hinings 1993). Managers who are in control rarely need to engage in symbolic gestures of change. But they may use new management ideas to consolidate or refocus their established culture. For example, this is how some organisations have used concepts like quality and the learning organisation. The idea of managing change by creating a sense of stability in the midst of change is one way to increase employee security.

Arguably, an emphasis on the importance of change linked to a continuing concern for competitive advantage has resulted in a susceptibility to the latest fads and fashions and to a transience which reflects an insecurity on the part of managers (Abrahamson 1996). They have lost confidence about what is the right thing to do. Change for its own sake, or change to reflect fashion, have become ends in themselves. The result, far from revealing managers riding the waves of change (Morgan 1988; Marchington *et al.* 1993) displays them floundering in a choppy turbulence. As they thrash around, uncertain about what to do, they leave in their wake a general climate of insecurity. As long as they remain susceptible to the whim of fashion, managers must accept some of the responsibility for insecurity. This type of insecurity extends well beyond job or employment insecurity, creating a more pervasive sense of insecurity about how best to act. Managers who are less confident about how to manage effectively display an uncertainty and insecurity that are infectious. Organisations need to recapture a sense of confidence and continuity in their approach to management of employees and employment relations. The development of an effective partnership between the organisation and its workforce may provide an appropriate context for achieving this and for developing the kind of psychological contracts that promote a broad sense of security that embraces employment security.

Conclusion

Management policy and practice have an impact on perceptions of job security, and research indicates what some of the key policy influences might be. On the positive side, there is a management agenda to promote employment security and organisational effectiveness. It is as yet a poorly understood and poorly researched agenda. Its components include guarantees of employment security, an emphasis on employability, a system of internal job transfer and a wider policy context that emphasises progressive human resource practices, a culture of employee involvement and careful attention to the psychological contract, perhaps reinforced by a framework for partnership. A few organisations have already incorporated it, with benefits to both employer and employees. Further research is needed to confirm its benefits.

Notes

1 It is, of course, possible to be critical of the 'management' of organisational culture and of the meanings of 'security' and 'employability' (see, for example, Willmott 1993; Legge 1995). However, from a more positivist, policy perspective, it can be argued that policies and practices more likely to be associated with a sense of subjective security and well-being are generally to be preferred to those that have the opposite effect.

2 When scaled, the Cronbach's alpha was 0.64. Scores on this scale were used in the regression analysis.

References

Abrahamson, E. (1996) 'Management fashion', *Academy of Management Review*, 21: 254–85.

Bridges, W. (1995) *Job Shift: How to Prosper in a Workplace Without Jobs*, Reading, MA: Addison-Wesley.

Bryson, A. and McKay, S. (1997) 'What about the workers?', in R. Jowell, J. Curtice, A. Park, L. Brook, K. Thomson and C. Bryson (eds) *British Social Attitudes: The 14th Report*, Aldershot: Ashgate.

Coupar, W. and Stevens, B. (1998) 'Towards a new model of industrial partnership: beyond the "HRM versus industrial relations" debate', in P. Sparrow and M. Marchington (eds) *Human Resource Management: The New Agenda*, London: Financial Times/Pitman Publishing.

Greenwood, R. and Hinings, C. (1993) 'Understanding strategic change: the contribution of archetypes', *Academy of Management Journal*, 26: 518–45.

Guest, D.E. (1987) 'Human resource management and industrial relations', *Journal of Management Studies*, 24, 5: 503–21.

Guest, D.E and Conway, N. (1997) *Employee Motivation and the Psychological Contract*, Issues in People Management 21, London: Institute of Personnel and Development.

Guest, D.E. and Hoque, K. (1996) 'Human resource management and the new industrial relations', in I. J. Beardwell (ed.) *Contemporary Industrial Relations: A Critical Analysis*, Oxford: Oxford University Press.

Guest, D.E. and Peccei, R. (1998) *The Partnership Company*, London: Involvement and Participation Association.

Hartley, J., Jacobson, D., Klandermans, B and Van Vuuren, T. (1991) *Job Insecurity: Coping With Jobs at Risk*, London: Sage.

Herriot, P. and Pemberton, C. (1996) 'Contracting careers', *Human Relations*, 49, 6: 759–90.

Legge, K. (1995) *Human Resource Management: Rhetorics and Realities*, London: Macmillan.

Mackenzie Davey, K. (1999) 'What is an organisation that it may learn? The learning organisation as metaphor and method', *The Psychologist*, forthcoming.

Marchington, M., Wilkinson, A., Ackers, P. and Goodman, J. (1993) 'The influence of managerial relations on waves of employee involvement', *British Journal of Industrial Relations*, 31, 4: 553–77.

Morgan, G. (1988) *Riding the Waves of Change: Developing Managerial Competencies for a Turbulent World*, London: Sage.

Morrison, E.W. and Robinson, S.L. (1997) 'When employees feel betrayed: a model of how psychological contract violation develops', *Academy of Management Review*, 22, 1: 226–56.

Peters, T.J. (1988) *Thriving on Chaos: Handbook for a Management Revolution*, London: Macmillan.

Smither, J.W. (1995) 'Creating an internal contingent workforce', in M. London (ed.) *Employees, Careers and Job Creation: Developing Growth-Oriented Human Resource Strategies and Programs*, San Francisco, CA: Jossey-Bass.

Storey, J. (1987) *Developments in the Management of Human Resources: An Interim Report*, Warwick Papers in Industrial Relations, 17, Coventry: Industrial Relations Research Unit, School of Industrial and Business Studies, University of Warwick.

Thomas, C. and Wallis, B. (1998) 'Dwr Cymru/Welsh Water: a case study in partnership', in P. Sparrow and M. Marchington (eds) *Human Resource Management: The New Agenda*, London: Financial Times/Pitman Publishing.

Willmott, H. (1993) 'Strength is ignorance; slavery is freedom: managing culture in modern organisations', *Journal of Management Studies*, 30, 4: 515–52.

8 Trade unions and the insecure workforce

Edmund Heery and Brian Abbott

Introduction

If employees in the industrialised world are becoming more insecure, then surely this reflects, at least in part, the decline of trade unionism, the primary institution upon which employees have relied for protective regulation at work. As union membership and coverage by collective bargaining have fallen in Britain, Australia, New Zealand, the USA, Germany and other countries, so worker vulnerability to offensive action by employers and exposure to hostile market forces has increased. In Britain, available evidence indicates that episodes of employer derecognition of trade unions have been followed by a decline in relative wages, greater use of contingent contracts and the imposition of a managerial regime characterised by tighter discipline, work intensification and closer scrutiny of individual employee performance (cf. Bacon 1999; Casey *et al.* 1997; Evans and Hudson 1994; Gall 1998; Metcalf 1994; Saundry and Turnbull 1996). Insecurity in its various manifestations, it seems, increases when the protective shield of trade unionism is removed.

While union decline may hasten the birth of an insecure workforce, the reverse may also be true and the shift towards more precarious and insecure employment presents trade unions with a series of challenges. On the one hand, the changing structure of the workforce poses a serious threat to unions because insecure workers are difficult to organise and represent. According to the 1996 Labour Force Survey (Cully and Woodland 1997: 235), the level of unionisation among those on temporary contracts is only 60 per cent of that of permanent employees, while Riley's (1997: 284) recent international review of the determinants of union membership highlights the consistent finding that part-time workers and the self-employed are less likely to join trade unions. On the other hand, however, growing insecurity may stimulate employee demand for union protection and provide unions with a representative opportunity. Some of the most militant and effective unions of the post-war era in Britain in mining, docks and the car industry built their strength through attempts to regulate systems of casual labour and piecework which rendered employment and earnings unpredictable (Durcan *et al.* 1983). More recently, evidence from *British Social Attitudes* (Bryson and McKay 1997: 37; Hedges 1994: 48) identifies a strong demand among union members to make the defence of job security a priority.

The main purpose of this chapter is to examine how unions, in Britain and in other countries, have responded to this seeming demand. Potentially, demand for union protection from a more insecure workforce might come from two sources. First, from existing union members who face a threat to their security from privatisation, competitive tendering, transfer of ownership, contractual change or redundancy. The trade union task in this context is to halt or mitigate a slide to more precarious employment and the erosion of employment standards amongst previously secure employees. Secondly, there is a demand for protection on the part of those employees on non-standard or contingent contracts of employment, whose numbers have grown in recent years, at least in certain sectors, and who have often been marginal to the concerns of trade unions in the past. The union task with regard to this group, which includes temporary, contract and agency workers, labour-only subcontractors and at least a proportion of part-timers, is to recruit and organise and develop a representative strategy which successfully articulates and advances the interests of these employees.

Both tasks can be performed in a variety of different ways. The first section of our chapter reviews the different approaches unions have developed to protect existing members from insecurity and extend union organisation to the insecure. This review is based on Hyman's (1996) typology of trade union 'identities' which describes a number of different forms of union representation, each of which derives from a particular conception of employee interests. A key distinction which Hyman draws is that between approaches to employee representation which are based on exclusive and inclusive definitions of employee interests and, throughout, our review is concerned with the extent to which attempts to promote the security of existing union members complement or conflict with attempts to organise the insecure. We are concerned, that is, with the degree to which the two tasks which unions face are compatible with one another.

The second half of our chapter is more speculative and is concerned with two possible implications for the role of trade unions of the emergence of a more insecure workforce. First, the dominant trend in Britain since the Second World War has been for trade union representation to become concentrated at the workplace. A defining characteristic of worker insecurity, however, is that employees become detached from particular places of work and we consider whether the emergence of a more contingent workforce implies a shift in the locus of union representation beyond the workplace. Second, worker in-security is associated with new patterns of division between employees as the use of different types of non-standard employment increases. These divisions between secure and flexible workers, moreover, are frequently based upon and reinforce more basic differences of sex, race and age. It can be argued, therefore, that the trend towards worker insecurity is simultaneously promoting a more diverse and fragmented workforce. The question which arises in this case is whether a more diverse workforce implies a structural reform of systems of union government which is directed both towards articulating and representing this new diversity and redistributing union resources from more to less secure workers.

Trade union identity and the insecure workforce

In a series of recent articles, Hyman (1994, 1996, 1997a, 1997b) has elaborated typologies of the strategic choices available to unions in the field of employee representation. Central to his argument is the claim that workers possess a wide range of diverse and often competing interests and that 'interest representation' involves an often difficult process of aggregation and the selection of priorities from across this field. Thus, there is scope for choice, and internal union conflict, over the definition of the union's constituency or who it will represent, over the range of employee concerns which the union will seek to address and over the methods it will use. Unions can choose, therefore, to be more or less inclusive in defining their constituency, more or less restrictive in the issues they pursue and can adopt strategies of representation based on member mobilisation or passivity (Hyman 1997b). Hyman uses the notion of 'trade union identity' (1994, 1996) to refer to the main patterns of choice with regard to interest representation taken by European labour movements and argues that five ideal typical identities encompass the current strategic repertoire. The first identity is that of the 'guild', in which the union constituency is narrowly defined in terms of an elite occupation, and the focus of representative effort is on preserving the relatively privileged position of a craft or profession. The second identity is the 'friendly society' which seeks to provide mutual insurance and representational and consumer services to individual employees. The third identity is that of the 'company union' which develops a productivity coalition with management and seeks, through cooperation, to enhance company performance and the pay and job prospects of members within a particular enterprise. The fourth identity is that of the 'social partner' which defines broadly both its constituency and workers' interests and seeks to promote social welfare and economic growth through dialogue with government. And the fifth identity is that of the 'social movement', which is again oriented towards a broad definition of its constituency and worker interests but which seeks to pursue these through mobilisation and campaigning.

Each of these identities, it can be argued, is likely to preference a particular response to the rise of insecure work, and below we use Hyman's framework as an instrument for reviewing the reaction of unions to the dual challenge of insecurity, to incumbent and contingent workers, described above. The five responses to insecurity that are likely to emerge from the separate identities are exclusion, servicing, partnership, social dialogue and mobilisation. These are described below, with illustrative examples. As strategy does not occur within a vacuum (Kelly 1997), moreover, for each response we have also described some of the limiting factors which serve to constrain choice.

Exclusion

Increased use by employers of a variety of forms of contingent labour, including temporary workers, subcontractors and agency staff, can represent a potent threat to both the security of existing employees and the power of their unions. One union response to insecurity, therefore, is to try and exclude these workers from employment, and perhaps also from union membership, and this has been a relatively common reaction to employer-led flexibility in Britain and in other industrial economies (Carré *et al.* 1994: 315; Delsen 1990: 262–4). At one level it can be seen in social distance between contingent and permanent employees, and informal workplace rules which deny union membership and representation to 'outsiders' (Adam-Smith 1997: 8; Allen and Henry 1997: 188–90; Geary 1992: 263; Heery 1998a: 364; Hunter and MacInnes 1991: 60). At another it can be seen in formal union policies which seek to exclude various categories of non-standard labour from the workplace. The latter may be a particular characteristic of the occupational unions which Hyman believes are likely to develop a 'guild' identity, and the NUT, for example, has tried to block the use of agency teachers in state schools. Formal policies of exclusion are not confined to occupational unions, however, and in Britain have been adopted by general unions, like the TGWU, and industrial unions, like the NUM, which have attempted to restrict the use of agency drivers and mining subcontractors, respectively. The defining feature of this response in all cases, however, is the identification of opposing interests between the hitherto secure and contingent workers and a determination to protect the jobs and pay levels of the former from external threat. Exclusion might also be justified, legitimately, on grounds that are wider than sectional self-interest, such as the need to maintain the coherence of a profession and quality of service, and in some cases is accompanied by attempts to denigrate the interests of outsiders. Prowse and Turner (1996: 155) report that in mining, subcontractors, who were mainly ex-British Coal employees who had taken redundancy, 'were regarded as having sold their jobs and, by returning to the pit, threatened the current and future employment of young people in the community . . . "the lads were classed as lepers" '.

While union policies to prevent the use of contingent labour can readily be identified, successful policies cannot, and the NUT, TGWU and NUM have all failed in their attempt to exclude agency and subcontracted labour.[1] These, and other unions, have lacked the bargaining power to prevent employers adopting new strategies of labour use, and the case of mining can again prove instructive. The growth of subcontracting in the industry stems from the defeat of the NUM in the great strike of 1984–5 and has been driven by intense competitive pressure, privatisation and the emergence of a more abrasive management style, high unemployment in mining areas and the creation of a pool of subcontract labour and the split between the NUM and UDM (Prowse and Turner 1996). While national policy in the NUM remains opposed to the use of subcontractors, at local level it is accepted as a *fait accompli* and they are actively recruited into the union. Other unions have altered national policy and the TGWU, BIFU and CWU have negotiated recognition agreements with employment agencies which allow the recruitment of agency labour, while the NUT has adopted an intermediate position and tried to regulate the terms of employment of agency staff, in order to prevent undercutting, while refraining from active recruitment. Exclusion, as a response to worker insecurity, seems to be weakening amongst British unions, therefore, and they are having to find ways of including new types of worker and integrating them with their existing members. Similar developments are in train in continental Europe and North America, where increases in the contingent workforce have forced unions to engage with their interests. As in Britain, accommodation has assumed a number of forms, including attempts to regulate the conditions of temporary and agency staff to prevent undercutting, seeking to obtain pro-rata pay and conditions for part-time employees through legislation and collective agreements, and making contingent workers a priority target for recruitment and organisation (Engberg 1993; Wever 1998).

Servicing

The recruitment of mining subcontractors by the NUM, according to Prowse and Turner (1996: 159), has been based in part on the provision of individual representative services and union success in securing compensation for injured miners. Attempts of this kind, to draw contingent workers into trade unionism through the provision of individual services, are apparent across a number of unions and reflect the fact that collective representation at the workplace may be difficult to achieve for agency, casual or self-employed workers because they are dispersed and often mobile. Examples include a Driver Care union benefit package offered by the TGWU, a discount mortgage scheme for workers on fixed-term contracts provided by the AUT and the special set of benefits for self-employed members developed by the AEEU (IRS 1997). Similar schemes have been launched in other countries (ILO 1998: 31–2) – most notably in the USA, where the AFL-CIO launched an 'associate membership' programme in 1985 to provide portable consumer benefits and advisory services, in return for reduced union subscriptions, to employees who were not covered by collective bargaining (Kochan *et al.* 1986: 223).

There is also evidence of unions adapting individual services to the needs of core members whose employment has become more precarious. In 1996, the FDA established a Prospects Register in conjunction with P-E International to find work for members made redundant (Heery 1997) and a number of other white-collar unions (e.g. BECTU, IPMS, STE) operate similar labour market services for members threatened by contracting out and redundancy. These unions also now provide contract advice and pay data for members on individual contracts who negotiate their own salaries and IPMS and EMA, in conjunction with the Open University, have launched an MBA in technology management which accords with the theme of 'employability' and provides a means for union members to update their human capital in an uncertain labour market (IRS 1997).

An important constraint faced by unions seeking to deploy this strategy of individual servicing is that many employees remain committed to a more collectivist conception of trade union purpose. Waddington and Whitston's (1997; see also Kerr 1992; Sapper 1991) survey of the reasons workers join trade unions indicates that, while 'support if I had a problem at work' is the primary reason given for membership, relatively few union members are decisively attracted by the kinds of consumer, advisory and labour market services which have been offered in recent years. The 'associate membership' programmes developed by American unions under the AFL-CIO initiative have also failed to contribute significantly to membership growth and had enrolled fewer than 100,000 members by the early 1990s (Fiorito and Jarley 1992). Member services may prove to be more important for workers on contingent contracts, who can rely less upon workplace representation, but Waddington and Whitston's survey differentiates only between full- and part-time workers and indicates only a slightly higher preference for individual servicing among the latter group.

Partnership

A third response to worker insecurity targets the employer and seeks to furnish existing union members with guarantees of future employment through a 'labour-management partnership' (Towers 1997: 219–27). Partnership agreements have attracted considerable attention from policy makers and academics in recent years and examples have been widely reported in both Britain and the USA. At their core is a joint commitment to promote the competitiveness of the enterprise which is underpinned on the one side by guarantees of employment security, employee voice, training and development and gain-sharing and, on the other side, by acceptance of a new 'high performance' work system (Guest and Peccei 1998). British companies which have concluded partnership agreements with unions include Rover, Welsh Water, United Distillers, Vauxhall and Blue Circle, while American examples include the extensively reviewed experiments at Saturn and NUMMI (Kochan and Osterman 1994; Marks *et al.* 1998; Towers 1997).

The degree of employment security afforded through partnership agreements varies, but generally falls short of an open-ended commitment. Rover's New Deal ends the practice of laying-off employees during downturns, provides a guarantee that unavoidable workforce reduction will not be achieved through compulsory redundancies and provides outplacement services to those who are made redundant (Towers 1997: 128). At Blue Circle, Vauxhall and United Distillers the guarantee of employment security takes the form of a three- or five-year commitment to maintain employment which is conditional on acceptance of modest pay increases and new working practices and which is reviewed at the end of the collective agreement (Marks *et al.* 1998: 213; *Observer*, 12 January 1997; *The Financial Times*, 24 April 1998). At Blue Circle the deal also includes a commitment to end contracting-out, but several other partnerships, including those at Welsh Water and Saturn, contain provision either for the use of temporary and agency workers or for two-tier employment, with lower pay and reduced security for new recruits (Towers 1997: 222–5). Indeed, the negotiation of partnerships may promote the security of existing union members by intensifying the insecurity of those outside. According to Hecksher (1988: 126–7; see also Standing 1997: 30), the essential feature of partnership is the externalisation of costs: 'the union and company protect their existing employees and members, but they pass off to the wider society the costs of absorbing business cycles; they draw a sharp line between those "inside" with full rights, and those who remain basically "outsiders"'.

Although partnerships have attracted a great deal of attention, they remain confined to a minority of companies and there seems to be a number of impediments to their diffusion. One possible impediment is the changeable nature of worker preferences and the fact that guarantees of employment security, which are highly valued when times are hard, may lose their appeal when economic conditions improve. Case study research on partnerships indicates some disenchantment over time as the costs to employees become more apparent and the benefit of secure employment either diminishes in salience or is taken for granted (Marks *et al.* 1998; Towers 1997: 224). A second impediment lies in the preference of employers and the fact that they may seek the benefits of partnership without recourse to collective negotiation with trade unions, which is particularly likely in a period of reducing union membership and bargaining power. There is evidence in Britain of some employers seeking to promote partnership directly with individual employees (Guest and Peccei 1998: 8) and the kind of high-trust exchange of secure employment for employee commitment, which lies at the heart of labour–management partnership, has long been a feature of anti-union 'welfare capitalism' in the USA (Jacoby 1997). Finally, the diffusion of partnership may be constrained by Anglo-Saxon systems of corporate financing and governance which place a premium on relatively short-term financial performance (Marginson and Sisson 1994: 29–33). Such a context is likely to reduce the plausibility of partnership from the perspective of unions and their members while reducing its attractiveness to managers anxious to retain the freedom to respond to market signals and use workforce reduction to maintain shareholder value.

Dialogue

The focus of union action in the fourth response to worker insecurity is the state, and consists of attempts by unions to influence government policy and secure changes in employment law in order to conserve the jobs of existing union members and reduce the insecurity experienced by workers on contingent contracts. In Britain, political action of this kind currently embraces three distinct union activities and in certain respects extends beyond the kind of 'social partnership' identified within Hyman's typology.

The first, and time-honoured, activity has been to use union influence within the Labour Party to secure changes in employment law which promote worker security. The TUC has made the issue of job insecurity central to its formal policy in recent years (Monks 1998a) and has lobbied to ensure it is addressed in the programme of the Labour Government elected in May 1997. To date, there are signs of considerable success and the *Fairness at Work* White Paper, setting out the Government's plans for employment legislation, lists a number of measures which are designed to address the issue of insecurity at work. The primary measures are the proposals to reduce the qualifying period for protection from unfair dismissal from two years to twelve months and to remove the cap on financial compensation when unfair dismissal occurs. The Government has also invited consultation on the abolition of clauses in fixed-term contracts which allow employees to waive their rights to protection from unfair dismissal and entitlement to statutory redundancy payments and the abolition of zero hours contracts. Running alongside these specific measures, moreover, are policies for a more general re-regulation of the labour market, with new or proposed rights for a minimum wage, trade union recognition and the representation of individuals in company grievance and disciplinary procedures.

The second activity has been to press for a similar extension of employment rights at the European level, the significance of which has increased since the signing of the Treaty of Amsterdam and Britain's acceptance of the European Union's Employment Charter (Taylor 1998). The primary objective at European level has been to extend employment rights enjoyed by permanent, full-time employees to those on non-standard contracts on a *pro rata* basis. Thus, in 1997 the European Trade Union Confederation negotiated a collective agreement on part-time workers with the European employers' organisations which has since been adopted as a European directive. The latter provides for the equal treatment of part-time workers across all dimensions of the employment relationship and guarantees equal access to pay supplements and bonuses, holidays, sick pay, occupational pensions and vocational training. Additional negotiations are currently underway to secure the same entitlements for workers on fixed-term contracts (Eironline 1998) and embody an attempt to promote the use of flexible labour without simultaneously creating a more insecure and vulnerable workforce.

The third activity is also derived from Europe and involves the strategic use of case law effectively to extend employee rights to legal protection at work. British unions have made particular use of European equality and business transfer legislation to challenge various aspects of domestic law, both to mitigate threats to employment security which arise from the spread of compulsory tendering in the public services and to extend legal protection to previously excluded contingent workers. Union-sponsored cases have secured the right of part-timers to access to company pension schemes, in advance of the Part-time Workers' Directive, and limited the capacity of employers to cut wages and conditions when public services are transferred to private ownership (Cavalier 1997; Heery 1998a). Through the *Seymour-Smith* case, moreover, unions have sought to challenge the use of qualifying periods in employment law on the grounds that they discriminate indirectly against women (TUC 1997: 12–13). The capacity of the European Court to override domestic legislation, therefore, has been used as a parallel route to address the issue of employment insecurity alongside the more established methods of political dialogue and pressure.

Reviews of the conditions under which effective social partnership between government and unions can emerge have identified several requirements, including institutional ties between trade unions and left-wing governments, ideological affinities between the two wings of the labour movement and the need of governments for union cooperation in economic management (Goldthorpe 1984). The constraint faced by British trade unions in trying to use a strategy of social dialogue to counter insecurity at work is that these conditions are only weakly present or declining in the present context. Thus, the period since the return of the Labour Party to office has been marked by considerable tension between the new Government and the trade unions, and it is apparent that the New Labour project being developed by Tony Blair affords only limited scope for trade unions in the development and implementation of employment policy. The economic strategy of the Government looks as much back to the Conservatives or to Clinton's USA as it does to partnership in Europe and there is a commitment to preserving the flexibility of the UK labour market, which has been apparent in the Government's refusal to concede the unions' demand to do away with all qualifying periods for employment rights, in the modest level at which the national minimum wage has been set and the qualifications which surround the new right of employees to be represented by a recognised trade union (Taylor 1997, 1998). New Labour's political strategy is equally lukewarm and, with its concern to build new bases of support amongst business and the private sector middle class, implies a continued distancing of the Party from its traditional base in the trade unions. On both wings of the labour movement there have been calls from some for an end to the formal tie between Labour and the trade unions (Heery 1997). The asymmetry in union and New Labour objectives, moreover, is compounded by the fact that the Government is not critically dependent on union cooperation, either to regulate industrial conflict or moderate wage inflation, both of which, ironically, appear to be dampened down by the very sense of job insecurity which the TUC is anxious to alleviate (OECD 1997: 129; Robinson, this volume). Given these constraints, it is likely that political action at European level and the strategic use of labour law will continue to be used by British unions as a means of compensating for a lack of influence in the politics of Whitehall.

Mobilisation

While trade unions can act as bargaining and servicing agents on behalf of their members and as political representatives, they can also assume the characteristics of a social movement. A defining feature of social movements is that they seek to mobilise members and supporters in pursuit of an explicitly moral demand for justice (Kelly 1998: 27–9) and the fifth response to insecurity has been to mobilise union members, other employees and wider public opinion against injustice at work. Social movement unionism, as it is increasingly described, has two connected aspects, both of which have been manifest to varying degrees in Australia, Britain, the USA, Canada and other industrial economies in recent years (Johnston 1994; Turner 1998). On the one hand, there are attempts to re-create trade unions as social movements, such that their purpose is defined in terms of the mobilisation of members, while on the other are attempts to submerge trade unionism in a broader social movement, such that the boundary of the labour movement becomes blurred and it takes its place within a progressive, campaigning network or alliance.

The first aspect of social unionism can be seen most clearly in attempts to extend trade unionism to the insecure workforce through aggressive organising campaigns. In the USA, the AFL-CIO's new leadership of John Sweeney, Richard Trumka and Linda Chavez-Thompson, elected in 1995, has sought to push organising to the top of the union agenda and has established a new organising department, committed $20 million to support large-scale organising drives, launched the 'Union Summer' programme, which places more than a thousand college students and young workers in organising campaigns, and sought a commitment from of its affiliates that 30 per cent of union expenditure henceforward will be dedicated to organising (Bronfenbrenner *et al.* 1998: 1–2). These initiatives at confederation level have been paralleled in several large international unions in North America, including IBT, SEIU, CWA and UNITE, and similar developments are in train in Australia and New Zealand (Cooper and Walton 1996; Oxenbridge 1997). Their explicit purpose has been to extend union membership to new groups within the labour market, who are often low-paid, vulnerable and employed on contingent contracts, and they embrace what has been described as a 'union-building' approach to organising (Bronfenbrenner and Juravich 1998), in which the union seeks not only to recruit new members but to mobilise them around grievances and develop effective workplace organisation.

In Britain, experiments with the organising variant of social unionism are less advanced but have been promoted via the TUC's New Unionism project. The latter was instituted in late 1996 with the aim of creating 'a culture of organising' across the trade union movement and extending union membership to those at 'the rough end of the labour market'. The major achievement to date has been the creation of an Organising Academy to train 'lead organisers' who will plan and head up organising campaigns initiated by TUC affiliates. The Academy opened its doors in January 1998 with an initial cohort of thirty-six trainees sponsored by sixteen separate unions and, through a mixture of training and extended campaign placements, has sought to inculcate a 'union-building' approach to organising across a new generation of British union organisers. Trainees are encouraged to develop campaigns through the involvement of workplace activists and the setting up of an organising committee within the targeted company, to base them around workplace grievances and to use a variety of 'actions' which mobilise members, raise the union profile and demonstrate its effectiveness. Many of the techniques in which they are trained have been borrowed from the repertoire of other social movements but in this case have been directed towards trade union organising. It is also notable that a high proportion of the campaigns to which trainees have been attached have been directed at unorganised or poorly organised workplaces with a high proportion of temporary, contract and agency labour.[2]

The second aspect of social unionism is the development of labour–community alliances which seek both to draw upon the resources of the community in the pursuit of union goals while simultaneously developing a broader notion of union purpose which embraces community and environmental objectives alongside improvements in the world of work. Once again, development of this approach has progressed furthest in the USA, where another notable initiative of the new AFL-CIO leadership has been the launch of the Union Cities campaign. The latter is based on a set of labour movement standards to which local Community Labor Councils (CLCs) and the unions in their jurisdictions can give a formal commitment to adopt. Assessment by a special AFL-CIO committee occurs on an annual basis and if the standards have been attained the CLC can be awarded 'Union City' status. The standards include: establishing a Street Heat rapid response team comprised of 1 per cent of local union membership which can be mobilised to support organising campaigns and local community political action; creating a grassroots political action committee to run local campaigns on labour and community issues and identify and support pro-labour political candidates; developing worker and family-friendly community standards for local industries and public investment; and lobbying local legislatures to adopt a Union City Charter which promotes the right of workers to organise. By the spring of 1998 130 CLCs had signed up for the Union Cities programme and about seventy of those were in the process of setting up Street Heat teams. The initiative relates directly to the issue of worker insecurity because its broad purpose is to promote higher labour standards across local labour markets and has stemmed, in part, from state-level labour–community alliances which have been directed at organising and protecting contingent workers (Wever 1996: 24)

In Britain, this kind of concerted attempt to promote grassroots labour–community alliances is less apparent but there have been a number of labour movement initiatives which seek to draw upon the support of local communities and other interest groups and which have been directed at countering threats to worker security. The policy of privatisation and compulsory competitive tendering for public services pursued by the last Conservative Government, for example, met with a number of attempts from unions to develop an alliance of service providers and users to try either to block or to deflect legislation. In the 1980s the trade unions assembled an impressive but ultimately unsuccessful alliance of employees, water consumers, professional bodies, environmental and amenity groups to campaign against water privatisation (Ogden 1991), while a similar campaign, which included a very effective lobby of back-bench Conservative MPs, was successful in halting the privatisation of the Royal Mail in the 1990s. There have also been campaigns against competitive tendering in local government and the health service, which, with similarly mixed results, have attempted to forge an identity of interests between union members and service users, essentially by focusing on the adverse effect on service quality of private sector provision (Foster 1996: 52–4; Foster and Scott 1998: 144–5). Finally, the TUC, since its formal relaunch in 1994, has developed a more active campaigning style, a distinctive feature of which has been the deliberate attempt to develop policy alliances with a wide range of interests and agencies. Its campaign for equal rights for part-timers in the mid-1990s, for instance, involved a series of joint projects with non-labour movement bodies, including joint research with the Institute of Management on the implications for business of harmonising part-time and full-time workers' conditions and the use of Citizens' Advice Bureaux (CABx) to disseminate information and advice to non-union, part-time workers (Heery 1998a: 360).

Perhaps the most significant constraint on the pursuit of union policy through mobilisation is the risk of counter-mobilisation either by employers or the state (Kelly 1998: 25). Despite an increased investment in organising, US trade union density has continued to decline, in large part because the state maintains a framework of employment law which is effectively anti-union (Adams and Markey 1997) and because US employers have increased their own investment in anti-unionism (Bronfenbrenner and Juravich 1998: 28). Mobilisation hinges on the willingness of employees to act collectively through their unions, and if the costs of action are increased, the likely effect will be quiescence, even where substantial grievances exist and workers are susceptible to union organising. In Britain, the success of attempts to organise contingent workers has yet to be evaluated, though the seemingly more favourable framework of public policy emerging under Labour and the absence of intense anti-unionism amongst larger British firms provide some grounds for optimism.

However, counter-mobilisation is not the only risk attached to social movement unionism – two other significant constraints are apparent. First, attempts to extend union membership to contingent workers through investment in organising have encountered internal opposition within unions in Britain, the USA, New Zealand and Australia (Oxenbridge 1997; Waldinger *et al.* 1998). Opposition has arisen from a number of sources but an underlying issue has been the transfer of resources from the representation and servicing of existing members towards the organisation of potential members. Secondly, the development of effective campaigning alliances between unions and other social groups can prove fraught with difficulty. The interests of union members do not necessarily coincide with those of consumers, environmentalists or community and ethnic groups, while unions and community organisations can find it difficult to work together because of their differing cultures, decision-making structures and modes of operation (Needleman 1998; Wrench and Virdee 1996). There are indications from the USA that community alliances can prove an effective means through which unions can act on behalf of insecure and vulnerable groups within the labour market, but this can also prove a testing and problematic method for unions to adopt.

Discussion

The five identities, identified by Hyman, are offered as ideal types of the main representative choices available to trade unions. While he acknowledges the schematic nature of his typology (1996: 54), the implication is that individual trade unions or, indeed, national labour movements will approximate to a particular identity. The problem with this assumption is that unions, and particularly the large general unions which increasingly dominate national labour movements (Streeck and Visser 1997), can develop complex strategies of representation which draw upon several 'identities'. Thus, in Britain, at the apex of the trade union movement, the TUC has responded to the issue of insecurity by seeking to position itself as the voice of part-time and contingent workers, developing new member services for a more flexible labour market, promoting 'partnership' agreements with employers which are designed to rebuild job security, seeking dialogue with government and the passage of new legislation to regulate employment contracts, and encouraging its affiliates to organise contingent workers through the New Unionism initiative (Heery 1998b). A similarly multiple response can be seen in the large general unions, like the TGWU and GMB, both of which have made a priority of recruiting contingent workers, espoused partnership with employers and been critical of the Labour Government for the limitations of its programme of protective labour law. Even relatively closed unions, like the NUT, moreover, have developed quite varied policies on job security and contingent work with the development of new services and campaigns on behalf of part-time and fixed-term contract teachers sitting alongside continued opposition to the use of agency labour.

To note multiple responses to the insecure workforce, however, is not to deny that choices have to be made and that tension can arise between different union strategies. At several points in the preceding review of union responses to insecurity a conflict of interest was noted between union policies which are broadly inclusive and which seek to extend representation to contingent workers and those which are exclusive and which have as a priority the preservation of the terms and conditions of existing members whose employment hitherto has been relatively secure. Putting it crudely, the trade union movement has to decide whether it will speak primarily for economic 'insiders', many of whom seemingly feel embattled, or whether it will accept a broader representative remit which encompasses the substantial proportion of employees with non-standard working arrangements.[3] In the remainder of this chapter we want to explore the implications for unions if the latter choice is made by looking, first, at the level at which unions can most effectively represent contingent workers and, secondly, at the systems of internal union government which might, and in some cases are, being put into place to ensure that the interests of these employees find expression.

Beyond the workplace

The dominant theme in the evolution of British trade unionism in the thirty years after the Second World War was the strengthening of workplace trade unionism (Batstone 1988; Terry 1995). In turn promoting and reflecting the decentralisation of collective bargaining, workplace trade union organisation became more sophisticated and extensive, and in many industries the workplace became the primary locus of trade union activity. Even today, the promotion or revival of effective workplace trade unionism remains a central concern of both trade union leaders and academic commentators. It can be seen in the encouragement of labour–management partnerships, which are designed to re-establish the relevance of workplace trade unionism in a period of management ascendancy and heightened competition, and in the critique of this policy adumbrated by those who favour militant shopfloor activism (Darlington 1995). It can also be seen in the TUC's policy on trade union recognition which is concerned primarily with legal support for the establishment of a union presence within an individual enterprise (Ewing 1996: 67)

While shop steward organisation remains a distinctive feature of British industrial relations, however, the period since 1980 has seen a decline of workplace organisation and greater appreciation of the disadvantages of a decentralised system of collective bargaining and worker representation (Ewing 1996; McIlroy 1997; Terry 1995). Decentralisation has been associated with a decline in coverage by collective bargaining, avoidance of unions by employers and an increase in income inequality and has tended to work to the benefit of those with bargaining power, while offering little to workers who are poorly organised or who are in a weak position in relation to their employers. An additional disadvantage is that a strategy of representation at workplace level, based on the development of permanent workplace organisation, is simply not plausible for many contingent workers who are not tied to a particular workplace or particular employer and who, in many cases, work at small work-sites in industries without an established union tradition.

In the USA, industrial relations are similarly decentralised and based on strong workplace trade unionism but there has been a growing appreciation that 'organising workers into enterprise-based bargaining units . . . may not always be the best strategy' (Cobble 1997: 295). Partly in response to the difficulties encountered in securing certification under the existing framework of employment law and partly in response to labour market change, American unions have begun to experiment with forms of representation which extend 'beyond the workplace'. The latter have included the associate membership programmes referred to above and a renewed emphasis on political lobbying at both federal and state levels to raise minimum wages (Towers 1997: 248; Wever 1996: 26). Perhaps the most significant development, however, has been the emergence of 'labour-market-wide organising' (Wever 1998: 395–7; see also Carré *et al.* 1994; Cobble 1991, 1994; Rogers 1995; Wial 1994). The latter involves attempts by US unions to organise workers across specific regional labour markets and regulate their terms and conditions through the revival of multi-employer collective agreements. Examples include the Justice for Janitors campaigns developed by the SEIU in Seattle, Denver, Portland and Los Angeles, the organisation of drywallers in Southern California, the organisation of hotel workers by HERE in Las Vegas and the SEIU's drive to unionise home care workers along the West Coast (Bronfenbrenner 1998; Cobble 1997; Waldinger *et al.* 1998; Wever 1998). The Union Cities initiative, launched by the AFL-CIO, is intended to extend this approach to organising and to prompt inter-union, cross-sectoral attempts to push up union membership and employment standards within local labour markets.

Available research reports suggest that these campaigns have the following characteristics. First, they are targeted at relatively low-paid workers in sectors with a high proportion of insecure and precarious employment and a predominantly female labour force. Second, they seek to organise workers across company boundaries and have been developed outside the National Labor Relations Board certification procedure. Third, and as a consequence, they seek voluntary recognition from all employers of the target workers, backed up by protest and other direct action, community pressure, political lobbying and corporate campaigns targeted at consumers and shareholders. Fourth, the objective is to secure a multi-employer collective agreement which sets a basic framework of employment conditions across the local labour market and provides a degree of economic security for hitherto vulnerable workers. Fifth, such agreements are intended to take labour costs out of competition and remove the incentive for individual employers to escape from or avoid trade union recognition. Sixth, there is an explicit attempt to combine improvement in employment conditions with a 'claim to advance the general good' (Rogers 1995: 371) by raising labour quality and productivity (in some cases through the establishment of jointly agreed training standards) and closing off the avenue of low-cost, low-wage competition. In Wever's (1996) terms, labour-market-wide organising aspires to solve a problem of social welfare (low pay and insecurity in local labour markets) while simultaneously addressing a problem of market failure (poor quality and low productivity in competitive product markets).[4]

In Britain the only directly equivalent initiative to labour market organising has been the 'Join the Union Campaign' developed by Battersea and Wandsworth Trades Council in London, which has run a number of successful, community-based projects to extend union organisation to companies providing privatised public services. There is evidence, however, of labour market change stimulating an analogous, though decidedly less militant, shift 'beyond the workplace' within the mainstream of the British trade union movement. This can be seen in the expansion of union services for their members, increased union concern with training provision and in the use of legal regulation as a means of harmonising the conditions of standard and contingent workers. It can also be seen, however, in incipient attempts to revive systems of joint regulation which extend beyond the individual enterprise.

A major theme in TUC policy in recent years has been the need to re-establish 'minimum standards' across the labour market which protect vulnerable employees while simultaneously protecting the 'good' employer from undercutting by the bad (TUC 1996a). Before the last election, the TUC set out a list of minimum employment standards, including access to education and training, a guarantee of job security, a minimum level of earnings, the right to representation at work, equal treatment, parental leave, the regulation of working time, and access to an occupational pension. The standards were justified in terms of the contribution they could make to competitiveness, as well as social justice, and were presented to employers as the basis for a developing partnership. Thus, in 1995 the TUC held a series of meetings with the main employers' and managers' organisations (the Confederation of British Industry, the Institute of Personnel and Development, the Institute of Directors, the Chambers of Commerce and the Federation of Small Businesses) which explored the prospects for the negotiation of voluntary framework agreements which would give effect to the standards. These meetings failed to bear significant fruit and it is likely that progress towards the joint regulation of labour market standards will depend on either national or European legislative initiatives which push employers towards acceptance. The joint involvement of employer and union representatives in recommending the national minimum wage through the Low Pay Commission provides a possible model and further developments may arise from the provision for the flexible implementation of European directives through national collective agreements.

The revival of multi-employer bargaining and its use to establish a framework of minimum employment standards may prove beyond the capabilities of British trade unionism, given the disorganisation of British employers and their commitment to labour market flexibility (Brown 1997).[5] The key point, however, is that the issue of insecurity at work and the need to accommodate the interests of contingent workers have prompted union interest, in both Britain and the USA, in systems of employment regulation which extend beyond the workplace and which incorporate multi-employer bargaining. Both labour movements, in their different environments and with differing emphasis, have moved to a position which acknowledges the limits to 'work-site unionism' and have developed a similar rationale, based on a dual appeal to social justice and economic competitiveness, for developing new forms of labour market regulation. According to cross-national research by the OECD (1997: 150), the percentage of workers reporting insecurity is inversely related to a number of institutional features of national labour markets, including the proportion of the workforce covered by collective bargaining and the degree of centralisation of the collective bargaining system. On this evidence, a shift in the locus of union organisation and action beyond the workplace appears a rational response to insecurity at work.

Representing diversity, redistributing resources

If the interests of contingent workers conflict, at least in part, with those of full-time, permanent employees, then the question arises as to how their separate interests can be effectively articulated within unions. In this section we consider two types of change in union government systems which have emerged as the issue of contingent work has become more significant. The first is the development of structures of representation within unions which have been designed to capture the specific interests of contingent workers. The second is a movement to centralise decision-making within unions in order to redistribute resources from core to previously peripheral groups of union members. Both developments, we suggest, representing diversity and redistributing resources, are necessary if unions are to respond adequately to the needs of part-time, temporary, agency and other types of non-standard worker.

In an analysis of women's participation in trade unions, Colgan and Ledwith (1996) employ a distinction between 'liberal' and 'radical' approaches. The former are distinguished by the removal of barriers to women's participation while leaving existing government structures intact, while the latter involve the creation of new structures of government, such as women's conferences, committees and officers, which are designed to achieve fair representation directly. Research on participation in union government by part-time workers in Britain (Lawrence 1994: 19; Rees 1992: 106) suggests that they do face considerable barriers in becoming active in their unions, and this is probably true of other workers with non-standard working arrangements. One response on the part of unions, therefore, has been to institute 'liberal' reform and to seek to remove some of these barriers to activism. Changes of this kind have been targeted primarily at part-timers, as the largest group of non-standard workers within unions, and have taken two main forms: the negotiation of facility agreements which release part-time union representatives for union work and the scheduling of union meetings so that part-timers can more easily attend (TUC 1996b; see also Roby and Uttal 1993). In some cases unions have also adopted a policy of job-sharing for branch and other elected representative positions.

Radical initiatives to promote participation by contingent workers appear to be much less common, and commissioned research for the TUC (1996b: 18–19) indicates that few British unions establish representative structures specifically for these groups. The distribution of contingent work, however, reflects differences in age, sex and ethnicity and union government structures which take account of these differences may also allow for the representation of contingent workers. In Britain, part-time work and homeworking remain predominantly female, while women are slightly more likely to have temporary employment; temporary work is more likely to be experienced by young workers, both male and female; and ethnic minority men and women are also more likely to experience temporary work and to be self-employed (Dex and McCulloch 1997: 64–70). A significant international trend in unions is the attempt to 'represent diversity', by establishing government structures to reflect the particular interests of women, ethnic minorities and the young (ILO 1998; Olney 1996; Wever 1998). In Britain, the TUC has recently strengthened the representation of women and black workers on its Executive Committee and has established a Youth Forum. Parallel developments, including reserved seats on union executives, the setting up of special committees and networks and the election of women's, black and young workers' representatives, have occurred across a significant proportion of its affiliates (Heery 1998a: 357; SERTUC 1997). The effectiveness of these structures in reflecting the interests of contingent workers remains uncertain, but it is through this more general attempt to accommodate diversity that unions have realigned their formal structures of government to reflect labour market change.

In addition to 'liberal' and 'radical' reform, unions have instituted two further changes to make policy more reflective of the interests of contingent workers. The first of these has been the use of market research and opinion-polling, to which there has been growing resort by the labour movement in recent years

(Hammarstrom 1994; Heery 1997). These techniques rest on a conception of the union member as a reactive consumer whose needs must be researched, analysed and reflected in appropriate policies and they have been used by unions to target groups of workers whose interests are not typically articulated through systems of representative democracy. In Britain, for instance, the TUC and several individual unions have used both focus group and survey research to identify the preferences of part-time workers, fixed-term contract staff and home-workers. The second method has been to rely on external voluntary agencies as a means of communicating with contingent workers and representing their views to the trade union movement proper. The decline of unions has been associated with an increasingly active role for voluntary agencies in advising and representing insecure workers and it has been suggested that institutions like the Citizens' Advice Bureaux (CABx) in Britain and the American Civil Liberties Union in the USA may replace unions across much of the labour market (Freeman 1995: 520; see also Abbott 1998). An equally likely scenario, however, is that unions will act in concert with agencies of this kind, employing the kind of networking described above. Thus, in Britain the TUC has used CABx to contact part-time workers and has relied on joint research to build up a picture of their condition and preferences (Heery 1998a), while in the USA organising campaigns directed at temporary and other contingent workers have been developed in cooperation with community organisations and conducted on a joint-agency basis (Wever 1998: 398–9).

A number of recent research studies of British trade unions have identified a process of centralisation which has embraced the strengthening of the position of general secretaries, the downgrading of intermediate levels of union government, together with financial reform and new management controls over union officers (Kelly and Heery 1994; Undy *et al.*, 1996; Willman *et al.* 1994). This process has been stimulated by a number of factors, but included amongst them has been a desire to shift union resources towards organising, including the organising of contingent workers. A striking feature of recent organising initiatives in Britain, the USA, Australia and other countries is that they have largely originated at the apex of the trade union movement within national confederations or amongst the full-time leadership of individual unions (Heery 1998b). The style of organising which has been favoured in many cases has been mobilising and bottom-up, but the initiative, paradoxically, has been top-down. The SEIU, for instance, which has pioneered new approaches to organising in the USA, was traditionally a highly decentralised union but has evolved a different, more centralised structure, 'which effectively redistributes resources from organised to unorganised workers' (Waldinger *et al.* 1998: 112). By way of illustration, its development of the Justice for Janitors initiative has been accompanied by the taking into trusteeship of a series of union locals (branches) which failed to back the campaign.

The reasons for this pattern of innovation remain uncertain but it is suggested that national union leaders have a more immediate interest in organising than do leaders at lower levels, particularly where organising is directed at new or poorly unionised employees (Fiorito and Jarley 1992). Local leaders and their members benefit from organising to the extent that it enhances bargaining strength and prevents undercutting of wages, but may resist where a sudden infusion of new members threatens to overturn the existing balance of political power (Waldinger *et al.* 1998: 113) or where it involves a transfer of resources away from member servicing. Union organising initiatives in both Britain and the USA have been partly funded by the 'empowerment' of existing members who have been encouraged to take greater responsibility for their own servicing. In unions, as in companies, however, 'empowerment' may appear a mixed blessing to those on the receiving end and the non-availability of officer support or representation may generate discontent, to which local union leaders have to respond. National leaders, in contrast, may have greater freedom to prioritise organising because their accountability to existing members is less immediate and they may also be more acutely aware of the costs of declining membership, in terms of diminished revenue, status and influence. Whatever the precise reason, however, the indication is that recent initiatives in unions to organise and embrace the interests of contingent workers have come largely from the centre. If unions are to represent the insecure workforce, this suggests, there must be a centralisation within systems of union government to permit cross-subsidy of activities and the redistribution of resources towards the representation of contingent workers.

Conclusion

The purpose of this chapter has been to review trade union responses to the dual problem of worker insecurity: the threat to the conditions of existing union members through delayering, redundancy and privatisation and the growth of a contingent workforce on the margins of the trade union movement. Perhaps the first point that ought to be stressed by way of conclusion is that in Britain, the USA and other countries the issue of insecurity has come to occupy a central place in the formal policy of trade unions. Notwithstanding the limits to labour market change identified by several contributors to this volume, unions have perceived a growing threat to members' employment and earnings and have aspired increasingly to organise and represent part-time, temporary, agency and other contingent workers. A second point to be emphasised is that the union response to insecurity has assumed a variety of forms, and policies which conform to each of Hyman's five identities can be readily identified within national labour movements but also within individual unions. In many cases, these policies can be regarded as reinforcing and amount to parallel union initiatives with regard to members (organising and servicing), employers (partnership) and government (dialogue). There are also tensions within union policy, however, which are most apparent in attempts to promote the security of existing members through policies of exclusion which rebound against union 'outsiders'.

This tension suggests that unions are faced with a strategic choice in responding to the insecure workforce. On the one hand, they can seek to rebuild the security of existing members through a renewal of 'work-site unionism', which may take the form of a productivity coalition with employers or conceivably of revived shopfloor militancy. The weaknesses of this approach, however, are that there are seeming barriers to the diffusion of labour–management partnerships, and that a decentralised response is likely to confirm the existing pattern of union membership and balance of power within unions. On the other hand, unions might adopt a more coordinated response to insecurity which seeks to extend membership to new categories of worker, including those on contingent contracts, and which seeks to regulate the external labour market, rather than management practice within individual firms. A necessary support for such a strategy appears to be a dual process of reform within unions in which internal systems of government come to reflect a diversity of member interests and control of resources is centralised in order to allow their redistribution towards the representation of previously poorly organised workers. Its primary weaknesses are that it might elicit both counter-mobilisation from employers and recalcitrance from those union members who effectively subsidise expansion into new areas. Such a strategy, once again, might be developed under the rhetoric of partnership and emphasise the mutual gains to be secured from the re-regulation of the labour market, or it might take a militant form in which the stress is on mobilising contingent workers and the forced regulation of obdurate employers. Increasingly, the choices available to unions are couched in these terms, of renewed resistance to business or accommodation and a search for mutual gains (see Bacon and Storey 1996; Claydon 1998; Kelly 1996, 1998; Monks 1998b). The issue of insecurity, however, raises another and perhaps more fundamental choice, that of whether unions will focus primarily on the work-site and accord priority to defending their existing, declining membership, or whether they will become more inclusive and encompassing in the interests they address and redirect their activity beyond the workplace.

List of Abbreviations

AEEU	Amalgamated Engineering and Electrical Union
AFL-CIO	American Federation of Labor-Congress of Industrial Organisations
AUT	Association of University Teachers
BECTU	Broadcasting, Entertainment and Cinematograph and Theatre Union
BIFU	Banking, Insurance and Finance Union
CABx	Citizens' Advice Bureaux
CWA	Communication Workers of America
CWU	Communication Workers' Union
EMA	Engineers and Managers' Association
FDA	Association of First Division Civil Servants
HERE	Hotel Employees and Restaurant Employees International Union
IBT	International Brotherhood of Teamsters
IPMS	Institution of Professionals, Managers and Specialists
NUM	National Union of Mineworkers
NUT	National Union of Teachers
SEIU	Service Employees International Union

STE	Society of Telecom Executives
TGWU	Transport and General Workers' Union
TUC	Trades Union Congress
UDM	Union of Democratic Mineworkers
UNITE	Union of Needle Trades, Industrial and Textile Employees

Notes

1 Casey *et al.*'s (1997) review of survey and case study evidence on employers' use of 'flexible labour' found that certain types of contingent contract, such as short-term contract workers and freelancers, are used less frequently where unions are strong. They also found, however, that few managers regard unions as a significant constraint on the use of flexible labour, which they explain in terms of a reduction of union power.
2 One of the authors, Edmund Heery, is part of a research group at Cardiff Business School which is engaged on an evaluation of the New Unionism project. Other group members are Rick Delbridge, John Salmon, Melanie Simms, Dave Simpson and Paul Stewart.
3 According to Dex and McCulloch (1997: 173), 'At least one quarter of men and one half of women of working age held non-standard jobs in 1994; these figures amount to over 5.5 million women and over 3.4 million men.' Estimates for the contingent workforce in the USA are provided by Cappelli (1995: 580).
4 The extent and significance of these organising campaigns are difficult to gauge because systematic statistics are not collected on union organising outside the National Labor Relations Board framework in the USA. The official policy of the AFL-CIO, however, is to encourage 'voluntary' organising of this kind. It can also be noted that increasingly academics in the USA have proposed models for the reform of the labour movement which are not workplace-based. Cobble (1991, 1994), for example, has advocated the revival of occupational unionism in which unions control labour supply and monitor occupational standards, while regulating pay and conditions through multi-employer bargaining. Such a model, she argues, is particularly appropriate for many of the new professional and semi-professional occupations which lie at the heart of the service economy. Wial (1994), in contrast, proposes a 'geographical/occupational model' in which multi-employer bargaining is used to set a uniform pay and benefit structure for loosely defined occupational groups within a localised geographical area. This kind of prescriptive model-building is not a feature of recent British work, but detailed proposals for the statutory reconstruction of sectoral collective bargaining have been put forward by a group of labour lawyers and trade unionists in a report for the Institute for Employment Rights (Ewing 1996).
5 Other obstacles exist as well, most notably a framework of collective labour law which seeks to confine trade unionism to the individual enterprise and which has outlawed institutions like the pre-entry closed shop and secondary action which have supported multi-employer bargaining in the past. Much of the Conservative reform of British employment law was borrowed from the USA, and those American commentators who favour occupational or geographical unionism have called for the abolition or reform of those aspects of US labour law which inhibit union action at the labour market level (Carré *et al.* 1994; Cobble 1994; Wial 1994).

References

Abbott, B. (1998) 'The emergence of a new industrial relations actor: the role of the Citizens' Advice Bureaux', *Industrial Relations Journal*, 29, 4: 257–69.
Adams, R.J. and Markey, R. (1997) 'How the state affects trade union growth: re-evaluating

New World departures from European models', in J. Brown (ed.) *The Role of the State in Industrial Relations*, Proceedings of the Fifth IIRA Regional Industrial Relations Congress, Dublin: Oak Tree Press.

Adam-Smith, D. (1997) 'Atypical workers – typical expectations: on temporary work, temporary workers and trade unions', *Employee Relations Review*, December: 3–9.

Allen, J. and Henry, N. (1997) 'Ulrich Beck's *Risk Society* at work: labour and employment in the contract service industries', *Transactions of the Institute of British Geographers*, New Series, 22, 2: 180–96.

Bacon, N. (1999) 'Union derecognition and the new human relations: a steel industry case study', *Work Employment and Society*, 13, 1: 1–17.

Bacon, N. and Storey, J. (1996) 'Individualism and collectivism and the changing role of trade unions', in P. Ackers, C. Smith and P. Smith (eds) *The New Workplace and Trade Unionism*, London: Routledge.

Batstone, E. (1988) *The Reform of Workplace Industrial Relations: Theory, Myth and Evidence*, Oxford: Clarendon Press.

Bronfenbrenner, K. (1998) 'From the bottom up: building unions and building leaders through organising and first contract campaigns', Paper presented at UCLEA/AFL-CIO conference, San Jose, California.

Bronfenbrenner, K., Friedman, S., Hurd, R.W., Oswald, R.A. and Seeber, R.L. (1998) 'Introduction', in K. Bronfenbrenner, S. Friedman, R.W. Hurd, R.A. Oswald, and R.L. Seeber (eds) *Organizing to Win: New Research on Union Strategies*, Ithaca, NY: ILR Press.

Bronfenbrenner, K. and Juravich, T. (1998) 'It takes more than house-calls: organising to win with a comprehensive union building strategy', in K. Bronfenbrenner, S. Friedman, R.W, Hurd, R.A. Oswald and R.L. Seeber (eds) *Organizing to Win: New Research on Union Strategies*, Ithaca, NY: ILR Press.

Brown, W. (1997) 'Bargaining for full employment', in J. Philpott (ed.) *Working for Full Employment*, London: Routledge.

Bryson, A. and McKay, S. (1997) 'What about the workers?', in R. Jowell, J. Curtice, A. Park, L. Brook, K. Thomson and C. Bryson (eds) *British Social Attitudes. The 14th Report: The End of Conservative Values?*, Aldershot: Ashgate.

Cappelli, P. (1995) 'Rethinking employment', *British Journal of Industrial Relations*, 33, 4: 563–602.

Carré, F.J., du Rivage, V. and Tilly, C. (1994) 'Representing the part-time and contingent workforce: challenges for unions and public policy', in S. Friedman, R.W. Hurd, R.A. Oswald and R.L. Seeber (eds) *Restoring the Promise of American Labor Law*, Ithaca, NY: ILR Press.

Casey, B., Metcalf, H. and Millward, N. (1997) *Employers' Use of Flexible Labour*, London: Policy Studies Institute.

Cavalier, S. (1997) *Transfer Rights: TUPE in Perspective*, London: Institute for Employment Rights.

Claydon, T. (1998) 'Problematising partnership: the prospects for a co-operative bargaining agenda', in P. Sparrow and M. Marchington (eds) *Human Resource Management: The New Agenda*, London: Financial Times/Pitman Publishing.

Cobble, D.S. (1991) 'Organising the postindustrial work force: lessons from the history of waitress unionism', *Industrial and Labor Relations Review*, 44, 3: 419–36.

—— (1994) 'Making postindustrial unionism possible', in S. Friedman, R.W. Hurd, R.A. Oswald and R.L. Seeber (eds) *Restoring the Promise of American Labor Law*, Ithaca, NY: ILR Press.

—— (1997) 'Lost ways of organising: reviving the AFL's direct affiliate strategy', *Industrial Relations*, 36, 3: 278–301.

Colgan, F. and Ledwith, S. (1996) 'Sisters organising: women and their trade unions', in S. Ledwith and F. Colgan (eds) *Women in Organisations: Challenging Gender Politics*, Basingstoke: Macmillan.

Cooper, R. and Walton, C. (1996) 'Organising and recruitment in australia: the response of unions to the "membership crisis"', paper presented at 'Organising for Success' Conference, Cornell University.

Cully, M. and Woodland, S. (1997) 'Trade union membership and recognition', *Labour Market Trends*, June: 231–40.

Darlington, R. (1995) 'Restructuring and workplace unionism at Manchester Airport', *British Journal of Industrial Relations*, 33, 1: 93–116.

Delsen, L. (1990) 'European trade unions and the flexible workforce', *Industrial Relations Journal*, 21, 4: 260–73.

Dex, S. and McCulloch, A. (1997) *Flexible Employment*, Basingstoke: Macmillan.

Durcan, J.W., McCarthy, W.E.J. and Redman, G.P. (1983) *Strikes in Post-War Britain: A Study of Stoppages of Work Due to Industrial Disputes 1946–73*, London: George Allen & Unwin.

Eironline (1998) 'UNICE opens door to negotiations on rights of fixed-term contract workers', www.eiro.eurofund.ie/servlet/ptconvert, European Foundation for the Improvement of Living and Working Conditions.

Engberg, E. (1993) 'Union responses to the contingent workforce', in D.S. Cobble (ed.) *Women and Unions*, Ithaca, NY: ILR Press.

Evans, S. and Hudson, M. (1994) 'From collective bargaining to "personal contracts": case studies from port transport and electricity supply', *Industrial Relations Journal* 25, 4: 305–14.

Ewing, K. (ed.) (1996) *Working Life: A New Perspective on Labour Law*, London: The Institute for Employment Rights and Lawrence & Wishart.

Fiorito, J. and Jarley, P. (1992) 'Associate membership programs: innovation and diversification in national unions', *Academy of Management Journal*, 35, 5: 1070–85.

Foster, D. (1996) 'Competitive tendering in local government: trade unions and organisational change', in D. Braddon and D. Foster (eds) *Privatization: Social Science Themes and Perspectives*, Aldershot: Dartmouth.

Foster, D. and Scott, P. (1998) 'Conceptualising union responses to contracting out municipal services, 1979–97', *Industrial Relations Journal*, 29, 2: 137–50.

Freeman, R.B. (1995) 'The future for unions in decentralized collective bargaining systems: US and UK unionism in an era of crisis', *British Journal of Industrial Relations* 33, 4: 519–36.

Gall, G. (1998) 'The changing relations of production: union derecognition in the UK magazine industry', *Industrial Relations Journal* 29, 2: 151–61.

Geary, K. (1992) 'Employment flexibility and human resource management', *Work, Employment and Society*, 6, 2: 251–70.

Goldthorpe, J.H. (1984) 'Introduction', in J.H. Goldthorpe (ed.) *Order and Conflict in Contemporary Capitalism*, Oxford: Clarendon Press.

Guest, D. and Peccei, R. (1998) *The Partnership Company*, London: Involvement and Participation Association.

Hammarstrom, P. (1994) 'Local and global: trade unions in the future', in J.R. Niland, R.D. Lansbury and C. Verevis (eds) *The Future of Industrial Relations: Global Change and Challenges*, London: Sage.

Hecksher, C. (1988) *The New Unionism: Employee Involvement and the Changing Corporation*, New York: Basic Books.

Hedges, B. (1994) 'Work in a changing climate', in R. Jowell, J. Curtice, L. Brook and D. Ahrendt (eds) *British Social Attitudes: The 11th Report*, Aldershot: Dartmouth.

Heery, E. (1997) 'Annual review article 1996', *British Journal of Industrial Relations*, 35:1, 87–109.

—— (1998a) 'Campaigning for part-time workers', *Work, Employment and Society*, 12, 2: 351–66.

—— (1998b) 'The re-launch of the Trades Union Congress', *British Journal of Industrial Relations*, 36:3, 339–60.

Hunter, L. and MacInnes, J. (1991) *Employers' Labour Use Strategies: Case Studies*, Employment Department Research Paper No. 87, Sheffield: Employment Department.

Hyman, R. (1994) 'Changing trade union identities and strategies', in R. Hyman and A. Ferner (eds) *New Frontiers in European Industrial Relations*, Oxford: Blackwell.

—— (1996) 'Changing union identities in Europe', in P. Leisink, J. Van Leemput and J. Vilrokx (eds) *The Challenges to Trade Unions in Europe*, Cheltenham: Edward Elgar.

—— (1997a) 'The future of employee representation', *British Journal of Industrial Relations*, 35:3, 309–31.

—— (1997b) 'Trade unions and interest representation in the context of globalisation', *Transfer*, 3, 515–33.

ILO (1998) *World Labour Report: Industrial Relations, Democracy and Social Stabiligy 1997–98*, Geneva: International Labour Office.

IRS (1997) 'At your service: what unions offer their members', *IRS Employment Trends*, 643, 5–10.

Jacoby, S. (1997) *Modern Manors: Welfare Capitalism since the New Deal*, Princeton, NJ: Princeton University Press.

Johnston, P. (1994) *Success While Others Fail: Social Movement Unionism and the Public Workplace*, Ithaca, NY: ILR Press.

Kelly, J. (1996) 'Union militancy and social partnership', in P. Ackers, C. Smith and P. Smith (eds) *The New Workplace and Trade Unionism*, London: Routledge.

—— (1997) 'Challenges to unions in Britain and Europe', *Work, Employment and Society*, 11:2, 373–6.

—— (1998) *Rethinking Industrial Relations: Mobilization, Collectivism and Long Waves*, London: Routledge.

Kelly, J. and Heery, E. (1994) *Working for the Union: British Trade Union Officers*, Cambridge: Cambridge University Press.

Kerr, A. (1992) 'Why public sector workers join unions: an attitude survey of workers in the health service and local government', *Employee Relations*, 14, 2: 39–54.

Kochan, T., Katz, H. and McKersie, R.B. (1986) *The Transformation of American Industrial Relations*, New York: Basic Books.

Kochan, T. and Osterman, P. (1994) *The Mutual Gains Enterprise*, Boston, MA: Harvard Business School Press.

Lawrence, E. (1994) *Gender and Trade Unions*, London: Taylor and Francis.

McIlroy, J. (1997) 'Still under siege: British trade unions at the turn of the century', *Historical Studies in Industrial Relations*, 1, 3: 93–112.

Marginson, P. and Sisson, K. (1994) 'The structure of transnational capital in Europe: the emerging Euro-company and its implications for industrial relations', in R. Hyman and A. Ferner (eds) *New Frontiers in European Industrial Relations*, Oxford: Blackwell.

Marks, A., Findlay, P., Hine, J., McKinlay, A. and Thompson, P. (1998) 'The politics of partnership? Innovation in employment relations in the Scottish spirits industry', *British Journal of Industrial Relations*, 36, 2: 209–26.

Metcalf, D. (1994) 'Transformation of British industrial relations? Institutions, conduct and outcomes 1980–1990', in R. Barrell (ed.) *The UK Labour Market: Comparative Aspects and Institutional Developments*, Cambridge: Cambridge University Press.

Monks, J. (1998a) 'Government and trade unions', *British Journal of Industrial Relations*, 36, 1: 125–35.

—— (1998b) 'Trade unions, enterprise and the future', in P. Sparrow and M. Marchington (eds) *Human Resource Management: The New Agenda*, London: Financial Times/Pitman Publishing.

Needleman, R. (1998) 'Building relationships for the long-haul: unions and community-based organisations working together to organise low-wage workers', in K. Bronfenbrenner, S. Friedman, R.W. Hurd, R.A. Oswald and R.L. Seeber (eds) *Organizing to Win: New Research on Union Strategies*, Ithaca, NY: ILR Press.

OECD (1997) *Employment Outlook*, Paris: Organisation for Economic Cooperation and Development.

Ogden, S. (1991) 'The trade union campaign against water privatisation', *Industrial Relations Journal*, 22,1: 20–34.

Olney, S. (1996) *Unions in a Changing World*, Geneva: International Labour Office.

Oxenbridge, S. (1997) 'Organising strategies and organising reform in New Zealand service sector unions', *Labor Studies Journal*, 22, 3: 1–27.

Prowse, P. and Turner, R. (1996) 'Flexibility and coal: a research note on workplace relations', *Work, Employment and Society*, 10:1, 151–60.

Rees, T. (1992) *Women and the Labour Market*, London: Routledge.

Riley, N-M. (1997) 'Determinants of union membership: a review', *Labour* 11, 2: 265–301.

Roby, P. and Uttal, L. (1993) 'Putting it all together: the dilemmas of rank-and-file union leaders', in D.S. Cobble (ed.) *Women and Unions*, Ithaca, NY: ILR Press.

Rogers, J. (1995) 'A strategy for labour', *Industrial Relations*, 34, 3: 367–81.

Sapper, S. (1991) 'Do members' services packages influence trade union recruitment?', *Industrial Relations Journal*, 22, 4: 309–16.

Saundry, R. and Turnbull, P. (1996) 'Mêlée on the Mersey: contracts, competition and labour regulation on the docks', *Industrial Relations Journal* 27, 4: 275–88.

SERTUC (1997) *Inching Towards Equality*, London: South East Regional Trades Union Congress.

Standing, G. (1997) 'Globalisation, labour flexibility and insecurity: the era of market regulation', *European Journal of Industrial Relations*, 3, 1: 7–37.

Streeck, W. and Visser, J. (1997) 'The rise of conglomerate unionism', *European Journal of Industrial Relations*, 3:3, 305–32.

Taylor, R. (1997) 'New Labour and the trade unions', *Transfer*, 3: 622–8.

—— (1998) 'Annual review article 1997', *British Journal of Industrial Relations*, 36, 2: 293–311.

Terry, M. (1995) 'Trade unions: growth, structure and policy', in P. Edwards (ed.) *Industrial Relations: Theory and Practice in Britain*, Oxford: Blackwell.

Towers, B. (1997) *The Representation Gap: Change and Reform in the British and American Workplace*, Oxford: Oxford University Press.

TUC (1996a) *Minimum Standards: Rebuilding Job Security*, London: Trades Union Congress.

—— (1996b) *Part of the Union? The Challenge of Recruiting and Organising Part-time Workers*, London: Trades Union Congress.

—— (1997) *General Council Report: Next Steps for the New Unionism*, London: Trades Union Congress.

Turner, L. (1998) 'Rank-and-file participation in organising at home and abroad', in K.

Bronfenbrenner, S. Friedman, R.W. Hurd, R.A. Oswald and R.L. Seeber (eds) *Organizing to Win: New Research on Union Strategies*, Ithaca, NY: ILR Press.

Undy, R., Fosh, P., Morris, H., Smith, P. and Martin, R. (1996) *Managing the Unions: The Impact of Legislation on Trade Unions' Behaviour*, Oxford: Clarendon Press.

Waddington, J. and Whitston, C. (1997) 'Why do people join trade unions in a period of membership decline?', *British Journal of Industrial Relations* 35, 4: 515–46.

Waldinger, R., Erickson, C., Milkman, R., Mitchell, D., Valenzuela, A., Wong, K. and Zeitlin, M. (1998) 'Helots no more: a case study of the Justice for Janitors campaign in Los Angeles', in K. Bronfenbrenner, S. Friedman, R.W. Hurd, R.A. Oswald and R.L. Seeber (eds) *Organizing to Win: New Research on Union Strategies*, Ithaca, NY: ILR Press.

Wever, K. (1996) 'Unions adding value: addressing market and social failures in the advanced industrial countries', unpublished manuscript.

—— (1998) 'International labor revitalization: enlarging the playing field', *Industrial Relations*, 37, 3: 388–407.

Wial, H. (1994) 'New bargaining structures for new forms of business organisation', in S. Friedman, R.W. Hurd, R.A. Oswald and R.L. Seeber (eds) *Restoring the Promise of American Labor Law*, Ithaca, NY: ILR Press.

Willman, P., Morris, T. and Aston, B. (1994) *Union Business: Trade Union Organisation and Financial Reform in the Thatcher Years*, Cambridge: Cambridge University Press.

Wrench, J. and Virdee, S. (1996) 'Organising the unorganised: "race", poor work and trade unions', in P. Ackers, C. Smith and P. Smith (eds) *The New Workplace and Trade Unionism*, London: Routledge.

Acknowledgements

Thanks to Derek Adam-Smith and Peter Turnbull for helpful comments on an earlier draft.

9 Job insecurity, psychological well-being and family life

Jane P. Nolan, Ines C. Wichert and Brendan J. Burchell

Introduction

All industrialised countries have experienced sizeable upheavals in their labour markets over the past two decades, and one of the most significant recurring themes in this upheaval has been the reduction of employee security. In this chapter we address three principal questions about job insecurity, from the perspective of social psychology. First, is job insecurity stressful, and if so, who is affected by stress and why? Second, how does job insecurity affect the motivations and attitudes of employees — does it make them more disciplined and hard working, or less motivated and satisfied? And third, how does job insecurity affect domestic and family relationships beyond the workplace?

In the 1970s and 1980s the main themes that concerned politicians, academics and the media centred firmly on the new distribution of work, and the sudden and dramatic rise in the rate of unemployment. The marked human misery that was associated with unemployment was widely researched (Warr 1987; Feather 1990). Over the past decade, however, attention has switched to less obvious but perhaps more pervasive and ultimately more damaging changes associated with job insecurity. There is now a considerable international literature which links job insecurity to its individual and social costs and this chapter will describe and synthesise this body of work.

Job insecurity and psychological well-being

Research on the relationship between job insecurity and well-being is mainly conducted in a stressor-stress-strain framework, where job insecurity is conceptualised as the stressor, or source of stress, which can lead to an appraisal of stress, which in turn can lead to certain strain outcomes. The latest definitions of stress take a psychological approach, in which stress is conceptualised as 'a dynamic interaction between the person and their work environment. When studied it [i.e. stress] is either inferred from the existence of problematic person-environment interactions or measured in terms of cognitive processes and emotional reactions which underpin those interactions' (Cox 1993: 13). These psychological models of stress have gained widespread acceptance and have been incorporated in the definitions of 'psycho-social hazards' and 'well-being' used respectively by the International Labour Organisation and the World Health Organisation (Cox 1993).

The psychological effects of stress are often visible in the form of decreased quality of life and decreased levels of psychological well-being. Van Vuuren *et al.* (1991) define psychological well-being as an umbrella term for a number of emotional and cognitive states, with a person's mental health, happiness, work and life satisfaction all being included. Signs of decreased psychological well-being include increased levels of anxiety and depression, a sense of uselessness, lack of self-confidence, and dissatisfaction with oneself and one's environment (Warr 1987). In studies on job insecurity, psychological well-being has been measured with a wide range of scales and indicators. Examples include the *General Health Questionnaire* (Burchell 1997; Ferrie *et al.* 1995; Roskies *et al.* 1993), job and/or life (dis)satisfaction measures (Lim 1996; Heaney *et al.* 1994), global measures of health (Kuhnert and Palmer 1991; Kuhnert and Vance 1992) and many other single- and multi-item measures.

The same is true for the measurement of job insecurity. Measurement scales range from single- and multi-item unidimensional scales to a number of multidimensional scales, the best known of which is the Ashford *et al.* (1989) Job Insecurity Scale (for a review, see Hartley *et al.* 1991). Single-item measures take three typical forms. Some ask respondents to say how secure their job is on a multipoint scale, from 'very secure' to 'very insecure'. Some ask respondents to rate the likelihood of losing their jobs and becoming unemployed within the next, say, twelve months. And some (often because they are using secondary datasets with no more direct measures of job security) use scales on which respondents have rated their level of satisfaction with their job security. These different methods of measuring job security tend to be highly correlated, and there is no evidence that differences in findings between studies are caused by differences in the way that job security has been measured.

Following psychological definitions of stress, most of these job insecurity scales emphasise the subjective experience of job insecurity, which is reflected in the self-completion nature of the scales. It is important to emphasise that, for the effects reported in this chapter, we are not so much interested in issues of objective stability in the labour market (as measured, for example, by turnover or tenure) but by individuals' perceptions of risk of loss of their job, or valued features of their job. Multidimensional scales can attempt to measure separately the level of risk of job loss (a 'cognitive' component) and the extent to which this is a source of anxiety and other emotional reactions (an 'affective' component).

In some instances it is useful to draw distinctions between different types of insecurity. For instance, Campbell (1997) distinguished between eight possible forms of insecurity, including income, working time, loss of the specific job and the inability to obtain any employment in the labour market as well as the threat of termination by the current employer. While this distinction is potentially very useful in guiding further research, few of the studies into the psychological effects of insecurity have made such distinctions.

While job insecurity has in the past been included as a stressor in compound measures of stress in the workplace, it is only more recently that studies have been concerned solely with job insecurity as a source of occupational stress. Most of these studies are of a cross-sectional nature and show a negative relationship between job insecurity and psychological well-being. This means that increased levels of job insecurity are related to decreased levels of psychological well-being. Van Vuuren *et al.* (1991), for example, report on findings from a series of studies on job insecurity in Israel and the Netherlands which show a positive relationship between job insecurity and both psychosomatic complaints and depression. Dutch employees with high levels of job insecurity reported more nervousness, guilt, sadness, fear and anger, as well as less pleasure and self-confidence, than employees who felt that their jobs were secure. Negative effects of job insecurity have also been found with respect to job dissatisfaction (Lim 1996), global health (Kuhnert *et al.* 1989), mood (Barling and Kelloway 1996), anxiety and sleep disturbances (Mattiasson *et al.* 1990).

These studies are based on different occupational groups and are not representative of the working population as a whole, but in Britain a large-scale representative sample is available through the British Household Panel Study (BHPS). The BHPS is a longitudinal survey of 5,000 randomly selected British households, in which all adult members in each household were interviewed on various aspects of their working lives on five data collection waves between 1990 and 1995. In an analysis of the BHPS data, Burchell (1997) reports findings similar to those mentioned above: that for each of the five data collection waves, there was a highly significant, positive relationship between satisfaction with job security and psychological well-being, as assessed by the General Health Questionnaire (GHQ). The relationship between lower satisfaction with job security and poorer health was still present even when demographic variables and other aspects of job satisfaction had been controlled for. However, Burchell found that the relationship between satisfaction with job security and psychological well-being was weaker for women in part-time employment and that those with higher levels of education were more susceptible to job insecurity: when better educated respondents felt secure they had better health than those with lower levels of education, but when they felt insecure they reported worse health.

Another study based on a large data set is Burchell's (1994) analysis of the Social Change and Economic Life Initiative (SCELI) survey. The latter covered six urban labour markets and addressed a wide range of issues, including people's past work careers and their current employment and unemployment experience. Burchell again found that across the sample, perceived job insecurity had a direct effect on the GHQ scores. Moreover, when the sample was broken down into five sub-groups on the basis of labour-market experience, the two most advantaged and secure groups had the highest psychological well-being, while respondents termed 'labour market descenders', who were characterised by their lack of perceived job security, had the lowest GHQ scores. The latter were not significantly different to those of the unemployed respondents in the sample.

The problem with cross-sectional evidence is that no cause–effect relationship can be established. There are, however, a growing number of longitudinal studies (Burchell 1994; Burchell 1997; Dekker and Schaufeli 1995; Ferrie *et al.* 1995) which support the findings of the cross-sectional studies mentioned earlier. One of these, the Whitehall II study by Ferrie *et al.* (1995), is of particular interest because it constitutes a 'natural experiment'. Baseline data were collected in 1985 in a period of job security and repeat data gathered in 1989, when jobs had come under threat as a result of the privatisation of London-based civil service departments. The research found that, at baseline, the staff of the departments to be privatised reported better mental health than those in other departments, but once the threat to jobs had been announced they reported a significantly greater deterioration in health between the two points of measurement. The GHQ scores for those whose jobs had come under threat were also worse than those for the remaining civil servants, though the difference was not statistically significant.

Longitudinal studies serve not only to confirm cross-sectional evidence but also to investigate the effects of chronic job insecurity, where job insecurity is experienced over a prolonged period of time, sometimes over a number of years. It could be argued that harmful stress is most likely where there has been a sudden and unexpected reduction in job security and that employees might adjust to persistent insecure work without any negative consequences for health and well-being. An alternative view, however, suggested by models by stress, would be that persistently high levels of insecurity are more likely to result in illness as the individual's capacity to cope with the stressor becomes exhausted over time (Lazarus and Folkman 1984).

The evidence indicates that the latter is the case: prolonged experience of job insecurity leads to increasingly impaired psychological well-being. Heaney *et al.* (1994) examined the effects of job insecurity in a sample of 207, mainly male, automobile manufacturing workers in the USA and found that chronic job insecurity was predictive of changes in job satisfaction and physical symptoms over time, over and above the effects of job insecurity at any one time. In addition, Burchell (1997), using BHPS data, found that the well-being of those in insecure work continued to decline throughout the period of insecurity, a finding which was not reproduced amongst the unemployed for whom deterioration tended to cease after a period of about six months (see also Dekker and Schaufeli 1995).

These findings from both cross-sectional and longitudinal studies are a powerful demonstration that, under certain circumstances, being in employment can be as stressful as being unemployed. Unemployment has been shown extensively to have detrimental effects on psychological health and well-being (Warr 1983; Dooley and Catalano 1988). Ferrie *et al.* (1995: 1269) conclude that 'the increasing levels of job insecurity, created by changes in the nature of employment relationships may lead to greater ill-health in the general population, beyond the *direct* effects of unemployment'.

Why is the experience of job insecurity so stressful?

One of the defining characteristics of job insecurity is the experience of uncertainty and ambiguity (Barling and Kelloway 1996; Heaney *et al.* 1994; Joelson and Wahlquist 1987; Jacobson 1987; Roskies and Louis-Guerin 1990). Lazarus and Folkman (1984) talk about the stressfulness of 'event uncertainty', which they define as the 'likelihood of an event occurring'. High levels of such uncertainty can have paralysing effects on the coping process. Warr (1987) supports this position by pointing out that predictability is important for the coping process, since it allows for the nature and timing of potentially noxious events to be anticipated. In addition, ambiguity, or the lack of situational clarity, can decrease a person's feelings of control and increase feelings of helplessness.

Employees who experience job insecurity do not know what to cope with since they do not know what to expect. The lack of control over the situation does not give the worker the chance to combat the experience of job insecurity (Dekker and Schaufeli 1995). Reduced ability to plan and control one's life in the experience of job insecurity may also add to the stressfulness of the experience (Burchell 1994). Joelson and Wahlquist (1987: 179) describe the experience of Swedish shipyard workers under threat of job loss as follows: 'It is a period of agony of varying strength. Rumours about possible decisions and actions are circulating. Reliable information is not available. You have to decide whether you should try to look for another job or not. Sometimes you have too little to do. You hover between hope and despair.' They found that the anticipatory phase (the period of insecurity) was perceived to be the most strenuous of the unemployment process, due to the prolonged uncertainty.

Dekker and Schaufeli (1995) point out that the certainty about one's job situation, even if that is the unpleasant certainty of having been made redundant, is less detrimental to workers' psychological well-being than a situation of prolonged job insecurity. Event uncertainty *per se*, i.e. the subjective probability of an event's occurrence, may be a greater source of anxiety and tension than the event itself (Lazarus and Folkman 1984). The number of studies which show that the anticipation of, or concern about, future job loss may be as traumatic as unemployment itself, is substantial and growing (Roskies *et al.* 1993).

An additional factor identified by Jacobson (1987), is that, in contrast to unemployment, job insecurity is of minimal social visibility. This means that unless there is strong evidence of imminent job loss, the affected employee is expected to continue working as usual. The insecure worker therefore has no special status and no opportunity to express dissatisfaction or seek help, and this can add to the experienced stress. Furthermore, a threat to the continuation of one's job means a threat to important 'identity-formatting factors' (Joelson and Wahlquist 1987), such as the provision of regular activities and the structuring of the day into working and rest periods, the contact and interaction with people at work and the definition of personal status. Finally, in times of economic instability and insecure employment, generally poor working conditions are tolerated due to the lack of alternative jobs. These poor working conditions add to the stressful experience of job insecurity. Exposure to long hours, arduous conditions and poor-quality work are all conditions which add to the stress experienced in insecure employment (Sutherland and Cooper 1988).

Demographic moderators of reactions to job insecurity

There are a number of personal, social and environmental factors which might influence the relationship between job insecurity and well-being. These factors are called *moderators*, as they affect, change or moderate the relationship between two or more variables – in this case job insecurity and well-being. Koslowsky (1998) points out that much of the research on occupational stress is aimed at identifying moderators, since they are helpful in explaining conflicting evidence. The failure of a researcher to replicate previous findings on a certain set of independent and dependent variables may be a sign of the influence of a moderator. We will first consider the role of demographic moderators such as occupational group, age and gender.

It has been suggested that managerial employees might be less affected by job insecurity and unemployment than other employees due to their greater organisational influence, financial resources, employment mobility and generally better coping resources (Roskies and Louis-Guerin 1990; Greenhalgh and Sutton 1991). Conversely, it has also been suggested that managers may react more strongly, due to their meritocratic 'you-get-what-you-deserve' attitude (Roskies and Louis-Guerin 1990). Research evidence to date, while still sparse, indicates that perceived job insecurity for managers is as stressful as for other workers.

Roskies and Louis-Guerin (1990) found that those managers who were insecure in their jobs showed poorer health, and that the level of distress increased proportionately with the level of insecurity. They further found that managers who perceived their jobs to be highly insecure had anxiety scores as high as those commonly found among the unemployed. Hallier and Lyon (1996), in their qualitative analysis of the experience of job insecurity in managers, reported reactions like severe shock, struggle to understand the reasons for being selected for possible redundancy, threat to self-esteem, and negative and emotional responses encompassing resentment, bitterness, anger, disbelief and humiliation.

In a comparison of reactions to job insecurity between white managerial employees and black production workers, Orpen (1993) found that, while white managerial employees felt more secure in their jobs than black production workers, there was a correlation between job insecurity and both anxiety and depression for both groups. This correlation was found to be stronger for the white managerial employees than the black production workers. Therefore, while fewer white managerial employees felt job insecurity than the black production workers, for those who did, the reactions to job insecurity were more severe.

Kuhnert and Vance (1992), on the other hand, investigating blue- and white-collar differences in reactions to job insecurity, found that for blue-collar workers, job insecurity was positively related to more symptoms on their global health measure (SCL-90-R) than for white-collar workers. For white-collar workers, job insecurity was positively related to depression, anxiety, obsessive-compulsive behaviour and interpersonal sensitivity, whereas for blue-collar workers job insecurity was, additionally related to anger-hostility and somatisation, distress arising from bodily dysfunctions including headaches, faintness or pains in the lower back (Kuhnert *et al.* 1989)

The public sector, a traditional stronghold of secure employment, has started to experience greater job insecurity as a result of pressure to control public expenditure. The main finding from research on the response of public servants is that they experience the same stressful reactions to job insecurity as do other occupational groups. Jacobson (1987), in his qualitative study of the reactions to job insecurity in male white-collar employees in an Israeli Government Ministry, identified a range of emotions, such as suspicion, external anger, helplessness, stress, self-blame, and demoralisation, similar to those reported by Hallier and Lyon (1996) in their work on managerial employees. Similar results have been reported for public sector employees in Australia (Dekker and Schaufeli 1995), the USA (Kuhnert and Palmer 1991) and Britain (Ferrie *et al.* 1995). Job insecurity has similar negative consequences for members of different occupational groups, therefore, and while some research points to significant differences between groups, findings are to a certain degree contradictory. The link between occupational status, job insecurity and mental health clearly requires further research.

While many studies do not explicitly state or conduct tests on gender differences with respect to the consequences of job insecurity, the few that do seem to suggest that men and women react differently to the experience of job insecurity. Ferrie *et al.* (1995), in the longitudinal Whitehall II study, found that in response to job insecurity, men showed a significant deterioration for self-rated general health, number of symptoms experienced over the previous two weeks, and number of health problems experienced over the last year. For women, on the other hand, there was 'only' a significant worsening in the number of reported symptoms. The authors concluded that, generally, changes in reported physical health were larger for men, whereas changes in psychological health were larger for women. Burchell (1994) found that on aggregate, men suffered more from job insecurity than women. More specifically, he found that, for men, the psychological benefits of re-employment, following unemployment, were moderated by the security of the job that they obtained. In other words, those who entered insecure jobs only showed a very small, non-significant improvement in psychological health, whereas those who entered secure employment showed a marked improvement in their GHQ score. For women, however, psychological benefits of re-employment occurred, regardless of how secure the new job was. Burchell (1994), referring to agency theory, points out that women might be less affected by job insecurity than men, since some rely on a male partner's wage as the main income for their household. Threats to their own job security may not be perceived as putting them in as much jeopardy.

Kuhnert and Vance (1992) found a moderating effect of age on the relationship between job insecurity and psychological well-being. While older employees reported that they would be less likely than their younger colleagues to find a

similar job elsewhere, they reported fewer adverse symptoms than younger colleagues. Kuhnert and Vance attribute these findings to changes in values, needs
and expectations in the older men. The previously cited study by Mattiasson *et al.*
(1990) on Swedish shipyard workers shows that other age-related factors, such as
being able to take early retirement and thereby avoiding financial worries, might
also play an important role in the reactions to job insecurity. Due to the small
number of studies, only tentative conclusions can be drawn about the importance
of age as a moderator at present.

Social and personality differences as moderators of reactions to job insecurity

A second type of potential moderator of reactions to job insecurity includes social
and personal differences, such as the ability to cope with stress, social support and
differences in personality. With regard to coping, the experience of job insecurity
may lead not only to a decrease in psychological well-being, but also to efforts to
cope with the situation (Klandermans *et al.* 1991). The concepts of stress and
coping are often seen as being inextricably linked. Lazarus and Folkman (1984:
141) define coping as 'constantly changing cognitive and behavioural efforts to
manage specific external and/or internal demands that are appraised as taxing
and exceeding the resources of the person', and differentiate between problem-
focused coping and emotion-focused coping. Problem-focused coping serves to
manage or alter the problem which causes distress, whereas emotion-focused
coping serves to manage or alter the emotional reactions associated with the
problem. Armstrong-Stassen (1994), investigating survivors' reactions to workforce reduction in a sample of telecommunication technicians, reported that
perceived job insecurity was significantly related to both control-coping (problem-
focused coping) and escape-coping (emotion-focused coping). Unfortunately, the
research only investigated the effects of these coping strategies on organisational
outcome variables, and not on psychological well-being. It was established, however that control-coping led to positive organisational outcomes such as higher
commitment and performance and lower intentions to leave, whereas emotion-
focused coping led to the reverse.

While the term 'social support' is widely used in everyday language and people
seem to have an intuitive feeling for what it means, there is no generally accepted
definition. House (1981: 26) defines social support as 'a flow of emotional concern, instrumental aid, information and/or appraisal (information relevant to self-
evaluation) between people', while Thoits (1995: 64) states that 'social support
usually refers to the functions performed for the individual by significant others
such as family members, friends, and co-workers'. Social support has been found
to be a very promising avenue for effective stress intervention and there is an
extensive literature which demonstrates the positive effects of social support on
health and well-being in a range of stressful situations and events (Berkman 1985;
Kessler and McLeod 1985).

The main debate in the social support literature is on how and where social support intervenes in the stressor-stress-strain process. There are two competing hypotheses: the buffering effect hypothesis and the main effect hypothesis. A buffering effect is present when the relationship between the job stressor(s) and employee health is weaker in the presence of strong social support than in the presence of weak social support. The buffering hypothesis proposes that support is beneficial for well-being mainly for persons under high levels of stress. The main effect hypothesis, on the other hand, states that social support is beneficial to health and well-being, irrespective of whether a person is under stress or not. Main effects are also often referred to as direct effects.

Beneficial effects of work-based social support in the experience of job insecurity have been reported by Lim (1996) who used mail survey data of MBA graduates in the USA. She found that social support from others at work can contribute significantly in buffering individuals against job dissatisfaction and other organisational outcome measures. Similarly, she found that non-work-based social support was effective in buffering against life dissatisfaction. However, she did not find any buffering effects for non-work support on job dissatisfaction and the organisational outcome measures in the study, and equally, no buffering effects for work-based support on life dissatisfaction. This finding, that work-based social support is more important than non-work social support in buffering stress at work, is in line with findings from studies on the effects of social support in other areas of occupational stress (Buunk 1990).

Another study which shows what role social support can play in the experience of job insecurity is that of Fried and Tiegs (1993), which examined the effects of emotional support from shop stewards. In contrast to many other studies, they conceptualised satisfaction with job security as a strain, along with burnout, helplessness and psychosomatic complaints. Role ambiguity and role conflict were conceptualised as the stressors. They found that higher support from a shop steward was related to higher satisfaction with job security. Therefore shop steward support had a main effect on satisfaction with job security. Only when there was a simultaneous increase in both stressors, role conflict and role ambiguity, was there a buffering effect of shop steward support on satisfaction with job security. What these and other studies indicate is that there is evidence for both main and buffering effects in the moderation of reactions to job insecurity.

In addition to the effect of social moderators, researchers have examined the moderating effects on job insecurity of a range of personality differences. The principal findings are as follows.

Mastery

Mastery has been defined as 'the extent to which one regards one's life/chances as being under one's own control in contrast to being fatalistically ruled' (Pearlin and Schooler 1978: 5). It is positively associated with the adoption of problem-oriented coping strategies (Fleishman 1984). In a study of redundancy survivors in the telecommunications industry in Canada, Armstrong-Stassen (1994) found that those survivors with a strong sense of mastery were more likely to engage in problem-oriented coping which, in turn, was associated with positive organisational outcomes.

Decision latitude

Karasek and Theorell's (1990) 'job strain model' proposes that perceptions of decision latitude (such as control of task in the workplace and discretion of skill use) moderate the impact of job strain on individual well being. More particularly, they demonstrate that high workload, low satisfaction and low workplace control are the best predictors of coronary heart disease. Using this framework in a study of South African miners, Barling and Kelloway (1996) have also shown that when perceived workplace control is low, job insecurity is positively associated with increased blood pressure, but unrelated when perceived workplace control is high.

Hardiness

Maddi and Kobasa's (1984) research on American executives underlined the importance of hardiness in moderating the stress of job insecurity. They define 'hardiness' as a belief that one's activities are intrinsically valuable, that one can control events and that change is a beneficial experience. However, not all research on the hardiness construct is in line with these findings (Funk 1992; Funk and Houston 1987).

Optimism

In a study of job insecure workers in Canada, Roskies *et al.* (1993) found that, after controlling for socio-demographic factors, those with an optimistic disposition were much less likely to perceive job insecurity as stressful than those inclined to pessimism. Optimism, however, did not, in this study, make a significant impact on the type of coping used. This suggests that personality may be particularly important in the appraisal of job insecurity as stressful. Where measures of pessimism and optimism have been included in other studies of job insecurity, pessimists – those who are generally predisposed to see the world in a negative way – report higher stress levels (Armstrong-Stassen 1994; van Vuuren *et al.* 1991; Jacobson 1987*).*

Workplace moderators of reactions to job insecurity

Kuhnert *et al.* (1989) examined the relationship between perceived job insecurity and employee health in two manufacturing organisations in the USA. They used a multidimensional measure of perceived job insecurity with five sub-scales (company concern for the individual; job permanence; job performance; company growth and stability; long-range perspective) and a global measure of employee health with four sub-scales (somatisation, depression, anxiety and hostility). When they examined the data at a global level they found that there was a negative relationship between job insecurity and psychological well-being. Furthermore, they found that there were no significant differences in the overall ratings of perceived job insecurity and health for the employees of the two companies.

However, when they looked at the data in more detail and examined the patterns of the different sub-scales, using canonical correlation analysis, they found a different pattern of results for the employees of the two organisations. In the first organisation, the job security canonical variate was primarily defined by the job performance sub-scale and was related to employee health, which was mainly defined by depression, interpersonal sensitivity and somatisation. In the second organisation, the job security canonical variate was primarily defined by long-range perspective, job permanence and company growth and was related to employee health, which was mainly defined by depression. Employee characteristics were assessed to be the same in both organisations, whereas management style and organisational climate were judged to be different. The first organisation was traditional and bureaucratic and the second one was jointly owned by management and the employees. Therefore, Kuhnert *et al.* concluded that organisational factors such as management style and organisational climate might moderate the relationship between job insecurity and well-being. The importance of organisational culture and climate has also been pointed out in Greenhalgh and Rosenblatt's (1984) model of job insecurity, which proposed that organisational culture influences employees' sense of powerlessness. Their work shows the potential importance of environmental workplace factors, which to date have received almost no attention in the study of job insecurity.

Stress management in the experience of job insecurity

Having shown the detrimental effects of job insecurity, we will now briefly talk about what can be done to reduce the stressfulness of the experience of job insecurity. As we have seen earlier, one of the most stressful aspects of the experience of job insecurity is the uncertainty and ambiguity associated with it. Equally, the importance of retaining a sense of control has been outlined as important when dealing with a stressful situation. Barling and Kelloway (1996) state that in the experience of job insecurity, informing individuals of the criteria to be used in making the lay-off decisions can reduce any negative effects and increase individual perceptions of workplace control. Ashford *et al.* (1989) also emphasise the importance of information by stating that organisations ought to take steps to provide people with adequate information with respect to likely future outcomes, thereby reducing their job insecurity. Consequently, managers should set norms that promote asking for information or help with problem-solving and the sharing of worries and concerns. Encouraging information-seeking will only reduce job insecurity, however, if relevant information actually exists.

In a similar vein, Kuhnert and Palmer (1991) point to the importance of good communication. They refer to an earlier study by Kuhnert and Lahey (1988) which found that employees in organisations which faced lay-offs or work shortages felt more secure when they were aware of the criteria on which such decisions were based and when they were given the information from management which was vital for them to assess their own position in the organisation.

The strategies outlined here are based on interviews with affected employees or have been inferred from findings that uncertainty, ambiguity and lack of information during periods of insecurity are perceived as stressful. However, none of these strategies has been tested with regards to their effectiveness in a so-called intervention study which employs systematic pre- and post-intervention tests to assess the effectiveness of the intervention. Unfortunately, such intervention studies are generally very rare in the occupational stress literature, and to our knowledge, they are non-existent at present in the job insecurity literature.

Discussion

The research reviewed in this section shows a fairly consistent pattern of results, which indicates the detrimental effects of the experience of job insecurity on psychological well-being. The evidence comes from both cross-sectional and longitudinal studies and demonstrates that perceived job insecurity has become a major concern for employees in different countries and across a range of occupational groups. However, a small number of studies exist which provide conflicting evidence in that they show either no link (Büssing and Jochum 1986; Depolo and Sarchielli 1986) or a positive link (Kinicki 1985; Swinburne 1981) between job insecurity and psychological well-being, and it must also be acknowledged that some of the research which does indicate an adverse effect suffers from methodological weaknesses and in many cases reports only modest statistical correlations. What this suggests is that further research is needed and there is a particular requirement for more detailed and disaggregated analysis, such as that found in studies by Burchell (1994) and Kuhnert *et al.* (1989). In our view, there is also a requirement for further research to be conducted on the basis of a set of universally recognised, validated and used measures of job insecurity and psychological well-being.

Work orientation: motivation and performance

There are numerous examples of employers attempting to increase motivation, performance or commitment by manipulating job security, but there is no consensus as to whether the relationships between job insecurity and these outcome measures are positive, negative or non-linear. A common assumption is that the threat of dismissal is one of the main tools available to employers to ensure that poor performance is eradicated, and the alleged positive effects of privatisation or downsizing have been cited in support of this belief. Conversely, a number of companies, such as United Distillers, Blue Circle and Welsh Water have recently offered increased job security to their employees as a means of boosting productivity (see Guest, this volume). The purpose of this section is to establish which of these competing assumptions has greatest validity and to review recent research which has explored the link between job insecurity and the orientations of employees to their work.

There are at least two ways in which job insecurity might affect the performance of an individual employee. There might be a *direct* relationship, whereby an employee decides to work harder to maximise their chances of retaining their employment (or conversely work less hard, because they do not foresee any future in their relationship with their current employer). Or there might be *indirect* effects, as job insecurity causes stress or dissatisfaction, which in turn increases (or decreases) productivity. We have already reviewed the literature which shows a link between job insecurity and stress, but the effect of that stress on performance is unclear. Sometimes it is theorised that stress and insecurity will be positively related, if stressors act as challenges or activators. Alternatively, stressors might act to interfere with performance. If these are both true, stress might enhance performance at low levels, but peak and then have a negative relationship — the classic inverted-U shape relationship.

Abramis (1994) explored the relationships between stressors, strains, performance and job insecurity, and went beyond many other investigators by testing for both linear and non-linear relationships. With a sample of US employees, he measured stressors (role ambiguity, role conflict, job insecurity), strains (job dissatisfaction, anxiety, depression, etc.) and performance (both social and technical, and by both self-report and from a 'significant other'). His findings suggest that the relationships between the stressors and both the strains and the performance measures were linear and negative — in other words, the lower the level of stressors, the better. However, if he had included other more positive stressors (such as demanding deadlines or high expectations), the findings might have been different. It is worth noting that job insecurity was found to have negative correlations with all the performance measures, and positive correlations with job dissatisfaction, anxiety and depression. However, being a simple cross-sectional design, we cannot with any confidence assert that job insecurity causes poor performance: poor performers might be well aware that their poor performance puts them at risk of job loss.

Most other research which has explored the direct relationship between job insecurity and performance reports similar findings. Thus, Armstrong-Stassen's (1993) study of Canadian production workers, facing a plant closure but where some jobs would be transferred to other plants, showed a moderate correlation between perceived job security and self-rated level of performance. Rosenblatt and Ruvio (1996) also found a relationship using a sample of Israeli teachers, though not only were the results again based only on self-report, but the correlations were very low, showing an exceedingly weak effect. An exception to this pattern of findings is to be found in Orpen's (1993) study of an Australian manufacturing plant, which showed no correlation between job insecurity and performance (both rated by their superiors).

As an alternative to measuring performance directly, several studies have used self-reported attitudes to work, such as job satisfaction and organisational commitment (Davy *et al.* 1997). Much of this work has focused on the impact of redundancy and in particular the effect of redundancy on 'survivors', those who keep their jobs. Following on from similar research in the USA (Brockner 1992; Brockner *et al.* 1985, 1986), Horsted and Doherty (1995) surveyed 170 personnel in financial services, a sector where many of the major employers have been 'rightsizing' through large-scale redundancy programmes. They found decreased motivation, morale, confidence and loyalty and increased stress, scepticism, anger and bitterness, which they labelled 'survivor syndrome'.

Brockner's (1992) research arrived at similar conclusions, although he emphasised that the legacy of redundancy programmes was contingent on the way in which they were managed. Typically, companies provided careful assistance for those who were 'outplaced', in the form of counselling and career guidance, but they ignored the survivors. If the survivors were kept informed, however, and led to believe that the redundancy programme was carefully managed and, most importantly, fair, then Brockner found that it could result in increased motivation among this group. Brockner *et al.* (1992) also found a non-linear, inverted-U relationship between job security and work effort in a sample of retail chain employees (survivors of recent redundancies) in the USA. Work effort was low for those with highest and lowest levels of job insecurity, but relatively high for those reporting moderate levels of job insecurity.

Hallier and Lyon's (1996) study of UK managers facing the threat of redundancy paints a more elaborate picture. Their sample of 42 men was selected by virtue of their contacting an employment agency following an announcement of imminent redundancies and they conducted five separate, semi-structured interviews with each manager over a twelve-month period. The earliest interviews were conducted in the period after the managers had received their warnings of impending redundancies. Widespread shock was characteristic of this stage, despite the fact that the managers had been aware of an ongoing 'downsizing' programme, and had in many cases overseen redundancy programmes for their subordinates. There was also a lot of searching for internal attributions for their own post having been chosen. Feelings of resentment, bitterness, anger and disbelief were commonly expressed during this period, as well as a deep questioning of the trust that they had placed in the employer. Their final psychological state was dependent, it was claimed, on their fate in the labour market. Some were reprieved by sideways movements into other management posts; some were demoted into engineering jobs (often alongside their old subordinates); some were 'outplaced' but soon found other jobs; and some remained unemployed for many months. In all but the reprieved group, there was a deep questioning of the trust which had previously been taken for granted in their relationships with their employers. Most felt that they would never return to the previous high levels of commitment to their jobs.

The evidence concerning the legacy of trust among survivors of redundancy programmes is therefore sparse, and suggests that the relationship is a complex one. It would be unwise to generalise from a small number of self-report studies on different types of employee, but it is important to consider the possibility that labour market insecurity may disrupt the tacit relationship between employer and employee. Many different traditions within the social sciences place great emphasis on the nature of the tacit understandings which govern the employment relationship, and it is frequently argued that violation of these understandings through reduced security may generate unforeseen, negative effects. For example, Alogoskoufis *et al.* (1995), in arguing against deregulating job security as a method of reducing unemployment, contend that security of employment lengthens the horizon of job-specific investment decisions and so encourages training and human-capital development. Similarly, in the transaction cost or institutionalist literatures, the cooperation which comes more easily to the traditional employment relationship, and which can be contrasted with other types of market transaction, is sometimes judged to be the very *raison d'être* of firms (Hodgson 1995). Once the relative permanence of that relationship is withdrawn, its very nature may change and it is notable that accountants Ernst and Young (1995) have blamed job insecurity in financial services for increased levels of fraud, as employment relationships have tended towards lower levels of trust.

Job insecurity and family life

We have seen that job insecurity can influence the psychological well-being of the individual; for the sake of clarity, much of this research focuses on the worker in isolation. Yet it is essential to appreciate that people are much more than just workers. Research consistently demonstrates the importance of the successful interaction of employment, family, friendships and leisure for general psychological well-being (Kahn 1981). The focus of this section will be the particular interactions between employment, job insecurity and family life. After defining families and the different ways in which women and men experience them, we will briefly outline some concepts and theories used to account for the links between work and family. Then we will examine evidence of the impact of job insecurity on both marital functioning and parent–child interactions, highlighting throughout the multivariate nature of influence.

How do we define a family in the late 1990s? Is the nuclear family of husband, wife and 2.4 children now a redundant stereotype? Families are certainly smaller than in the past, childbearing is occurring later, more people cohabit before marriage (if they marry at all), divorce rates in the UK are at their highest levels, there are large increases in the numbers of families maintained by women, more mothers working outside the home (often in part-time employment), increasing numbers of people are living alone, or choosing not to have children, and issues such as homosexual marriage and adoption are no longer taboo subjects (Scott *et al.* 1993). However, while the nuclear family is less dominant than it used to be, it still remains, in public opinion at least, the 'desirable' state for the rearing of children. In most Western countries, many continue to advocate family roles for women, particularly when they have young children (Scott *et al.* 1993). Gershuny and Roberts (1988) also point out that although men have increased their involvement in domestic tasks and child care, this has only been by a small amount. We will see the influence of such family roles on the experience of job insecurity, and how, in some ways, adherence to 'traditional' divisions of labour can sometimes exacerbate the stress of job insecurity. First, however, it is necessary to outline some of the concepts used to account for the way in which work and family overlap.

One of the most generally used concepts is 'spillover'. Kanter (1977) emphasises the way in which women's and men's emotional experience at work influences the dynamics of family life. In this approach there are no boundaries to an individual's behaviours and moods, so if one is unhappy in work then one will be unhappy at home. Most research tends to focus on the spillover of negative work experiences into the family (Barling 1990). Spillover, however, can be positive or negative and can occur in either direction, that is, from family to work, as well as work to family. An alternative concept sometimes used is 'compensation'. This suggests that what, in some way, may be missing for an individual in the work role may be compensated for in out-of-work activities. While there is some evidence to support this view, by far the majority of the research supports the 'spillover' hypothesis (Zedeck 1992).

These broad concepts do, however, tend to lack detailed analysis of the processes underlying the 'transfer' of experience from one area of life to another. Greenhaus and Beutell (1985) suggest that there are three distinct ways in which this transfer occurs. First, the amount of time spent at work by definition reduces the time and energy available for family, potentially producing conflict. Secondly, work stressors can preoccupy the individual even when they are not at work, and this psychological strain can undermine family relationships. Thirdly, the behaviour considered appropriate in one role may not be appropriate for another. For example, the emotional distance required in some workplaces may be unsuitable when interacting with children. Although, for the sake of clarity, these distinctions are useful, they are necessarily interrelated, as we shall see below. The interaction between job insecurity and family relationships has been considered in two ways: links to marital functioning, and associations with parent–child relationships. We will examine each of these areas in turn.

Marital functioning

Barling (1990) suggests that marital functioning can be categorised into activities which are behavioural (e.g. verbal aggression, such as argument), affective (e.g. feelings towards the spouse), or cognitive (e.g. commitment to the relationship). Research findings seem to suggest that these elements have different influences on spouses' levels of satisfaction with their marriage (Broderick and O'Leary 1986). Barling and Macewen (1992) suggest that the effects of work on family, or of family on work, are mediated by these activities. Using self-report measures in a random sample of 180 married couples in Canada, at least one of whom was employed, they found that while job insecurity had no direct effect on marital satisfaction, it was significantly correlated with reduced concentration (cognitive response). This, in turn, was correlated with depression, reduced marital satisfaction, reduced sexual satisfaction (affective responses) and increased psychological aggression (behavioural response). This study is interesting, because it begins to unpack particular aspects of psychological well-being and family functioning which are influenced by job insecurity. However, it is somewhat unique in this respect. Most studies of the impact of job insecurity focus on other ways in which job insecurity influences family functioning and, in particular, have examined the belief that job insecurity is related to long hours and that this, in turn, is linked to reductions in marital functioning.

It has been established that British employees now work among the longest and most unsocial hours in Europe (Office for National Statistics 1998). While some suggest that this style of working is entered into voluntarily (Guest and Conway 1997), others indicate that working long hours, particularly among middle management grades, can be linked to the increasing job insecurity associated with the UK's 'flexible' labour market (Beatson 1995). Wheatley (1992) suggests that the introduction of new technologies, redundancies and trends towards multi-skilling can often lead to 'work overload'. Employees sometimes find that the new tasks they are expected to perform are too difficult and/or they simply have too much work to do within their contracted hours. In addition, 'survivors' in organisations which have experienced redundancies can sometimes increase their work effort, in spite of low morale (Brockner *et al.* 1993). Thus employees may work longer hours than is strictly necessary, in an attempt to be 'visible' in the organisation and to try and reduce their chances of being the next in line for redundancy. Cooper and Williams (1994) label this phenomenon 'presenteeism', and have suggested that it is particularly prevalent amongst managerial employees. However, in a study of manual and lower non-manual grade workers in Finland, Kinnunen and Mauno (1998) also suggest there are links between job insecurity, increased work effort and longer hours.

But does working long hours adversely affect family life? Results from a questionnaire survey of British companies seems to suggest that it does (Austin Knight (1995) in Sparks *et al.* 1997). Forty-seven per cent of respondents reported that their family life had suffered because of long hours, and a quarter of women claimed to have put a relationship at risk due to work. In a survey of 6,000 British parents from the National Child Development Study (a birth cohort study of all those born during one week in 1958), Ferri and Smith (1996) demonstrate that when men work more than fifty hours a week their involvement in joint family activities (e.g. family meals and outings) is severely reduced. This study also demonstrates that lack of male involvement in the family can be significantly detrimental to mothers' psychological well-being, and corrosive to family cohesiveness. In a questionnaire study of Canadian dual-earner couples, moreover, Galambos and Walters (1992) found that when wives work long hours, their husbands are likely to experience more depression and anxiety than those whose wives work shorter hours. Thus, spouse support is important for both husbands and wives, and working long hours can obviously undermine the spouse's ability to provide this.

Kinnunen and Mauno (1998) used self-report data from a sample of 501 employees in three areas of the Finnish economy considered particularly vulnerable to job insecurity (the public sector, manufacturing for export and supermarket retailing) to suggest that moderate levels of job insecurity may have led to increased work-effort, which, in turn, meant their participants experienced more family/work conflict than under normal circumstances. They also found that this effect held for *both* spouses, which they explained by reference to social expectations in Finland: that is, that women and men should participate equally in the workplace, and therefore one would expect conflicts to be experienced equally by both partners.

We have seen, then, that there may be some links between job insecurity, long hours and conflict between work and family. While long hours at work can lead to psychological stress, the actual threat of job loss itself should not be under-estimated in creating difficulties for both the worker and their spouse. What other evidence is there of stress 'spillover' into marital relationships?

One of the first studies to examine the impact of job insecurity on the family in the postwar period was carried out by Voydanoff and Donnelly (1988). They surveyed a probability sample of 410 married people from the city of Dayton in the USA using a telephone questionnaire. Interestingly, their participants showed the influence of traditional gender roles on the evaluation of job insecurity as a family stressor. For husbands experiencing job insecurity, their marital dissatisfac-tion, rather than being associated with job insecurity itself, was often associated with the adoption by their wife or children of 'bread-winning roles'. Moss and Brannen (1987) emphasise that men are also often pressured into conforming to appropriate gender roles – in this case that they alone should be the 'primary' breadwinner – and that they often experience stress when their roles are threatened.

For wives in this study, however, it was their husband's level of job insecurity, rather than their own, which was negatively correlated with their personal level of marital and family satisfaction. Rook *et al.* (1991) suggest that one reason that wives may experience their husband's job stressors as psychologically distressing, is that some women expend much time and energy in trying to support husbands in their work. Men often rely heavily on their wives to provide emotional support, and this 'burden-of-care' can become very stressful at times when the husband is experiencing extra, work-related stress. It has also been suggested that the empathy women experience for their husbands may mean that they often experi-ence his disappointment as if it were their own (Riley and Eckenrode 1986; Belle 1987).

Other studies, however, have indicated that husbands too can experience their wife's job insecurity as detrimental to marital satisfaction. Larson *et al.* (1994) studied a stratified random sample of 111 couples, at least one of whom worked on a US university campus (as either a blue-collar or a white-collar employee) experiencing severe financial cutbacks. They showed that job insecurity was associated with reduced psychological well-being and marital satisfaction not just in the worker but also in their spouse. Using self-report methods they found that husbands' stress was significantly related to lower marital adjustment (e.g. agreements on family finances), less role clarity (e.g. agreement on family responsibilities) and less affectiveness (e.g. showing an interest in the spouse). For wives, all of these outcomes were significant, with the addition of poorer communication, decreased problem solving and reduced behaviour control (e.g. 'breaking the usual rules'). Wives, therefore, experienced a greater range of marital dissatisfaction than did their husbands.

However, the relationship between job insecurity and the family is a multi-faceted one. While workers and spouses are both prone to the stress associated with insecurity, those couples who are most vulnerable are those with young children (Larson *et al.* 1994; Hughes and Galinsky 1994; Kinnunen and Mauno 1998). While we have emphasised that people are more than just workers – they are spouses and parents too – there is a huge variation in the degree to which both employers and organisational 'cultures' acknowledge this, especially during uncertain times.

Drawing on data from both questionnaires and in-depth interviews with 220 managers in the UK, Simpson (1998) suggests that during restructuring, rivalry may develop amongst project teams, which can lead to the development of uncooperative and insular cultures. In such circumstances, women managers with families sometimes had to find surreptitious ways of resisting the culture, often fearing to be seen as 'lacking commitment' if they gave family reasons for leaving work.

However, these sorts of circumstances, what Collinson and Collinson (1995) call 'macho' cultures, do not just make life difficult for mothers. Cooper and Lewis (1993) suggest that fathers often have to be deceptive in such cases too, making excuses for absence to colleagues which specifically do not mention their parenting commitments. In a recent British survey carried out for the Institute of Management, 45 per cent of male managers claimed that not seeing enough of their children was a major source of stress (Charlesworth 1996). In addition, men often experience even less support for their parenting role from the workplace than women do (Hass and Hwang 1995*)*. Galinsky *et al.* (1996) suggest that working parents experienced greater levels of work/family conflict, more stress and less effective ways of coping when they were in jobs which were insecure, had low levels of autonomy and high output demands. Examining self-report data from a nationally representative sample of 2,958 US employees, they also found that those parents, both mothers and fathers, who fared better were those in supportive workplaces with both supervisors and colleagues who were sympathetic to their caring responsibilities as mothers and fathers.

So, if job insecurity can interfere with spouse relationships and parenting responsibilities, the next question which needs to be considered is whether it is also associated with marital dissolution or divorce. Using data from 943 interviews drawn from a randomised survey carried out in the UK during 1986, Lampard (1994) found that being in an insecure job at the time of marriage was associated with a significantly greater risk of marital dissolution later on. Lampard does not consider precisely why this should be because his main concern lay with the relationship between unemployment and divorce. However, he does suggest that, as the psychological stress associated with insecurity may be similar to that experienced in unemployment (see Burchell 1994), it is possible that it is the increase in stress which heightens the risk of marital dissolution.

Lampard is sensitive to the considerable literature which suggests that male unemployment (on which the bulk of the research is based) is often only a trigger for divorce in those couples who were relating poorly prior to the onset of unemployment (see also Mattinson 1988). Further evidence of this pattern is available from research carried out both during and after the 1930s' Depression in the USA which suggested that the presence of certain family characteristics such as adaptability, cohesion, and willingness to take on non-traditional family roles can buffer families against strain during periods of economic uncertainty and unemployment. This longitudinal research followed 185 Californian children born during 1920 and 1921 through until their sixties. Using questionnaires, and, in the early stages, interviews with parents, Liker and Elder (1983) suggested that families who were more rigid and 'traditional' in their outlook on divisions of labour in the household were more likely to experience marital breakdown. More recently, Hughes and Galinsky (1994) studied a sample of 523 married full-time employees from a major US company and found that the combination of high pressure for output combined with job insecurity led to marital tension, particularly when there was little spouse support in the performance of household tasks. The characteristics of the family, therefore, may exacerbate the experience of job insecurity, particularly where it is constituted through 'traditional' gender roles.

Parenting

We have seen then that job insecurity is associated with impaired marital functioning. The next important question to consider is whether or not job insecurity influences the relationship between parents and children. In reviewing the literature on the impact of parents' work on their children's psychological well-being, Barling (1990) emphasises that the evidence suggests that it is the parental work experience which affects children's behaviour, not their employment status. Voydanoff (1990) also suggests that any psychological impact will depend on the characteristics and behaviours of both parents and children. So, once again, we need to be sensitive to the multi-faceted nature of any relationship between job insecurity and parent–child interactions.

In a Canadian study of children from ten elementary schools, Stewart and Barling (1996) used self-report measures to explore the effects of fathers' job insecurity on children's behaviour. While the results showed that job insecurity had no direct effect on parenting style or children's behaviour, job insecurity was negatively correlated with job satisfaction. Other studies in Canada (Barling 1986) found that fathers' low job satisfaction was associated with children's conduct problems and hyperactivity. Voydanoff and Donnelly (1986) found that fathers' job insecurity was positively related to the number of children's problems as perceived by mothers. And Margolis and Farran (1984) found that children whose fathers were insecure in their employment had a higher risk of illness than those whose fathers perceived themselves as secure. Kelly *et al.* (1985) suggest that this relationship is indirect, in that economic strain can lead to parental health difficulties, which, in turn, may impact on children's physical well-being.

There are again some pertinent findings from questionnaire studies of US children from the 1930s Depression. During this period, men's involvement with their children reportedly dropped (La Rossa and Reitzes 1993). In one study, 111 families and their children (born in 1928–9) were studied through until the 1970s. Fathers who were in insecure employment and experiencing economic strain during the 1930s exhibited inconsistent parental discipline, which, in turn, was associated with difficult behaviour and temper tantrums in children. In addition, fathers were more likely to be rejecting of daughters than sons, especially if the daughters were perceived by their fathers to be physically unattractive. The daughters of rejecting fathers were also found to have lower employment aspirations than other girls (Elder *et al.* 1984, 1986). More recently, Barling *et al.* (1998) studied 134 Canadian undergraduates (now aged 18). Using self-report data, they found that those students who strongly identified with fathers who had themselves been in insecure jobs during the mid-1980s had less 'humanistic' work beliefs than other students. That is, they were less inclined to believe that they could find fulfilment through work than students whose fathers had not experienced job insecurity. No effect was found for mothers. This demonstrates the subtle ways in which job insecurity for fathers may have a 'knock-on' effect on the work attitudes of the next generation.

So, job insecurity may influence fathers' parenting which, in turn, can influence children's psychological well-being and their own work attitudes. Much more work is needed, however, on the way in which job insecurity affects parental interaction and on how that influences parenting behaviour. There is also a need for more research on the influence of mothers' job insecurity on children, an issue which so far has been neglected.

Discussion

It has been suggested then, that job insecurity is associated with marital dissatisfaction and is stressful not only for the individual worker, but also for their spouse and children. This may occur via long hours at work, concentration difficulties and depression, and/or communication difficulties. We have also seen the influence of 'traditional' gender roles on the experience of job insecurity. In some studies (Voydanoff and Donnelly 1988) we see that the wives of men in insecure jobs experience more marital dissatisfaction than their husbands, which has been explained in terms of women's traditional empathic, nurturing role in the family (Rook *et al.* 1991). Men, however, appear to experience more marital dissatisfaction from their wives' 'non-traditional' participation in the economy, perhaps perceiving this as a threat to their bread-winning identity (Moss and Brannen 1987).

However, research has also identified significant cultural and temporal differences in the relationship between insecurity and family functioning, and Kinnunen and Mauno's (1998) Finnish study demonstrates that both women and men may experience job insecurity as a source of family/work conflict. In addition, some women are prepared to risk relationships for work (Austin Knight 1995) and Hughes and Galinsky (1994) suggest that spouse support is an import- ant moderator for job insecurity for both men and women (see also Ferri and Smith 1996; Galambos and Walters 1992). Data from the 1930s suggest that the ability to adapt to 'non-traditional roles' may well buffer families against the impact of job insecurity.

These studies, therefore, demonstrate the way in which broader cultural norms of 'appropriate' family roles can influence the impact of job insecurity as a psy- chological stressor. They also demonstrate the ways in which those beliefs are geographically specific yet still subject to individual negotiation. Indeed, Orthner (1995) goes so far as to suggest that family members are becoming increasingly unsure of the behaviour that is expected of them, despite the continuing presence of cultural norms. Thus, in certain groups, a sense of ambiguity and insecurity may permeate modern family roles, as well as modern workplaces. This idea, however, while interesting, remains speculative and is in need of empirical investigation.

It has been emphasised throughout this chapter that influences on psycho- logical well-being and marital satisfaction are multiple and that a combination of life events, other than job insecurity or gender differences, leads to stress. The presence of young children seems important, as does the role of social support in the workplace and personal characteristics such as optimism and pessimism. Barling (1990) points out that the statistically significant associations between employment and family are often modest; no single variable is powerful enough to explain much of the variance. It is an amalgam of employment, family and personal characteristics which together reduce psychological well-being and marital satisfaction and it is important to be alert to these issues and avoid the easy slide into 'economic' or 'social' determinism.

On a methodological note, the majority of studies reviewed above are based on self-report questionnaires used in cross-sectional designs. It is not possible to estab- lish causal relationships in this sort of design, no matter how sophisticated the statistical technique used (Spector 1994). For example, the association between job insecurity, depression and marital functioning may well be bi-directional and circular in nature. That is, depression may be due to a 'third variable' such as a general predisposition to pessimism, which, in itself, may create marital difficulties and heighten the worker's perception of their level of job insecurity. Critically, too few of the studies reviewed had a measure of the quality of marital or family functioning prior to the onset of job insecurity. In addition, the use of question- naire self-report is a technique that is open to method bias problems such as social desirability effects (when the participant responds with what they think is an 'appropriate' answer, something which may in itself account for some of the gender differences reported). However, these are perennial methodological dif- ficulties and such qualifications are rehearsed in an almost ritualistic fashion (Howard 1994). The pragmatics of conducting expensive, longitudinal data col- lection and the bias problems associated with all methods means that the self- report cross-sectional design will probably remain prominent in organisational behaviour and family research, as will the presence of methodological caveats such as this.

As a closing comment, it is worth highlighting some important gaps in the literature which need further exploration. How, for example, does job insecurity affect types of family which do not conform to the 'nuclear' stereotype, such as the extended networks of some ethnic groups? There is little research that looks at ethnicity and job insecurity. In addition, one of the biggest changes in family structure – the huge increase in families maintained solely by women – needs to be considered. What will be the impact on single parents of 'welfare to work' campaigns in the UK and the USA? Will they find themselves in a cycle of insecure employment and benefit claims? There is also little work on women's job insecurity and its relationship to parent–child interactions. Indeed, in the UK, there is hardly any direct research at all on the impact of job insecurity on the family, and most of the studies quoted in this chapter are drawn from the USA and Canada. Other areas of concern include the influence of job insecurity on family formation: does it in some way disrupt early adult relationships, or influence the delay of, or even abstinence from, child-bearing? All of these and many other questions remain unanswered. What we hope is clear, though, is that work experiences and family experiences are intricately related. The 'insecure worker' is not a socially isolated creature.

Conclusion

This chapter has considered some of the personal and social outcomes of job insecurity, and the story is not a happy one. There is considerable evidence, for different types of employees in different countries, of serious problems caused by job insecurity, for individuals and their families. However, there is little evidence of any compensating increase in motivation or productivity; in fact job insecurity might, in some cases, be responsible for bringing with it a deterioration in the psychological contract between employer and employee.

And there might be other more long-term effects of job insecurity. For instance, the spending patterns of insecure employees may be more cautious, leading to a slowdown in the economy, and their house-buying behaviour, in particular, may be different, exacerbating the instability of the housing market (Burchell 1999). It may even be the case that, as individuals are caught in a long-term cycle of insecure work and unemployment, they take on the characteristics of the socially excluded and both experience and help reproduce a wide range of social problems (*ibid.* 1999).

The bulk of available evidence suggests that job insecurity is a major source of private misery and public dysfunction. Under these circumstances, governments, trade unions and employers must ensure that their policies and actions are carried out with full awareness of the implications for job security. The search for employment regimes which maximise both flexibility and security should be one of our highest priorities in the quest for profitability combined with a good quality of life.

References

Abramis, D.J. (1994) 'Relationship of job stressors to job-performance – linear or an inverted-U?', *Psychological Reports*, 75, 1 (Part 2): 547–58.

Alogoskoufis, G., Bean, C., Bertola, G., Cohen, D., Dolado, J. and Saint-Paul, G. (1995) *Unemployment, Choices for Europe: Monitoring European Integration 5*, London: CEPR.

Armstrong-Stassen, M. (1993) 'Production workers' reaction to a plant closing: the role of transfer, stress, and support', *Anxiety, Stress and Coping*, 6: 201–14.

—— (1994) 'Coping with transition: a study of layoff survivors', *Journal of Organizational Behavior*, 15: 597–621.

Ashford, S.J., Lee, C. and Bobko, P. (1989) 'Content, causes and consequences of job insecurity: a theory-based measure and substantive test', *Academy of Management Journal*, 32: 803–29.

Austin Knight (1995) *Long Hours Culture*, London: Austin Knight.

Barling, J. (1986) 'Fathers' work experiences, the father–child relationship and children's behavior', *Journal of Occupational Behavior*, 7, 61–6.

—— (1990) *Employment, Stress and Family Functioning*, Chichester: John Wiley and Sons.

Barling, J. and Kelloway, E.K. (1996) 'Job insecurity and health: the moderating role of workplace control', *Stress Medicine*, 12: 253–9.

Barling, J. and Macewen, K.E. (1992) 'Linking work experiences to facets of marital functioning', *Journal of Organizational Behavior*, 13: 573–83.

Barling, J., Dupre, K.E. and Hepburn, C.G. (1998) 'Effects of parents' job insecurity on children's work beliefs and attitudes', *Journal of Applied Psychology*, 83: 112–18.

Beatson, M. (1995) *Labour Market Flexibility*, Sheffield: Employment Department Research Series, No. 48.

Belle, D. (1987) 'Gender differences in the social moderators of stress', in C. Barnett, L. Beiner and G. Baruch (eds) *Gender and Stress*, New York: Free Press.

Berkman, L.F. (1985) 'The relationship of social networks and social support to morbidity and mortality', in S. Cohen and S.L. Syme (eds) *Social Support and Health*, London: Academic Press.

Brockner, J. (1992) 'Managing the effects of layoffs on survivors', *California Management Review*, 34, 2: 9–28.

Brockner, J., Davy, J. and Carter, C. (1985) 'Layoffs, survivors' guilt, motivation, affective and attitudinal consequences', *Organisational Behaviour and Human Decision Processes*, 36, 2: 113–27.

Brockner, J., Grover, S., Reed, T.F. and Dewitt, R.L. (1992) 'Layoffs, job security and survivors' work effort: evidence of an inverted-U relationship', *Academy of Management Journal*, 35, 2: 413–25.

Brockner, J., O'Malley, M., Reed, T. and Glynn, M. (1993) 'Threat of future layoffs, self esteem and survivors' reactions: evidence from the laboratory and the field', *Strategic Management Journal*, 14: 153–66.

Brockner, J., Greenberg, J., Brockner, A., Bortz, J. and Carter, C. (1986) 'Layoffs, equity theory and work performance: further evidence of the impact of survivors' guilt', *Academy of Management Journal*, 29, 2: 373–84.

Broderick, J.E., and O'Leary, K.D. (1986) 'Contributions of affect, attitudes and behavior to marital satisfaction', *Journal of Consulting and Clinical Psychology*, 54: 514–17.

Burchell, B. (1994) 'The effects of labour market position, job insecurity, and unemployment on psychological health', in D. Gallie, C. Marsh and C. Vogler (eds) *Social Change and the Experience of Unemployment*, Oxford: Oxford University Press.

—— (1997) 'Job security and psychological well-being: preliminary analyses of the British Household Panel Survey', paper presented at the JRF Work and Opportunity Workshop, 16–17 October.

—— (1999) 'The unequal distribution of job insecurity, 1966–1986', *International Review of Applied Economics*, forthcoming.

Büssing, A. and Jochum, I. (1986) 'Arbeitsplatzunsicherheit, Belastungserleben und Kontrollwahrnehmung. Ergebnisse einer quasi-experimentellen Untersuchung in der Stahlindustrie', *Psychologie und Praxis*, 30: 180–91.

Buunk, B.P. (1990) 'Affiliation and helping interactions within organisations: a critical analysis of the role of social support with regard to occupational stress', in W. Stroebe and M. Hewstone (eds) *European Review of Social Psychology. Volume 1*, Chichester: John Wiley and Sons.

Campbell, I. (1997) 'Beyond unemployment: the challenge of increased precariousness in employment', *Just Policy*, 11: 4–20.

Charlesworth. K. (1996) *Are Managers under Stress? A Survey of Management Morale*, London: Institute of Management.

Collinson, D. and Collinson, M. (1995) 'Corporate liposuction and the re-masculinisation of management', Keynote address at Gender and Life in Organisations Conference, University of Portsmouth.

Cooper, C.L. and Lewis, S. (1993) *The Workplace Revolution: Managing Today's Dual-Career Families*, London: Kogan Page.

Cooper, C.L. and Williams, S. (1994) *Creating Healthy Work Organizations*, Chichester, John Wiley and Sons.

Cox, T. (1993) *Stress Research and Stress Management: Putting Theory to Work*, HSE Contract Research Report 61, London: Health and Safety Executive.

Davy, J.A., Kinicki, A.J. and Scheck, C.L. (1997) 'A test of job security's direct and mediated effects on withdrawal cognitions', *Journal of Organizational Behavior* 18, 4: 323–49.

Dekker, S.W.A. and Schaufeli, W.B. (1995) 'The effects of job insecurity on psychological health and withdrawal: a longitudinal study', *Australian Psychologist*, 30: 57–63.

Depolo, M. and Sarchielli, G. (1986) 'A socio-cognitive approach to the psychology of unemployment', in G. Debus and H.W. Schroiff (eds) *The Psychology of Work and Organisation*, North Holland: Elsevier Science.

Dooley, D. and Catalano, R. (1988) 'Recent research on the psychological effects of unemployment', *Journal of Social Issues*, 44: 1–12.

Elder, G.H., Caspi, A. and Van Nguyen, T. (1986) 'Resourceful and vulnerable children: family influences in stressful times', in R.K. Silbereisen, K. Eyforth and G. Rudinger (eds) *Development as Action in Context*, New York: Springer-Verlag.

Elder, G.H., Liker, J. and Cross, C. (1984) 'Parent-child behavior in the Great Depression: life course and intergenerational influences' in P.B. Baltes and O.G. Brim (eds) *Life-span, Development and Behavior*, volume 6, New York: Academic Press.

Ernst and Young (1995) 'Report on job insecurity and fraud in the financial services', cited in the *Guardian*, 16 January.

Feather, N.T. (1990) *The Psychological Impact of Unemployment*, New York: Springer-Verlag.

Ferri, E. and Smith, K. (1996) *Parenting in the 1990s*, London: Family Policy Studies Centre.

Ferrie, J., Shipley, M. Marmot, M.G., Stansfeld, S. and Smith, G. (1995) 'Health effects of anticipation of job change and non-employment: longitudinal data from the Whitehall II study', *British Medical Journal*, 311: 1264–9.

Fleishman, J. (1984) 'Personality characteristics and coping patterns', *Journal of Health and Social Behaviour*, 25: 229–44.

Fried, Y. and Tiegs, R.B. (1993) 'The main effect model versus buffering model of shop steward social support: a study of rank-and-file auto workers in the USA', *Journal of Organizational Behavior*, 14: 481–93.

Funk, S.C. (1992) 'Hardiness: a review of theory and research', *Health Psychology*, 11: 335–45.

Funk, S.C. and Houston, B.K. (1987) 'A critical analysis of hardiness scales' validity and utility', *Journal of Personality and Social Psychology*, 53: 572–8.

Galambos, N.L. and Walters, B.J. (1992) 'Work hours, schedule inflexibility and stress in dual-earner spouses', *Canadian Journal of Behavioural Science*, 24: 290–302.

Galinsky, E., Bond, J.T. and Friedman, D.E. (1996) 'The role of employers in addressing the needs of employed parents', *Journal of Social Issues*, 52: 111–36.

Gershuny, J. and Roberts, J. (1988) 'Historical changes in the household division of labor', *Demography*, 25: 537–52.

Greenhalgh, L. and Rosenblatt, Z. (1984) 'Job insecurity: towards conceptual clarity', *Academy of Management Review*, 9: 438–48.

Greenhalgh, L. and Sutton, R. (1991) 'Conclusion', in J. Hartley, D. Jacobson, B. Klandermans and T. van Vuuren (eds) *Job Insecurity – Coping with Jobs at Risk*, London: Sage.

Greenhaus, J.H. and Beutell, N.J. (1985) 'Sources of conflict between work and family roles', *Academy of Management Review*, 10: 76–88.

Guest, D.E. and Conway, N. (1997) *Employee Motivation and the Psychological Contract*, London: Institute of Personnel and Development.

Hallier, J. and Lyon, P. (1996) 'Job insecurity and employee commitment: managers' reactions to the threat and outcomes of redundancy selection', *British Journal of Management*, 7: 107–23.

Hartley, J., Jacobson, D., Klandermans, B. and van Vuuren, T. (eds) (1991) *Job Insecurity – Coping with Jobs at Risk*, London: Sage.

Hass, L. and Hwang, P. (1995) 'Company culture and men's use of family leave in Sweden', *Family Relations*, 44: 28–36.

Heaney, C.A., Israel, B.A. and House, J.S. (1994) 'Chronic job insecurity among automobile workers: effects on job satisfaction and health', *Social Science and Medicine*, 38: 1431–7.

Hodgson, G.M. (1995) 'Corporate culture and evolving competencies: an old institutionalist perspective on the nature of the firm', paper presented to the CBR seminar, Cambridge, 8 March.

Horsted, J. and Doherty, J. (1995) *Survivors' Syndrome Survey*, Cranfield: Cranfield Human Resources Centre, Working Transitions Working Paper.

House, J. S. (1981) *Work Stress and Social Support*, London: Addison-Wesley.

Howard, G.S. (1994) 'Why do people say nasty things about self-reports?', *Journal of Organizational Behavior*, 15: 399–404.

Hughes, D. and Galinsky, E. (1994) 'Work experiences and marital interactions: elaborating the complexity of work', *Journal of Organizational Behavior*, 15: 423–38.

Jacobson, D. (1987) 'A personological study of the job insecurity experience', *Social Behaviour*, 2: 143–55.

Joelson, L. and Wahlquist, L. (1987) 'The psychological meaning of job insecurity and job loss: results of a longitudinal study', *Social Science and Medicine*, 25: 179–82.

Kahn, R.L. (1981) *Work and Health*, New York: Wiley.

Kanter, R.M. (1977) *Work and Family in the USA: A Critical Review and Agenda for Research and Policy*, New York: Russell Sage Foundation.

Karasek, R. and Theorell, Y. (1990) *Healthy Work Stress: Productivity and the Reconstruction of Working Life*, New York: Basic Books.

Kelly, R.F., Sheldon, A.W. and Fox, G.L. (1985) 'The impact of economic dislocation on the health of children', in J. Boulet, A. M. Debritto and S.A. Ray (eds) *Understanding the Economic Crisis*, Ann Arbor, MI: University of Michigan Press.

Kessler, R.C. and McLeod, J. D. (1985) 'Social support and mental health in community samples', in S. Cohen and S. L. Syme (eds) *Social Support and Health*, London: Academic Press.

Kinicki, A.J. (1985) 'Personal consequences of plant closings: a model and preliminary test', *Human Relations*, 38: 197–212.

Kinnunen, U. and Mauno, S. (1998) 'Antecedents and outcomes of work–family conflict among employed women and men in Finland', *Human Relations*, 51: 157–77.

Klandermans, B., van Vuuren, T. and Jacobson, D. (1991) 'Employees and job insecurity', in J. Hartley, D. Jacobson, B. Klandermans and T. van Vuuren (eds) *Job Insecurity – Coping with Jobs at Risk*, London: Sage.

Koslowsky, M. (1998) *Modelling the Stress-Strain Relationship in Work Settings*, London: Routledge.

Kuhnert, K.W. and Lahey, M.A. (1988) 'Technological Innovation and its impact on employee well-being', paper presented at the National Meeting of the Operations Research Society of America/Institute for Management Science, Washington, DC.

Kuhnert, K.W. and Palmer, D.R. (1991) 'Job security, health and the intrinsic and extrinsic characteristics of work', *Group and Organization Studies*, 16: 178–92.

Kuhnert, K.W. and Vance, R.J. (1992) 'Job insecurity and moderators of the relation between job insecurity and employee adjustment', in J. C. Quick, L. R. Murphy and J. J. Hurrell (eds) *Stress and Well-being at Work*, Washington, DC: American Psychological Association.

Kuhnert, K.W., Sims, R.R. and Lahey, M.A. (1989) 'The relationship between job security and employee health', *Groups and Organization Studies*, 14: 399–410.

Lampard, R. (1994) 'An examination of the relationship between marital dissolution and unemployment', in D. Gallie, C. Marsh and C. Vogler (eds) *Social Change and the Experience of Unemployment*, Oxford: Oxford University Press.

La Rossa, R. and Reitzes, D.C. (1993) 'Continuity and change in middle-class fatherhood, 1925–1939 – the culture-conduct connection', *Journal of Marriage and the Family*, 55: 455–68.

Larson, J. H., Wilson, S. M. and Beley, R. (1994) 'The impact of job insecurity on marital and family relationships' *Family Relations*, 43: 138–43.

Lazarus, R.S. and Folkman, S. (1984) *Stress, Appraisal and Coping*, New York: Springer-Verlag.

Liker, J. and Elder, G. H. (1983) 'Economic hardship and marital relations in the 1930s', *American Sociological Review*, 48: 87–105.

Lim, V. K. G. (1996) 'Job insecurity and its outcomes: moderating effects of work-based and non-work-based social support', *Human Relations*, 49: 171–93.

Maddi, S. and Kobasa, S. G. (1984) *The Healthy Executive: Health under Stress*, Homewood, IL: Dow Jones-Irwin.

Margolis, L. H. and Farran, D. C. (1984) 'Unemployment and children', *International Journal of Mental Health*, 13: 107–24.

Mattiasson, I., Folke, L., Nilsson, J. A., Theorell, T. (1990) 'Threat of unemployment and cardiovascular risk factors: longitudinal study of quality of sleep and serum cholesterol concentrations in men threatened with redundancy', *British Medical Journal*, 301: 461–6.

Mattinson, J. (1988) *Work, Love and Marriage: The Impact of Unemployment*, London: Duckworth.

Moss, P. and Brannen, J. (1987) 'Fathers' employment', in C. Lewis and M. O'Brien (eds) *Reassessing Fatherhood: New Observations on Fathers and the Modern Family*, London: Sage.

Office for National Statistics (1998) *Social Trends 1998*, London: HMSO.

Orpen, C. (1993) 'Job dependence as a moderator of effects of job threat on employees' job insecurity and performance', *Psychological Reports*, 72: 449–50.

Orthner, D. (1995) 'Families in transition: changing values and norms', in R. Day, K. Gilbert, B. Settles and W. Burr (eds) *Research and Theory in Family Science*, London: International Thomson Press.

Pearlin, L.I. and Schooler, C. (1998) 'The structure of coping', *Journal of Health and Social Behaviour*, 19: 2–21.

Riley, D. and Eckenrode, J. (1986) 'Social ties: costs and benefits within differing subgroups', *Journal of Personality and Social Psychology*, 51: 770–8.

Rook, K., Dooley, D. and Catalano, R. (1991) 'Stress transmission: the effects of husband's job stressors on the emotional health of their wives', *Journal of Marriage and the Family*, 53: 165–77.

Rosenblatt, Z. and A. Ruvio (1996) 'A test of a multidimensional model of job insecurity: the case of Israeli teachers', *Journal of Organizational Behavior*, 17: 587–605.

Roskies, E. and Louis-Guerin, C. (1990) 'Job insecurity in managers: antecedents and consequences', *Journal of Organizational Behavior*, 11: 345–59.

Roskies, E., Louis-Guerin, C. and Fournier, C. (1993) 'Coping with job insecurity – how does personality make a difference?', *Journal of Organizational Behavior*, 14: 617–30.

Scott, J., Braun, M. and Alwin, D. (1993) 'The family way', in R. Jowell, L. Brook, L. Dowds and D. Ahrendt (eds) *International Social Attitudes, the 10th BSA Report*, Aldershot: Dartmouth.

Simpson, R. (1998) 'Organizational restructuring and presenteeism: the impact of long hours on the working lives of managers in the UK', *Management Research News*, 21: 19–20.

Sparks, K., Cooper, C., Fried, Y. and Shirom, A. (1997) 'The effects of hours of work on health: a meta-analytic review', *Journal of Occupational and Organizational Psychology*, 70: 391–408.

Spector, P. (1994) 'Using self-report questionnaires in OB research: a comment on the use of a controversial method', *Journal of Organizational Behavior*, 15: 385–92.

Stewart, W. and Barling, J. (1996) 'Fathers' work experiences affect children's behaviors via job-related affect and parenting behaviors', *Journal of Organizational Behavior*, 17: 221–32.

Sutherland, V.J. and Cooper, C.G. (1988) 'Sources of work stress', in J.J. Hurrell Jr., L.R. Murphey, S.L. Sauter and C.L. Cooper (eds) *Occupational Stress: Issues and Developments in Research*, London: Taylor & Francis.

Swinburne, P. (1981) 'The psychological impact of unemployment on managers and professional staff', *Journal of Occupational Psychology*, 54: 47–64.

Thoits, P. A. (1995) 'Stress, coping, and social support processes: where are we? What next?', *Journal of Health and Social Behaviour*, Extra Issue: 53–79.

van Vuuren, T., Klandermans, B., Jacobson, D. and Hartley, J. (1991) 'Employees' reactions to job insecurity', in J. Hartley, D. Jacobson, B. Klandermans and T. van Vuuren (eds) *Job Insecurity – Coping with Jobs at Risk*, London: Sage.

Voydanoff, P. (1990) 'Economic distress and family relations: a review of the eighties', *Journal of Marriage and the Family*, 59: 1099–115.

Voydanoff, P. and Donnelly, B. (1986) *Economic Distress and Mental Health: Coping Strategies and*

Social Supports, Report submitted to the Office of Program Evaluation and Research, Ohio Department of Mental Health.

—— (1988) 'Economic distress, family coping, and quality of family life' in P. Voydanoff and L.C. Majka (eds) *Families and Economic Distress: Coping Strategies and Social Policy*, Beverly Hills, CA: Sage.

Warr, P. (1983) 'Work, jobs and unemployment', *Bulletin of the British Psychological Society*, 36: 305–11.

—— (1987) *Work, Unemployment and Mental Health*, Oxford: Oxford University Press.

Wheatley, M. (1992) *The Future of Middle Management*, Corby: Institute of Management.

Zedeck, S. (1992) 'Introduction: exploring the domain of work and family concerns', in S. Zedeck (ed.) *Work, Families and Organisations*, San Francisco, CA: Jossey-Bass.

10 Insecurity and housing consumption

Richard M. Walker

Introduction

Britain has witnessed significant social and economic changes over the last two decades, which have generated substantial inequalities in British society (Barcley 1995). Part of this growth in inequality can be traced back to restructuring in the housing and labour markets, which raises concern about insecurity in the field of housing consumption. This chapter explores how restructuring in the housing market has produced a range of new and unanticipated problems, which are indicative of growing inflexibility in the housing market. Unemployed households, for example, which are not able to command a wage high enough to raise income above that derived from welfare benefits, remain welfare dependent, while members of households may be unable to relocate to obtain employment elsewhere because of regional differences in the cost of housing. The chapter will review a range of evidence which indicates that, in addition to inflexibility in the housing market, we can now talk of the 'insecure housing consumer' alongside the 'insecure worker'. The argument is pursued through an examination of restructuring in the housing and labour markets, and seeks to demonstrate how changes in each sphere have interacted and generated a series of complex problems. The chapter concludes by considering a number of possible housing policy solutions to the problems of deregulation which would help to overcome housing market inflexibility and address the needs of the increasingly insecure housing consumer.

Restructuring the housing market

The spheres of housing production and consumption have clearly moved towards a more market-oriented system over the last two decades, leading to new forms of organisation and financing. This process is seen in reduced government intervention and a greater role for private or semi-private agencies (Clapham 1996) and has impacted on all forms of housing tenure. Thus, Table 10.1 shows an increase of over 10 percentage points in owner-occupation in Britain since 1981, and a reduction of over 11 percentage points in local authority renting.

The figures in the table mask some variation between the countries of Great

Table 10.1 Dwellings by tenure in Great Britain 1981–1996, percentages

	1981	1986	1991	1995
Owner-occupation	56.4	61.5	66.0	66.7
Privately rented	11.1	10.0	9.3	10.0
Housing association	2.2	2.6	3.2	4.0
Local authority	30.3	25.9	21.2	18.9

Source: Wilcox 1997

Britain. For example, owner-occupation had risen in Scotland from 36.4 per cent in 1981 to 57.9 per cent by 1995, and in Wales from 62.4 per cent to 71.3 per cent during the same period. These increases in owner-occupation took place primarily during the 1980s and were generated by ideological promotion, ongoing subsidies and the expansion of mortgage availability and greater access to credit. Lower-income households have been brought into this form of tenure through a variety of government initiatives to sponsor low-cost home ownership. The most successful of the latter has been the sale of council homes to sitting tenants through the right-to-buy legislation first introduced in the Housing Act 1980. A range of discounts are offered to tenants, which can amount to up to 70 per cent of the open market value of the dwelling, and by 1996 1.27 million homes had been transferred to owner-occupation through this medium in England alone. The resultant stock and social difficulties which have emerged in many areas, however, have led the current Labour Government to review the policy and consider reducing the discount.

Absolute increases in owner-occupation were also achieved by a range of government policies which have limited the production of new social housing by local authorities. Between 1980 and 1996 the number of new units of rented housing produced annually by local authorities in England fell from over 67,000 to 530. The task of providing new social housing was transferred largely to housing associations through the Housing Act 1988, and formed part of the Conservative Government's process of marketising public services (Le Grand and Bartlett 1993). Housing associations have produced between 10,000 and 31,000 new homes a year since 1989, though a large proportion of the total increase in this tenure has been a product of the transfer of local authority housing to housing associations. As Table 10.2 makes clear, however, the growth of housing association provision has not been sufficient to compensate for the decline in public sector housing, and the size of the total social housing sector (housing association and local authority) has fallen by nearly one fifth since 1981. Although there has been variation between regions, moreover, this pattern of substantial overall decline in social housing provision has been seen across the country.

Private renting also underwent a decline in the period 1981–95 (see Table 10.1), though registered some growth in the early 1990s as a result of the collapse in the owner-occupied market. The overall decline has occurred despite the promotion of this form of tenure by Conservative governments in the 1980s and

Table 10.2 Changes in regional provision of social housing in Great Britain 1981–1995

Region	Stock of dwellings (000s)						Percentage change in provision		
	April 1981			December 1995			1981–1995		
	Public sector	Housing association	All social housing	Public sector	Housing association	All social housing	Public sector	Housing association	All social housing
North	478	37	515	341	54	395	−28.7	45.9	−23.3
Yorkshire & Humberside	601	27	628	458	65	523	−23.8	140.7	−16.7
North West	720	53	773	533	118	651	−26.0	122.6	−15.8
West Midlands	615	40	655	451	85	536	−26.7	112.5	−18.2
East Midlands	413	19	432	303	43	346	−26.6	126.3	−19.9
East Anglia	190	13	203	122	44	166	−35.8	238.5	−18.2
Greater London	851	134	985	646	198	844	−24.1	47.8	−14.3
Rest of South East	885	60	945	517	223	740	−41.6	271.7	−21.7
South West	366	27	393	239	74	313	−34.7	174.1	−20.4
England	5,118	410	5,528	3,609	902	4,511	−29.5	120.0	−18.4
Wales	298	11	309	208	43	251	−30.2	290.2	−18.8
Scotland	1,031	33	1,064	695	90	785	−32.6	172.7	−26.2

Source: Wilcox (1997)

1990s, through the Business Expansion Scheme, which offered tax breaks for institutional investors, and the setting up of Housing Investment Trusts in 1996. Running alongside this direct promotion of the sector has been a policy of deregulation through reductions in security of tenure and the lifting of rent control on new lettings, which aims to make private renting a more attractive proposition to landlords. Despite these measures, however, a substantial revitalisation of private sector renting has not been achieved, and its long-term decline, from a 90 per cent tenure share at the turn of the century, has not been halted. Moreover, it is anticipated that private renting will decline further as the owner-occupied market recovers from the slump of the early 1990s and properties developed under the Business Expansion Scheme are sold.

The socio-economic composition of both the social rented sector and owner-occupation have been redefined through tenure restructuring. The majority of right-to-buy purchasers were from semi-skilled and skilled households and their departure from social renting means that this tenure is now characterised by poverty and populations of low income and economically inactive households. By 1995–6 only a quarter of social housing tenants had connections with the labour market. Social rented housing now houses those in greatest need and the process of concentrating the most vulnerable households in social housing, coupled with the sale of the best quality stock through right-to-buy, has led to the residualisation of this sector (Forrest and Murie 1991). Social renting has become the tenure of last resort and is now stigmatised; the widening gap between the incomes of home owners and renters, both public and private, is demonstrated clearly in Table 10.3.

The expansion of owner-occupation through ideological support, tax breaks and low-cost home ownership policies has also led to changes in owner-occupation: 8 per cent of home owners with a mortgage were economically inactive, permanently sick or unemployed in 1995–6, up from 5 per cent in 1981; 4 per cent were in part-time work in 1995–6 as against 1 per cent in 1981; and home owners constituted 23 per cent of households in the lowest income decile

Table 10.3 Average incomes of household heads by tenure in Great Britain (£ per week), 1972–1995

Tenure	1972	1980	1988	1992	1995
Owners:					
Outright owner	25	81	157	194	236
With mortgage	39	142	267	320	361
Tenants:					
Local authority	22	58	93	110	122
Housing association	—	66	94	120	137
Private – unfurnished	19	60	110	149	173
Private – furnished	21	87	161	170	223

Source: Wilcox (1997)

(Wilcox 1997). The expansion of owner-occupation across all social classes has resulted in a large number of marginal home owners who face difficulty in sustaining their tenure in the face of a relatively high risk of the head of household becoming unemployed and not being able to meet mortgage payments or adequately maintain their homes (Hogarth *et al.* 1996).

Changes in tenure have been achieved through a restructured subsidy system for renting and reductions in subsidy for owner-occupation since the early 1990s. These reforms, initiated by the Conservatives, and in the main continued under Labour, have been predicated on a belief in free markets. In owner-occupation, regulation has been reduced to allow financial institutions to compete freely with each other for customers. In renting, subsidy changes were aimed at removing distortions in the market to allow social and private landlords to compete more freely. This has been done by relaxing the controls on private renting and by redirecting the subsidy provided for social renting away from the production of housing towards individual housing consumers. As a consequence, local authorities have experienced a reduction in revenue subsidies, while housing associations have seen reductions in capital subsidies. The outcome of subsidy reductions has been a rise in the level of rents for social housing rents by over 100 per cent. In England, average local authority rents stood at £19.01 per week in 1988–9 but had risen to £40.05 by 1996–7, while new housing association assured tenancy rents rose from £24.50 per week in 1989 to £50.13 per week in 1996. Rents in the housing association sector, now the main provider of new social housing, currently stand 25 per cent higher than those in local authorities and there has also been an increase in rents in the private sector, which stood on average at £94.00 week in 1996 (Centre for Housing Policy 1997). These increases in the cost of renting, moreover, have occurred at the dame time as the average earnings of tenants have declined in relation to those of owner occupiers (see Table 10.3).

Renters who need help meeting their housing costs, because of unemployment or low incomes, are eligible for housing benefits. The consequence of transferring subsidy from bricks and mortar to personal subsidies has led to the cost of housing benefit rising from £5.7 billion in 1990–1 to an estimated £13.5 billion in 1998–9. Conservative Government concerns about these growing costs, up to the end of their term in office in 1997, led to a range of measures which limited the amount of housing benefit which can be paid. For example, housing benefit payments to single people are limited to the cost of a room in a shared house, not the cost of a single occupancy unit, and regional ceilings have been introduced beyond which housing benefit is not payable. The latter change has particular implications for the private rented sector, where high rents could lead landlords to refuse to provide accommodation for people on housing benefit. The current Labour administration is also concerned with the cost of subsidy and considering limiting the amount of housing benefit paid to entitled households. Proposals include restricting housing benefit to 90 per cent of total housing costs in order to encourage households to search for more affordable accommodation. If implemented, this change would make the British housing benefits system similar to those which operate in other European countries (Kemp 1998).

Subsidies to home ownership have also been reduced since the early 1990s and in 1999 mortgage interest tax relief (the MIRAS system) was abolished. The Conservative administration also reduced welfare payments to unemployed home owners from 1995. This latter change has placed the responsibility on owner occupiers (whether new entrants or those moving households) to take out private insurance to cover housing costs in the early months of unemployment (Williams 1995).

These processes of tenure restructuring, with their greater reliance on market mechanisms, have reinforced the dominance of owner-occupation. For the majority of households it is the only real tenure alternative. The private rented sector is not strong and social housing in many parts of the country is in short supply and has become a stigmatised tenure of last choice. Yet, whilst home ownership has expanded, subsidies have fallen and additional costs have been placed on home owners. The outcome of these reforms has led some commentators to describe the housing market as increasingly inflexible (Clapham *et al.* 1995; Ford and Wilcox 1994; Maclennan 1994). It is this inflexibility, particularly with regard to choice of tenure, which has interacted with labour market change and exacerbated the shift towards more insecure employment. Accordingly, we now turn to a review of parallel changes in the labour market.

The restructuring of the labour market

The shift to the management of supply, rather than demand, with an emphasis upon free markets, which has been apparent in housing policy is also visible in other policy arenas. The Conservative Government's labour market policies were intended to create a supply of cheap and flexible labour and were developed from the guiding assumption that high levels of long-term unemployment originated in distortions or inflexibility in the labour market. Accordingly, at the centre of policy were initiatives to deregulate the labour market and improve its efficiency through the reduction of union power, the removal of Wages Councils and other protective legislation and the break up of public sector monopolies (Gibb 1994). These developments have had fundamental implications for the housing system and have served to exacerbate insecurity in housing consumption.

Unemployment has been falling in recent years, although policies of labour market deregulation have failed, to date, to return the British economy to full employment. Continuing high levels of unemployment have two implications for housing and housing policy. First, as noted above, the unemployed are concentrated in social renting, which has implications for welfare benefits at the household and state levels, the management of the housing stock and the formulation of policies to bring social housing and its tenants back into the mainstream of society. For the foreseeable future there will be continuing demand for social rented housing, particularly from long-term unemployed households (Clapham *et al.* 1995; Maclennan 1994; Walker 1997). Second, though unemployment rates are lower for home owners than for other tenures, the dominance of home ownership means that a large number of home owners are likely to become unemployed during the course of any one year. Wilcox and Ford (1997) note that during 1997–8, even with falling levels of unemployment, at least half a million home-buying households were likely to have one mortgage-holder experience unemployment during the year and that the average period of unemployment was 25 weeks. A more flexible labour market, coupled with an extension of home ownership down the family income scale, means that increasing numbers of home owners will experience unemployment which, in turn, will pose a threat to their tenure.

Alongside continued high levels of unemployment, the flexible labour market has been characterised by extensive use of non-standard labour, including self-employment, part-time work and various forms of temporary and fixed-term contract (Clapham *et al.* 1995; Ford and Wilcox 1994). Of particular concern is the impact of forms of insecure employment on people newly entering the labour market and the longer-term impact this will have on their housing careers. It has been suggested that home ownership is a particularly problematic form of tenure for households with less secure jobs and fixed-term and temporary contracts (Maclennan 1994; Wilcox and Ford 1997).

Finally, there is evidence of growing inequality in the labour market and of a widening gap between households with access to work and those who are excluded from employment or who enjoy only limited access (Central Statistical Office 1996). Research for the Commission for Social Justice (1994) revealed the growing gap between 'work-rich' households, with one and a half or two jobs, and 'work-poor' households with no job at all. These differences in access to work, unsurprisingly, map onto differences in housing tenure, and five out of six of dual-earning households are owner occupiers; half of all home owners are below retirement age (Wilcox and Ford 1997). There has also been a relative increase in the number of those on low incomes: the number of men and women in either full or part-time employment whose income falls below the Council of Europe's decency threshold increased from 38.1 per cent in 1987 to 48.1 per cent in 1995, equating to 9.94 million people (Wilcox 1996). This low-income segment of the population is likely to face particular problems in maintaining home ownership (Maclennan 1994), while welfare-dependent renters and owners may become trapped within poverty and unemployment and be effectively excluded from the labour market (Clapham *et al.* 1995; Ford and Wilcox 1994; Maclennan 1994; Walker 1997).

During the 1980s and 1990s the labour and housing markets have become inexorably intertwined. Changes in the labour market now have a significant impact upon the experiences of housing consumers and their capacity to main-tain their homes or regain employment once unemployed. Though knowledge has existed about these interconnections, it was not until the housing market boom–bust of the late 1980s that these were fully appreciated or studied (Glass 1994). The shift in government policy during the 1980s and 1990s to supply-side management, which is being continued in many respects by the Labour administration, leads to a range of questions about the productive potential of the economy and the need for policy reform to address the uncertainty which has arisen from restructuring and to address issues of inflexibility in the housing market.

Housing consumers' experiences

The cyclical nature of the housing market was vividly demonstrated in the late 1980s' boom and bust which emanated from the deregulation of the mortgage finance market. The latter fuelled the rapid expansion of private home ownership in the 1980s, which came to an abrupt end as the Conservative Government raised interest rates and increased the cost of home ownership. The housing market went into decline and transactions fell from 2,148,000 in 1988 to 1,136,000 in 1992, and by 1996 had risen only to 1,243,000. For housing consumers the critical change in the housing market was the sharp increase in costs as interest rates rose steeply to a peak of 15 per cent in 1990. The cost of an average mortgage rose to a high of 28.1 per cent of average income for first-time buyers in 1990, though has fallen subsequently to 17.4 per cent today, its lowest level since 1983. The difficulty of affording housing with high interest rates, which affected first-time buyers, also affected other households and led to an increase in house repossessions. In 1996 repossessions were still running at 42,560 per annum (down from 75,540 in 1991), nearly 170,000 households were up to six months in mortgage arrears (down from 274,000 in 1991) and nearly half a million households were still in negative equity (down from 1,768,000 in 1992) (Wilcox 1997).

Many home owners are now apprehensive about this form of tenure and feel that it has become more risky, particularly with the limited interest in mortgage rescue schemes and the perception of mortgage lenders' propensity to freely repossess. There is also evidence that many have blamed the Conservatives for their predicament and have felt that insufficient was done to guarantee the security of those who were encouraged to enter this form of tenure for the first time. Feelings of insecurity among homeowners have been compounded by the reduction in the availability of social renting, which has effectively removed the safety net for those who get into mortgage difficulties (Holmans 1995). Perhaps the most vivid demonstration of rising insecurity in the realm of housing consumption, however, can be seen in the rise of homelessness. In the decade 1987–96 there were over 1.5 million homelessness acceptances in Great Britain, whilst street-homelessness has become a familiar sight in every city and town.

Housing market uncertainty has also been exacerbated by government reductions in financial support for home ownership, described above. Though these policies were in part introduced to stop the housing market booming again (and to reduce government expenditure), the costs of reduced welfare support to home owners, when replaced by private insurance, equates to 1 per cent on the monthly costs of mortgages. When linked to a more flexible labour market, with increased uncertainty and reduced job tenure, the likely effect will be increased problems of arrears in the future, particularly as the take-up of private insurance has been low (Wilcox 1996). A survey by Ford and Kempson (1997) indicated that only a third of home buyers had taken out mortgage payment protection insurance between

October 1995 and October 1996, whilst only one in five existing mortgagees already had such cover. The recent experience of many home owners, therefore, is of growing insecurity as risk and costs have been transferred from the state to individual consumers. As a consequence, a large proportion of households has faced some form of housing problem, and general awareness of housing insecurity has risen.

Housing consumption and the productive potential of the economy

Supply-side restructuring has impacted negatively upon the housing market and many households, whilst distortions in the housing market have not been removed. Traditionally housing has been seen as contributing towards economic inflexibility, as the interactions between housing subsidies, social security and taxation create work disincentives and the organisation of the system restricts geographical mobility. An alternative approach, however, suggests that the productive potential of the economy can be increased through greater public investment in housing. This theme has been pursued through new growth theory which argues that national economic prosperity can be increased and social needs met through greater public investment and government intervention (Kitson *et al.* 1997). Public investment in infrastructure can create the conditions which make private investment worthwhile again, raising the productive potential of the economy (Garcia-Mila and McGurie 1992; Ford and Poret 1991). This view challenges the assumptions that public investment crowds out private investment, or that the latter is inherently superior, and argues, instead, that poverty, inequality and economic difficulties can be overcome at relatively low cost through government-led job creation in housing, education, health and the environment (Kitson *et al.* 1997).

Within the field of housing policy, Clapham *et al.* (1995) have sought to demonstrate the benefits which can accrue from increased public sector investment. They argue that the latter can be used to address issues of supply and stock condition and can create employment opportunities. According to their calculations, a £1 billion public investment in housing in 1995–6 would have directly created 15,400 jobs in year one, rising to 31,700 in year two if the level of investment was sustained. The creation of employment in the construction industry, moreover, would generate spin-off employment in other sectors of the economy. Clapham *et al.* also calculate that much of the additional investment would be recouped through taxation and a reduction in benefit payments and that there would be only a minimal impact on the retail price index. Action of this kind has also been proposed because of its potential to regenerate local communities and revive areas of depressed social housing, effectively bringing them back from the social margin (Taylor 1995).

To date, three demand-side policies have been put in place by the New Labour Government which have the potential to impact on housing consumption. These are the Welfare-to-Work programme, which aims to reduce the number of long-term unemployed people through a mixture of direct government support and business activity, the National Minimum Wage and the reform of the welfare benefits system to a tax credit system. Action has also been taken within the housing sphere and local authorities have been given access to the capital receipts they have banked from the right-to-buy programme, but were previously prevented from using for new investment in social housing. In addition, a New Deal for Communities initiative has been launched to address problems of social exclusion in council housing estates. If these initiatives are to prove effective in addressing the problems faced by the insecure housing consumer, they must deal with four critical housing issues: labour mobility, disincentives to work, and the links between housing and employment and housing, disrepair and health.

Labour mobility

The restructuring of social housing subsidies described above was promoted, in part, by labour market economists seeking to increase labour mobility within the UK, in order to overcome regional differences in economic growth and transfer labour from areas of high unemployment to areas with job vacancies (Hughes and McCormick 1990). It was argued that propensity to move was lower within the social rented sector because of inefficient and unresponsive allocation mechanisms (Hughes and McCormick 1990; Minford *et al.* 1987). However, arguments have been presented both historically (Johnson *et al.* 1974) and more recently (Forrest *et al.* 1991; McGregor *et al.* 1992) to suggest that social status and income affect mobility and job search patterns, and have a more pervasive influence on the propensity to move than housing tenure. Forrest *et al.* (1993), in their study of mobility patterns in the South East of England, identified income as critical in explaining the higher mobility of managers and professionals in comparison with that of lower-income groups. Evidence presented above has indicated the ways in which financial restructuring has led to a concentration of unemployment in social housing and restructured household composition across all tenures. This suggests lower levels of labour market participation, especially in social renting, and reduced possibilities for labour mobility. Additionally, rising or falling house prices further hamper mobility (Maclennan 1997).

In order to increase labour mobility it has been argued that there must be an increase in the supply of private renting (Maclennan 1994) and/or social rented housing (Clapham *et al.* 1995; Forrest and Murie 1994). However, there has been little direct action on either front. The Conservative Government's creation of Housing Investment Trusts to attract new institutional investors into the sector was unsuccessful and private renting is unlikely to expand in any meaningful way to allow for labour mobility. The Labour Government has allowed local authorities to spend over £350 million up to 2001 on housing investment, but this is unlikely to be ploughed into new social rented housing as stock condition problems are sufficiently severe for this to represent the first call on investment. Moreover, the Housing Corporation, which funds housing associations in England, has seen substantial reductions in its budget for new social housing and, although it is looking to channel resources to regions of high demand, the provision of new homes is likely to be limited.

Poverty and unemployment traps

Low-income and unemployed households face disincentives to work, through unemployment and poverty traps. These are products of the interaction between the systems of welfare and taxation, and are seen most clearly in the rented sector. The unemployment trap affects unemployed households who, as they enter employment, have benefits withdrawn and pay taxes. Their income in work may be less than on benefits. Thus, there is a hurdle which households have to jump to gain a disposable income that is higher than their current benefit levels, which stands above average male manual wages. For households in work, the poverty trap can mean that the disposable income from increasing earnings may be lost through deductions of income tax and National Insurance and the withdrawal of welfare benefits. The extent of the poverty trap is dependent upon rent levels, and the higher the rent the wider the range of incomes the trap catches. At its extreme, the poverty trap can result in a marginal tax rate of 97 per cent.

Similar problems exist within the owner-occupied sector. Unemployed households in receipt of income support currently get help with their mortgage interest costs. However, they do not receive the equivalent of any form of in-work housing benefit. Thus, if they take up a low-paid job and, as a result, lose the support they had been gaining for their mortgage, they can face an absolute reduction in their disposable income (Ford *et al.* 1996). The expansion of owner-occupation has compounded this problem as it has brought more lower-income and economically inactive groups into the tenure (Wilcox 1996), whilst further government economy measures compound the difficulties. Policy debate over these disincentives has centred around increased producer subsidies in the rented sector (Clapham *et al.* 1995; Ford *et al.* 1996) and the introduction of a form of housing benefit for home owners (Webb and Wilcox 1991). The case for measures of this kind is supported by behavioural studies (Bradshaw and Millar 1991; Ford *et al.* 1996) which highlight the social recognition or satisfaction from work, a factor which is often overlooked in economic analysis (Kitson *et al.* 1997).

Government action through the introduction of a minimum wage and the shift to working family tax credits might be expected to address disincentives to work. However, the extra income which households are likely to obtain through such policies does not address the fundamental problem of high rents and will probably be insufficient to overcome all difficulties. For example, the poverty trap is deep and broad, and the higher the rent, the wider the range of incomes it catches. For the average housing association rent of £50.13 the trap extends to the average male manual workers' earnings of £14,600 at 1995 levels. The impact of the trap is such that a family with two children earning £280 per week is only £33.31 better off than if they were earning just £60 per week (Clapham *et al.* 1995). Such a family would also have to pay for the full costs of school meals, health services charges and travel to work and other related costs. Thus current labour market, welfare and taxation reforms do not address these difficulties, whilst proposals to reduce payment of housing benefit below 100 per cent could exacerbate the problem. However, an immediate alleviation of this problem could be achieved by reducing rents, and in the local authority sector a 10 per cent cut in rents is estimated to cost only £100 million over the next decade.

Housing and employees

The vast majority of housing consumers are home owners in employment. Though the previous arguments have been directed at typically unemployed social renters, recent work by Walker (1997) illustrates ways in which housing problems experienced by employees can affect their employment and exacerbate uncertainty. The research took the form of a questionnaire survey undertaken in a multinational corporation during 1995 which collected information on employees' housing problems experienced over the last three years. It indicated that 29 per cent of employees reported that they had experienced some form of housing problem of a financial or social kind, referred to as welfare housing problems (see Table 10.4). The most commonly reported issue was neighbour nuisance, though a significant minority of employees faced financial problems or where threatened with, or had experienced, homelessness.

Problems were more prevalent amongst three groups of households. First, employees with a low gross household income – 36 per cent of employees with gross household income under £20,000 reported problems, as against a quarter of households with incomes over £35,000. Second, households who spent a larger proportion of their income on housing costs. Of those spending up to 30 per cent of their household income on housing, problems were reported by 27 per cent of employees, as against 42 per cent for those spending over 61 per cent. Specific

Table 10.4 Welfare housing problems experienced over the last three years

Welfare housing problems	Employees experiencing problems %	All employees %
Problems with neighbours	79	23
Mortgage arrears	11	3
Problems with landlord	6	2
Other problems	8	2
Being told you have to move out	5	1
Rent arrears	4	1
Repossession/threatened with	3	1
Eviction/threatened with	2	1
No problems	n.a	68
Not stated	n.a.	3
Base	725	2,501

Source: Walker (1997)

housing problems also increased in line with increases in the proportion of housing income spent on housing. For example, financial difficulties were more likely to be experienced as the proportion of income spent on housing costs increased. Third, social and private renters were more likely to face difficulties than owners with the exception of neighbour nuisance (81 per cent of home owners as against 64 per cent of renters) and arrears (12 per cent of home owners as against 1 per cent of renters). Fifty per cent of renters experienced a housing problem within the last three years as against 24 per cent of owner occupiers. In particular, problems with the landlord, arrears, being told you have to move out and repossession or eviction figured highly amongst renters.

The employees' experience of housing problems identified problems which could lead to severe stress. One in ten of the employees who had experienced housing problems was made homelessness and one quarter had to use temporary accommodation as a result of their housing problems. Homelessness has the capacity to cause major disruption in people's personal and work lives. The experiences of staying in temporary accommodation, such as bed and breakfast hotels, left employees feeling insecure and uncertain about their housing, and adversely affected their work. Of the employees experiencing financial difficulties, mortgage arrears created particular problems, with employees often finding mortgage lenders difficult to deal with or unsympathetic. Cases of mortgage arrears clearly indicate the tension between the spheres of home and work. Neighbour disputes could also be severe and caused major disruption to people's lives, particularly in cases of harassment, which prompt a minority of individuals to move home. Such action, in turn, could lead to financial hardship and the need to work overtime in order to acquire sufficient resources to relocate. Employees felt that housing problems affected their work lives and performance in a variety of ways. One in ten employees with housing problems said that housing was their main cause of worry, and while some of the problems reported related to wider processes of social change (e.g. neighbour nuisance), several were indicative of the way in which a poorly resourced system of housing does not allow for the productive potential of the workforce to be realised.

Housing and health

The issues raised by the extension of market mechanisms into the housing system extend beyond the immediate concerns of the supply of social rented housing and labour market policies and embrace the link between housing quality, disrepair and health. Research indicates a variety of ways in which housing problems affect the lives of people individually, yet which have macroeconomic impacts, and indicates that 'bad housing is dangerous to your health' (Best 1995: 61). The relationship between poor housing and health are independent of income, smoking, unemployment, cooking and washing facilities and the presence of pets (Hopton and Hunt 1996), whilst as housing problems worsen, so does health (Platt *et al.* 1989). The relationship between housing and health is seen at its worst amongst people who are homeless, for whom there is a greater range and frequency of health problems (Stern *et al.* 1989). For households in temporary accommodation, problems include overcrowding, lack of access to reasonable hygiene facilities, lack of kitchen equipment so that people rely on nutritionally unsatisfactory take-aways, stress, which can impact on relationships, and increased risk of accidents (Robinson *et al.* 1996). In combination, these problems can have long-term effects and can lead to isolation, insecurity, uncertainty, stress and poor mental health.

Concern over the link between poor housing and health is compounded by the extent of disrepair in the housing stock. It is estimated that at least £7 billion needs to be spent to bring the current owner-occupied sector back to basic levels of fitness (Leather *et al.* 1994) and that £12 billion is needed to repair the public sector stock. If the health problems associated with poor housing are to be addressed then clearly there must but greater investment, particularly in the social housing sector (Best 1995).

Conclusion

This chapter has reviewed the implications for housing consumption and housing policy of a switch to a market-dominated system. A critical effect of this change has been a growing perception, and for some households, the reality of uncertainty and insecurity as a result of housing and labour market change. A number of these phenomena have operated independently, such as the externality impact of housing conditions. However, many are interrelated, such as labour mobility and disincentives to work. The driving force for these changes has been the parallel deregulation of the housing and labour markets, promoted by Conservative administrations of the 1980s and 1990s, which were based on an assumption about the efficacy of free markets. The extent, depth and permanence of housing market restructuring, and the way in which the housing and labour markets have become intertwined, mean that many of the problems highlighted have become permanent features of the housing landscape. It is clear that housing consumption has become more insecure – more households now experience homelessness than at any time since records have been collected, volatility in the housing market means that the costs of owner-occupation can vary substantially, affordability is an issue in all tenures and the reduction in the size of the social rented sector means that the safety net has reduced, while the quality of social rented housing is often poor.

The growth of insecure employment (Gregg and Machin 1994), together with the evidence presented here about the prevalence of housing problems amongst lower-income households, suggests that many people facing severe housing problems are also likely to experience labour market flexibility. For example, the growth of non-traditional forms of employment, typified in the construction sector where there has been a substantial growth in the informal economy and where the vast majority of people work on short-term and insecure contracts, can be expected to lead to a range of access and financial housing problems (Walker 1997). Housing problems, which impact on work performance or health, cost government through increased benefit bills, increased NHS costs and the increased demand for social housing.

There are, however, a range of housing market policies which could be developed to help alleviate the problems faced by the insecure housing consumer and allow the housing market to adapt to labour market flexibility. First, greater stability needs to be brought to owner-occupation to reduce the likelihood of mortgage arrears and negative equity, and the emphasis in macroeconomic policy in maintaining low inflation can help to ensure that housing costs remain afford-able. However, shortages of supply in ownership and renting can lead to house price inflation, particularly during periods of economic growth. Stability can be achieved through the expansion of the rented sector, to reduce the impacts of home loss on employees, to provide them with a cushion if needed (Munro *et al.* 1998), and to increase labour mobility, particularly where provision of social renting provides access to home ownership through the right-to-buy programme (Forrest and Murie 1994). An additional measure could be the introduction of greater flexibility into mortgage provision, in order to accommodate greater variety in patterns of work.

Second, the introduction of a mortgage benefits scheme would place home owners on a more secure footing if they experience unemployment. This would put them on the same basis as renters and give them access to a greater range of in-work benefits which would mean that they would be able to sustain their tenure. Webb and Wilcox (1991) have argued that the costs of such as scheme are low and could have been funded from the recent reductions in mortgage interest tax relief. Third, the problems of disincentives to work can be addressed through reductions in social sector rents. Such a reform would be both simpler than reforming the welfare benefits and taxation system and, in the local authority sector, cheaper.

Fourth, Maclennan (1997) reflects general housing concerns when he calls for a 'housing market policy' to develop more comprehensive housing planning and provide information for investors and consumers on the local housing market. Such a policy would require greater intervention by government and its agencies to develop knowledge and understanding of the private sector (rental and owner-ship) in order to ensure that local intervention was targeted where needed – at households with low income and high housing costs. More systematic housing market information may also help individual households in dealing with uncertainty.

This chapter has indicated a range of complex interactions that exist within and across the housing system which act to heighten the perceptions and realities of uncertainty and insecurity. Its overriding message is the pressing need for a well-resourced housing system which meets the requirements of the insecure housing consumer. This, in turn, implies greater state intervention and investment to ensure that disrepair does not affect people's health and stop them functioning in the labour market, that housing is sufficiently affordable and flexible to cope with labour market flexibility and to allow people to enter work without being penalised financially. Such investment in housing would also increase the productive potential of the economy and alleviate a range of problems centred on the basic human need for adequate housing.

References

Barcley, P. (1995) *Inquiry into Income and Wealth, Volume 1*, York: Joseph Rowntree Foundation.

Best, R. (1995) 'The housing dimension', in M. Benzeval, K. Judge, and M. Whitehead (eds) *Tackling Inequalities in Health: An Agenda for Action*, London: King's Fund.

Bradshaw, J. and Millar, J. (1991) *Lone Parent Families in the UK*, London: HMSO.

Central Statistical Office (1996) *Regional Trends 31*, London: HMSO.

Centre for Housing Policy (1997) *JRF Index of Private Rents and Yields*, York: Joseph Rowntree Foundation.

Clapham, D. (1996) 'Housing and the economy: broadening comparative housing research', *Urban Studies*, 33: 631–47.

Clapham, D., Walker, R.M., Meen, G., Thake, S. and Wilcox, S. (1995) *Building Homes Building Jobs: Housing and Economic Recovery*, London: National Housing Forum.

Commission for Social Justice (1994) *Social Justice: Strategies for National Renewal*, London: Vintage.

Ford, J. and Kempson, E. (1997) *Bridging the Gap? Safety Nets for Mortgage Borrowers*, York: Joseph Rowntree Foundation.

Ford, J., Kempson, E. and England, J. (1996) *Into Work? The Impact of Housing Costs and the Benefits System on People's Decision to Work*, York: Joseph Rowntree Foundation.

Ford, J. and Wilcox, S. (1994) *Affordable Housing: Low Incomes and the Flexible Labour Market*, London: National Federation of Housing Associations.

Ford, R. and Poret, P. (1991) *Infrastructure and Private Sector Productivity*, Paris: OECD.

Forrest, R. and Murie, A. (1991) *Selling the Welfare State: The Privatisation of Public Housing*, London: Routledge.

—— (1994) 'The dynamics of the owner-occupied housing market in Southern England in the late 1980s: a study of new building and vacancy chains', *Regional Studies*, 28: 275–89.

Forrest, R., Murie, A., Doogan, K. and Burton, P. (1991) *Labour Mobility and Housing Provision: A Review of the Evidence*, Bristol: Working Paper 98, Bristol: School for Advanced Urban Studies, University of Bristol.

Forrest, R. and Murie, A. with Gordon, D., Burton, P., Doogan, K. and Franklin, A. (1993) *New Homes for Home Owners: A Study of New Building and Vacancy Chains in Southern England*, London: HMSO.

Garcia-Mila, T. and McGurie, T. (1992) 'The contribution of publicly provided inputs to states' economies', *Regional Science and Urban Economics*, 22: 229–41.

Gibb, K. (1994) *Labour Market Flexibility and Housing in Britain*, Glasgow: Centre for Housing Research and Urban Studies, University of Glasgow.

Glass, N. (1994) *Housing and the Economy*, Harry Simpson Memorial Lecture, York: Joseph Rowntree Foundation.

Gregg, P. and Machin, S. (1994) 'Is the UK rise in inequality different?', in R. Barrell (ed.) *The UK Labour Market*, Cambridge: Cambridge University Press.

Hamnett, C., Harmer, M. and Williams, P. R. (1991) *Safe as Houses: Housing Inheritance in Britain*, London, Paul Chapman.

Hogarth, T., Elias, P. and Ford, J. (1996) *Mortgages, Families and Jobs: An Exploration of the Growth of Home Ownership in the 1980s*, Warwick: Institute for Employment Research, University of Warwick.

Holmans, A. (1995) *Housing Demand and Need in England 1991–2011*, York: Joseph Rowntree Foundation.

Hopton, J. and Hunt, S. (1996) 'The health effects of improvements to housing: a longitudinal study', *Housing Studies*, 11: 271–86.

Hughes, G.A. and McCormick, B. (1990) 'Housing and labour mobility', in J. Ermish (ed.) *Housing and the National Economy*, Andover: Avebury.

Johnson, J., Salt, J. and Wood, P. (1974) *Housing and Migration of Labour in England and Wales*, Farnborough: Saxon House.

Kemp, P. A. (1998) 'Housing allowances in comparative perspective', paper given at the European Network for Housing Research, CECODHAS, NETHER Conference Social Housing Management in Europe, Nunspeet, the Netherlands.

Kitson, M., Michie, J. and Sutherland, H. (1997) 'The fiscal and distributional implications of job generation', *Cambridge Journal of Economics*, 21: 103–20.

Le Grand, J. and Bartlett, W. (eds) (1993) *Quasi-Markets and Social Policy*, London: Macmillan.

McGregor, A., Munro, M., Heafey, M. and Symon, P. (1992) *Moving Job, Moving House: The Impact of Housing on Long Distance Labour Mobility*, Discussion Paper No. 38, Glasgow: Centre for Housing Research, University of Glasgow.

Maclennan, D. (1994) *A Competitive UK Economy: The Challenges for Housing Policy*, York: Joseph Rowntree Foundation.

—— (1997) 'The UK housing market: up, down and where next?', in P. Williams (ed.) *Directions in Housing Policy: Towards Sustainable Housing Policies for the UK*, London: Paul Chapman.

Minford, P., Peel, M. and Aston, P. (1987) *The Housing Morass: Regulation, Immobility and Unemployment*, London: Institute for Economic Affairs.

Munro, M., Madigam, R. and Memery, C. (1998) 'Choices in owner-occupation', in P. Taylor-Gooby (ed.) *Choices in Public Policy*, London: Macmillan.

Platt, S., Martin, C., Hunt, S., and Lewis, C. (1989) 'Damp housing, mould growth and symptomatic health state', *British Medical Journal*, 298: 1673–8.

Robinson, F., Spencer, S., Wood, M. and Kiethley, J. (1996) *More Than Somewhere To Live: Housing's Impact on Healthy Communities*, London: National Housing Forum.

Stern, R., Stilwell, B. and Heuston, J. (1989) *From the Margins to the Mainstream: Collaboration in Planning Services with Single Homeless People*, London: West Lambeth Health Authority.

Taylor, M. (1995) *Unleashing the Potential: Bringing Residents to the Centre of Regeneration*, York: Joseph Rowntree Foundation.

Walker, R.M. (1997) *Bad for Business: Company Employees and their Housing Problems*, London: Shelter.

Webb, S. and Wilcox, S. (1991) *Time for Mortgage Benefits*, York: Joseph Rowntree Foundation.

Wilcox, S. (ed.) (1996) *Housing Review 1996/97*, York: Joseph Rowntree Foundation.

—— (ed.) (1997) *Housing Review 1997/98*, York: Joseph Rowntree Foundation.

Wilcox, S. and Ford, J. (1997) 'At your own risk', in S. Wilcox (ed.) *Housing Review 1997/98*, York: Joseph Rowntree Foundation.

Williams, P. (1995) 'A shrinking safety net for a changing market', *Housing Review 1995/96*, York: Joseph Rowntree Foundation.

Index